The
Elements
of John Updike

Alice
and
Kenneth
Hamilton

THE ELEMENTS OF JOHN UPDIKE

WILLIAM B. EERDMANS / PUBLISHER

Grateful acknowledgment is made to the publisher, Alfred A. Knopf, Inc., for use of quotations from the copyrighted works of John Updike, and to *The Paris Review* for use of quotations from "The Art of Fiction," in issue no. 45 (Winter 1968) of *The Paris Review*.

To
David,
Andrew,
and Margaret

PREFACE

THIS STUDY HAS BEEN UNDERTAKEN BECAUSE OF OUR conviction that John Updike is one of the most elegant and most serious authors of our age. The artistry of his style is widely recognized, but the seriousness of what he has to say is not so generally admitted. So we have concentrated upon attempting to give an outline of his thought as this emerges from his poems, articles, short stories, and novels.

The temptation to turn aside from exposition to technical criticism has been continually present, but we have tried to resist it. We have said no more about Updike's literary technique than was necessary for explaining how he presents his ideas. Similarly, we have made no effort to place Updike in the context of contemporary literature, or to assess the influence upon him of other writers, past or present. Only those authors from whom he has drawn ideas directly, or whom he has mentioned as being particularly important to him in the formation of his own opinions, have received attention. And in general our aim has not been to strive after any type of completeness, but simply to lay down some guide lines that might help readers to approach Updike's work with some degree of sympathetic understanding.

Our interpretations, of course, are our own responsibility. They may be mistaken in emphasis, incomplete, or even wrong. Every would-be expositor of another person's thinking runs the risk of misrepresenting the author's thoughts because of insensitivity, mistaken presuppositions, ignorance, or personal shortcomings. Our main reason for believing that we have not wholly misread what Updike has communicated through his work is that the "elements" which we have described stand out so strongly and consistently that they seem to demand consideration. Furthermore, whenever Updike speaks in his own person about his convictions and his views on the writer's role, his statements agree with the ideas that appear, in their own right, in his stories and poems.

After our manuscript was completed and ready for press an extremely important interview with Updike appeared in the *Paris Review*. A number of footnotes have been added referring to statements by Updike in this interview having a direct bearing on conclusions to which we had come through our reading of his works, but for which there was no "objective" confirmation. We find particularly revealing, however, Updike's remark in the interview that he is reluctant to speak *about* his works when what he has to say has been said *in* them.

We do not apologize for our enthusiasm. It is with the most intense excitement that we have in the course of our investigation suddenly realized the implications of apparently simple statements in Updike's work. Yet our despair has equalled our excitement. For each time that we have caught an allusion that made us understand the dimension of a thought, we have been made aware of how often we may have *failed* to open "the same door" through which Updike walks.

Our thanks must be given first of all to the Canada Council and to the William B. Eerdmans Publishing Company for grants that allowed us to visit Mr. Updike and his family, and also his parents, Mr. and Mrs. Wesley Updike. Those days we remember with pleasure. Then, too, we owe our thanks to many others who have shown us great courtesy and helped us immensely in our work. To our colleagues and students for patience and toleration as we wrote. To Raymond C. Wright and his staff at the library of the University of Winnipeg; to the librarians at the University of Manitoba; to the librarians at the Houghton and Widener libraries of Harvard — especially to those in the Archives Room of the Widener. And, not least of all, to our friend Dr. C. L. Bennet of Dalhousie University. As editor of the *Dalhousie Review* he has kindly consented to our using in the book an adaptation of the article "Between Innocence and Experience."

ALICE HAMILTON
KENNETH HAMILTON

The University of Winnipeg

CONTENTS

JOHN UPDIKE'S LIFE AND WORKS: SOME DATES

1932　John Updike born in Shillington, Pennsylvania.

1945　Family moves to the farm near Plowville.

1950　Updike enters Harvard.

1951　Begins to write and draw for the *Lampoon*.

1953　Marries Mary Pennington.

1954　Graduates *summa cum laude* in English.

1954-55　At Ruskin School of Drawing and Fine Arts,
Oxford, England.

1954　First short story published in *The New Yorker* ("Friends
from Philadelphia").
Three poems published in *The New Yorker* ("Duet with
Muffled Drums," "Player Piano," "The Clan").

1955-57　Joins the staff of *The New Yorker*.

1957　Moves to Ipswich, Mass.

1958　*The Carpentered Hen and Other Tame Creatures.*

1959　*The Poorhouse Fair.*
The Same Door.

1960　*Rabbit, Run.*

1962　*The Magic Flute,* with Warren Chappell.
Pigeon Feathers.

1963　*Telephone Poles and Other Poems.*
The Centaur.

1964　National Book Award for *The Centaur.*
Updike elected to the National Institute of Arts and Letters.
Visits the Soviet Union on a State Department cultural
exchange.
(*Olinger Stories.*)
The Ring, with Warren Chappell.

1965　*Assorted Prose.*
(*Verse.*)
Of the Farm.
"Dog's Death."

1966　*The Music School.*

1968　*Couples.*
"Bath After Sailing"

11

KEY TO ABBREVIATIONS OF UPDIKE'S BOOKS

AP	*Assorted Prose*
C	*Couples*
CH	*The Carpentered Hen*
MS	*The Music School*
OS	*Olinger Stories*
OTF	*Of the Farm*
PF	*Pigeon Feathers*
RR	*Rabbit, Run*
SD	*The Same Door*
TC	*The Centaur*
TP	*Telephone Poles*
TPHF	*The Poorhouse Fair*

1

BETWEEN INNOCENCE AND EXPERIENCE

An Introduction to Updike's Style of Storytelling

JOHN UPDIKE'S FIRST COLLECTION OF VERSE, THE CAR-
pentered Hen and Other Tame Creatures,[1] contains a series of poems
called "A Cheerful Alphabet of Pleasant Objects: to David for his
edification." Cheerfully, the "Alphabet" begins with this poem:

> *APPLE*
>
> *Since Time began, such alphabets begin*
> *With Apple, source of Knowledge and of Sin.*
> *My child, take heart; the fruit that undid Man*
> *Brought out as well the best in Paul Cézanne.* (p. 70)

The tone of the verse, with its mocking bow to convention and its
light mimicry of heavy moralism, is strongly reminiscent of Hilaire
Belloc's rhymes for children.[2] Like Belloc, Updike believes both religion and art to be subjects a child ought to be introduced to without
false solemnity — they are far too important for that. Pre-Adamic
innocence and Post-Impressionism alike are notions to be added as
early as possible to the intellectual luggage of the boy who is setting
out to explore the interesting world into which he has been born.

Things found in the created world, all the way from A to Z, are
interesting just because they are themselves. Paul Cézanne, for ex-

---

[1] New York, 1958.

[2] Belloc's *Cautionary Verses* are used with telling effect in Updike's *Rabbit,
Run. See below,* pp. 149-50.

ample, took endless pains to record the appleness of apples. Man alone is uncertain of his own nature and can live in contradiction to it. The poem for "C" of "A Cheerful Alphabet" refers to that difference:

COG

Not for him the darkly planned
Ambiguities of flesh.
His maker gave him one command:
Mesh. (p. 71)

Although the ordered structures of the physical universe are endlessly fascinating to him and receive his admiring attention,[3] the ambiguities of flesh are what bring out the best in John Updike. His work constantly takes up the theme of man as the Adam who awakens to a knowledge of his fallen state and to a realization of the immensity of the issues of good and evil.

Perhaps the best way into Updike's writings is to see how he handles this theme in one particular instance. And so this chapter will concentrate upon one of his short stories, "You'll Never Know, Dear, How Much I Love You."

This story appeared first in *The New Yorker* for June 18, 1960, when Updike had already to his credit a number of stories. It was included in the second volume of his short stores, *Pigeon Feathers,*[4] and it was printed later in the paperbound collection *Olinger Stories.*[5] Thus it is a thoroughly representative work, and has the added advantage of belonging to the "Olinger" cycle of stories about growing up in a small Pennsylvania town, a cycle that has a special place in the author's affection.[6] It also displays, quite admirably, several characteristic features of Updike's literary technique.

*   *   *

"You'll Never Know, Dear, How Much I Love You" tells of a child standing between innocence and experience. By the end of the story the child has passed from a stage of intuitive knowledge

---

[3] See, for instance, the recent poem, "The Dance of the Solids," in the *Scientific American,* January 1969, pp. 230-31. This poem is to appear in the forthcoming volume *Midpoint and Other Poems.*

[4] New York, 1962.

[5] New York, 1964.

[6] "... if I had to give anybody one book of me it would be the Vintage *Olinger Stories"* — Updike in an interview with Charles Thomas Samuels, "The Art of Fiction, XLIII: John Updike," in the *Paris Review* (No. 45, Winter 1968, pp. 85-117), p. 93. (The interview is referred to hereafter as *Art.*)

"You'll Never Know, Dear ..." is the opening story in the Olinger collection, which arranges the stories not in the order of writing but according to the age of the central character in each, going from childhood through to young manhood.

into a new stage of understanding concerning his place in the world. The experience is a painful one.

The story is set in Olinger, although the text refers simply to "the town" without further elucidation. Ben, a young boy of ten, wants to go to the fair. This is not a local fair — as in Updike's novel *The Poorhouse Fair* — but a carnival run by strangers. It is held in a vacant lot, littered with mud and straw, behind the old icehouse. "Now, now, gather your pennies," is the urgent command of the fair (*PF*, p. 172). The last hour of daylight is fading before the coming of the artificial glitter of the night. The boy feels he is being held back by the poverty, slowness, and sadness of his parents.

Ben is thus aware of a sense of urgency driving him on. His fear is that he will be left behind while everyone else goes to the fair. His needs are clear to him: to be exalted; to find sweetness; to find light. Where, when, and how to get them, and how to distinguish the true from the false, is his problem. He has to guide him only an instinctive feeling for what he wants, and the "plenty" of fifty cents in his hand with which to purchase ecstasy.

From the outside, the fair seems to promise exaltation. Ben sees the balloon about to take off and the Ferris wheel about to lift from the earth (p. 173). But, once inside the fair, he is at first disappointed. There are no real gypsies, there is no real magic. Popcorn, merry-go-rounds, softballs, and plaster Virgins are available, but do not tempt him. He notices a thickset man with tattooed arms standing by a wheel of fortune and crying, "Hey, uh winneh. Hey, uh winneh, evvybody wins" (p. 174). But few seem to be winning. He wishes there were more people around to bring gaiety. Feeling that his fifty-cent piece must be broken into smaller pieces "to merge in the tinsel and splinters of strewn straw" (p. 174), he buys, for ten cents, a mass of pink, furry candy-floss — sticky sweetness that can enter his body — and is the richer with *three* coins change.

There is magic in the fair, after all. Ben now has triple wealth. And immediately he is granted triple sweetness in three girls wearing white-spangled cowboy costumes, who come onto a lighted stage and offer for nothing their song of love: "You Are My Sunshine." As they sing "The other *night,* dear, as I lay *sleep*ing, I dreamt I *held* you in my *arms,*" he is enthralled by the "unbearable rising sugar of the chorus that makes his scalp so tight he fears his head will burst from sweet fullness" (p. 175). The act that follows, though, makes him uneasy. A skeleton of a man, peeping down inside his baggy pants, tells dirty jokes to nice fat ladies from the town. Although these last look so safe and pleasant, their shaking laughter seems to reveal a "treacherous stratum" under the mud and straw.

Ben finds himself thinking of the words of the song: "Please don't *take* my *sun*shine a*way*" (p. 175).

Then he walks over to the wheel of fortune to offer his all at the shrine of chance. The boy's sense of urgency and longing for sweetness and light have brought him to the fair at the age of ten. Ten cents of his half dollar has gone for floss. The rest of his money he loses, playing the lucky "7" on the wheel. He never changes his fidelity to this number, nor his faith in this game that has promised that everyone is a winner. The tinseled wheel is to him "a moon-faced god." Ben can sense "puzzled pressure" radiating from the man who spins the wheel and thinks that this man is about to say something drastic to him, but he still feels impelled to lose or to gain, to give his devotion to the god of chance and change.

And then the tattooed man at the wheel shatters Ben's little universe. He demands to know how old Ben is and whether his father is rich. He forces on the boy six nickles, withholding one lucky-seventh coin delicately held between thumb and finger for Ben to see. After slipping the retained coin into his pouch, the man orders the boy never to come back to the game of chance.

Ben is oppressed by a sense of "waste" and bitterness, the injustice of being able to have candy-floss for ten cents but nothing at all for the dime that was not returned. To him at the moment "the lost dime seems a tiny hole through which everything in existence is draining" (p. 178). The lights of the fair become blurred by the tears in his eyes as he moves to leave the fair. Updike ends his story with a single sentence of comment: "Thus the world, like a bitter coquette, spurns our attempts to give ourselves to her wholly" (p. 178).

* * *

"You'll Never Know, Dear . . ." is a *short* story — only seven pages in *Pigeon Feathers* — but it exhibits most of the features Updike's readers have come to expect. The narrative is naturalistic. The setting is in a time and place falling within the author's own experience. There is a genuine dramatic development within the story, but it is subtle rather than violent, and concerned more with inward mood than with outward action.[7] Imagery is abundant. And comment outside the narrative line is minimal.

Although Updike obtrudes no verbal obstacles to be surmounted before his stories can be understood, it is one thing to follow his words and another to grasp his deeper meaning. What he intends to say to us has to be discovered from the precise way in which

---

[7] "I try instantly to set in motion a certain forward tilt of suspense or curiosity, and at the end of the story to rectify the tilt, to complete the motion" — Updike (*Art*, p. 96).

the story is told. Some pointers to this meaning are plainly displayed. Others are more obliquely introduced. So reading becomes a kind of treasure hunt, where the prize is the discovery of a richness and complexity in the text which casual attention would leave unrecognized and unappreciated.

The title "You'll Never Know, Dear ..." provides the first clue to the way in which Updike has organized his story. The song of the fair, "You Are My Sunshine," serves to unify the narrative and to identify explicitly its theme as one of dream-and-awakening. Ben's dream is of uniting himself utterly with the world of sweetness and light to be found at the fair. When he first becomes conscious of the "treacherous stratum" underlying the mud and straw upon which the world of the fair is built, it is the plaintive words of the song that revolve in his head: *please don't take my sunshine away.* His plea is that he not be awakened from a dream he fears may dissolve. His final disgrace before the crowd at the fair, when he is "exposed" by the tattooed man, is actually a recapitulation of the verse he has heard:

> The other night, dear, as I lay sleeping,
> I dreamt I held you in my arms.
> When I awoke, dear, I was mistaken.
> And I hung my head and cried.

Ben's dream belongs to the night ruled by the "moon-faced god" of the wheel of fortune. Ben wakes, hangs his head, and cries.

The song of the fair also tells us the cause of Ben's awakening. Updike does not explicitly quote the relevant words, but he expects the reader to recall them:

> You told me once, dear, you really loved me,
> And no one else could come between.
> But now you've left me and love another.
> You have shattered all my dreams.

The man at the stall appears to Ben in the guise of "humanity clouding the space between them that should be unobstructed" (p. 176). The tattooed man *comes between* Ben and his love, the world of the fair, which is ruled over by the god of the wheel of fortune. Sent away by this intervening figure, Ben feels deserted by the world he has wooed with such singleminded fidelity, and his dreams are shattered.

Dreams are limitless, but the waking world is strictly bounded by finite actualities; and it is other people — humanity — who call us back to the limits of the actual. (Hence the persuasiveness of Sartre's famous epigram in *No Exit:* "Hell is other people.") When Ben first encounters "the stare of heartbreaking brown blankness" of the man at the wheel of fortune, he is aware that the man "seems to elucidate with paralyzing clarity Ben's state: his dungarees, his fifty cents, his ten years, his position in space, and above the particulars the immense tinted pity, the waste, of being at one little place instead of everywhere, at any time" (p. 174). If the song of the fair describes Ben's dream and the disillusionment of his awakening, it is the thickset figure of the tattooed man who represents the human condition that Ben has to learn to accept realistically instead of romantically. "Humanity" cannot be ignored.

Ben comes to the fair to escape from the poverty, sadness, and slowness of adults. He wants to be where everything is dominated by fortune and chance, which is why he comes to the tinseled wheel and plays always on the lucky 7 — the magic number, symbol of the perfect and the unlimited. The man at the stall will not let him stay there, where infinite freedom beckons, and with seeming cruelty brings him back to his position in space and makes him admit his poverty and littleness. And it is the man's deliberately retaining the coin which he drops in his pouch that hurts Ben most sorely. "They" pretend to feel sorry for you because you are little, so Ben thinks, and then "they" cheat you (p. 178). Ben had yearned for the infinite, only to find his whole dream world draining down a hole precisely the size of a dime.

Nevertheless, when "humanity" forces Ben to turn back from the quest for the infinite and to face the finitude of actual living, the lesson — though harsh — is not unjust. Ben realizes early on in the story that his parents have given him, as his sum to go to the fair, one nickel for each year of his life (p. 173). In holding back a dime, the man at the stall makes the boy pay double for the year of his knowledge. He brings the unwelcome news that experience is a costly commodity, that there is a price to pay for leaving the innocence of childhood behind and seeking to enter "the world."

In ending his story by comparing "the world" to a "bitter coquette" Updike might seem to be preaching cynicism. Is the passage from innocence to experience simply the shattering of a dream and the awakening to a limited existence where you must spend much and gain always less than you expect? Updike has an answer to this question, though he does not spell it out in so many words. The answer is given in his picture of "humanity." The figure of the man at the stall is an enigma to Ben, who hears in fascination his announcement that everyone is a winner, and who feels uneasy under his stare of "heartbreaking brown blankness." Ben sees the tattoo marks on the man's arm: a fish, an anchor, and "the queer word PEACE." When the man drops the retained coin into his pouch he first pauses, so that Ben can read the word PEACE before he counts his change and finds that he has been — as he thinks — "gypped."

Ben is too young to know that the tattoo marks are Christian symbols, signs familiar to the early Christians in the catacombs. Yet that is what they are: the fish represents Christ, the anchor represents faith, and the word PEACE was the greeting of the early Christian community. The enigma presented by humanity is not to be deciphered by one possessing no more than Ben's small stock of knowledge of existence, and it is misread as much by those who pass from disillusionment into cynicism as by those who are in the thrall of romantic illusions. Indeed, there is a quality of self-forgetfulness in those who seek to worship at the shrine of a god, even if the god be a false one, that is absent in those who think themselves wise in the ways of "the world" and pride themselves on not being taken in by it.

Standing between innocence and experience, Ben is at the point where the future is open. He can stop at the stage of partial knowledge, the stage of disillusionment and distrust, or he can go on to a more complete knowledge, a knowledge of joy found through sorrow. The man at the stall has forced the mature truth on the immature boy, namely, that fortune's lie, "Hey, uh winneh, evvybody wins," is not necessarily false. The paradoxical reality is that gain is loss and loss is gain for those who can endure the shattering of dreams and the taking away of sweetness and light. Permanently marked on humanity's arm is the shorthand message of One who has overcome "the world": "My peace I give to you, not as the world gives . . ." (John 14:27).

* * *

"You'll Never Know, Dear" contains within itself, as do Updike's other stories, all the clues needed to grasp its meaning. However, we must bring to it the equipment needed to recognize and follow up those clues. We have to be familiar with Christian symbols, for example, and know our way around the New Testament. And it helps if we remember the lyrics of popular songs well enough to be able to pick up, after being given the words of one verse, the echoes of another.

Updike expects his readers to be literate. He assumes that references to world literature — to the Bible, to Boethius, to Beatrix Potter — will be recognized without being laboriously spelled out. In the greater part of Updike's work, indeed, there is a dialogue between the story he tells and other stories on the same theme that have established themselves within our cultural heritage and have helped to shape the Western imagination. Sometimes this dialogue is explicit; more often it is not.[8] In "You'll Never Know, Dear" the theme of the world as a fair inevitably harks back to the classic presentation of Vanity Fair in Bunyan's *The Pilgrim's Progress*.[9] Yet a more intimate link seems to exist between Updike's story and James Joyce's "Araby," from *Dubliners*, which itself contains clear reminiscences of Bunyan.

Critics have remarked that Updike's early stories have much the same flavor as *Dubliners*, and Updike shows an intimate knowledge of Joyce's works.[10] The resemblances between "Araby" and "You'll Never Know, Dear" are very strong in subject matter, situation, and even in some incidental details. If the points of contact between these two stories are coincidental only, or the result of wholly unconscious recollections of "Araby," that would be most surprising. But even if Joyce's story in no way influenced Updike, the convergences and divergences in their treatment of a common theme still make a comparison of the pair informative.

"Araby" tells of a boy (unnamed) who, like Ben, arrives late at a fair he has been eagerly anticipating and has been held back from reaching earlier by the slowness of adults.

He comes hoping to buy a gift for the sister of a school friend, a girl he worships with childish devotion. But the fair, though it carries the exotic name of "Araby," proves to be a most commonplace affair set in a big, unbeautiful Dublin hall. The boy sees nothing he can buy at the bazaar. Disillusioned, he is ashamed and angry with himself and the world.

Thus both Joyce and Updike write of a boy at a fair who sets out with urgency and expectation only to find disappointment and frustration. And like Ben, Joyce's boy holds three coins in his hand when he begins to look round the stalls. But at that moment, whereas

---

[8] In the *Paris Review* Updike is asked why *The Centaur*, which makes a constant parallel between the life of a Pennsylvania high school teacher and the Greek myth of Chiron, is his only work in this "mode." Updike replies that it is not. He is then asked why, if he has used such parallels elsewhere, he has not made them more explicit. Updike comments: "I don't think basically such parallels should be obvious. I think books should have secrets, like people do. I think they should be there as a bonus for the sensitive reader, or there as a kind of subliminal quivering" (*Art*, p. 104).

[9] The Vanity Fair episode in *The Pilgrim's Progress* is quite explicitly drawn upon by Updike for the subject of one of his poems, "Mr. High-Mind" (*CH*, pp. 42-43).

[10] Updike refers to Joyce when speaking of authors who, like himself, have derived special inspiration from memories of their own youth. See *Art*, p. 94. For a technical discussion of Joyce's art by Updike see the essay "Questions Concerning Giacomo" in *The New Yorker* (April 6, 1968), pp. 167-68, 171-74. In this essay Updike suggests that Joyce presented his characters better in *Dubliners* than elsewhere.

the Olinger boy feels himself infinitely rich after changing his money, the boy in "Araby" considers that he has already been robbed. He has had to pay for transport to the fair and then was forced to spend one shilling of his original two shillings to get in, for there was no cheap admission price for children. And he finds nothing worth buying with the sixpence and two pennies he has left to spend.

What has drawn the Dublin boy to the fair is the magic that he felt must materialize out of its romantic name. Like Ben, he comes to give rather than to get. Yet all his expectations are based on a wholly ideal vision, one that must inevitably vanish at the touch of hard reality. He sees himself in relation to his pure and remote love as a devotee with a chalice in his hand and prayers and praises on his lips. He will bring back, so he has promised, "something" from Araby. The disillusioning experience lies in the passage from the ideal Araby to the actual Araby, from fancy to fact. Araby proves to be no magical or sanctified place. It contains nothing worthy of being a love-offering. The large hall, in its near emptiness at this late hour, reminds him of a church after the service has ended. The girl looking after the stall that he approaches speaks with a foreign, English voice; and he hears her say to another adult a sentence in which the word "fib" sounds emphatically. Vanity Fair has dragged down the ideal to the level of a common lie.

Joyce's story draws on both Bunyan and the Bible to make its effects. The boy's passage from innocence to experience is marked by references to the Garden of Eden, where man's first fall from innocence took place, and also to the money-changers in the Temple — symbolic of the invasion of the sacred by the profane. The boy entering Araby, like Bunyan's pilgrims entering Vanity Fair, is conscious of the "foreign" language spoken there. (Bunyan describes how Christian and Faithful, because they speak the language of Zion, are not understood by the men of the fair.) In this alien environment Joyce's boy sees himself as one "driven and derided by vanity," which is a description applying precisely to the experience of Bunyan's pilgrims.

Joyce makes use of Christian parallels solely to present the opposition between two antithetical approaches to reality. For him it adds up to the same thing whether we label the contrast otherworldliness-worldliness, sacred-profane, idealism-cynicism, utopianism-realism, or innocence-experience. We are dealing in every case with the human desire to live in a world of dreams that is frustrated by the actual world contradicting those dreams. Updike also tells the story of this perennial human experience. *You have shattered all my dreams* is the desolate lesson which Ben learns from the song of the fair. At the same time, "You'll Never Know, Dear" is a far more

complex story than "Araby" because Updike's boy is not the singleminded romantic that Joyce's boy is, but one whose sensitivity is
far more open to the actual world around him in spite of his lack
of experience of its ways. This complexity makes itself felt in the
tone of Updike's story which, though it has its own pathos, contains too many touches of irony to be as directly pathetic as "Araby."
Instead of a head-on collision between the ideal and the actual,
"You'll Never Know, Dear" presents a dialectical relationship between the two.

For the boy in "Araby" the uncomplicated truth is that money
does not buy dreams. His ignorance is made wise, to his own shame,
because he is young enough and vain enough to think such a purchase
possible. His first contact with actualities defeats him. Ben too meets
an initial shock of disappointment over the lack of magic in a half-
empty fair; yet, instead of despairing, he continues to search. *Seek
and you shall find.* Ben's faith in the fair is childish and naive, but
at the same time has the quality of perseverance indicative of all
genuine faith. The boy is rewarded, for a short while, and this makes
his final disillusionment all the more bitter. Nevertheless, his consciousness has never been one of simple self-satisfaction or of hope
unclouded by fear. He has been acutely aware of the "treacherous
stratum" underlying the world of the fair; he has been acutely aware
that the happiness he has found in that world may be taken from
him. When he finds everything pouring down a tiny, dime-sized hole,
his fears are agonizingly confirmed. His tears climax the working out
of those dualities in existence that he has already discovered. He
realizes that choices in life are never simple or free from risk, but
he is too young to estimate the full complexity of living and to continue through loss to gain. As Updike says in *Rabbit, Run,* it takes
"the mindful will to walk the straight line of a paradox" (p. 237).
Ben has the will, but not the mind to help him in his moment of
exposure by the tattooed man at the stall.

The interplay of dualities and the experience of life as a series of
paradoxes bulk large in Updike's fiction. This is the result of his
viewing the world in the perspective of Christian faith. Taking such
a stance, he does not simply use Christian motifs (as Joyce does)
in order to point to the universality of the fall from the ideal to
the actual, from the sacred to the profane. He sees existence as that
which simultaneously hides and reveals the truth about itself, since
truth ultimately lies beyond the bounds of space and time and yet
must be grasped by creatures who are temporally and spatially limited. Thus he regards the passage from innocence to experience as
neither a triumph nor a disaster, as neither a casting off of foolish

illusion nor a fall from eternity into time. Insofar as innocence means an intuition of the eternal and the sacred, men should never travel so far away from it that they cannot return to the vision it gives;[11] and, insofar as experience means encounter with the actual world in all its ambiguity and complexity, men should never turn away from it under the impression that they can somehow escape the risks inherent in the human condition.

On one level, "You'll Never Know, Dear" is a realistic story of a ten-year-old's disappointment when he is forced to leave a child's imaginative universe and return to the factual one inhabited by adults. He had hurried to get away from a life that was slow, poor, and sad. The tinseled world of the fair provided a momentary glimpse into the land of heart's desire. But "they" would not allow him to remain there, calling him back to his poverty and sending him walking slowly and sadly home. In his own experience, Ben recapitulated the rapture and disillusionment described in the song of the fair.

On another level Updike's story is a parable of the human condition. It tells of man's infinite desires and of his persistent illusion that he can make a deal with fate in order to achieve their realization. Updike's suggestion is not that our dreams are too large but that they are misplaced. We rightly seek the eternal and the sacred, but we seek them in the wrong way, imagining that through the intensity of our willing we must be granted fulfilment; whereas we will find our peace, not in devotion to the god of chance, but in the paradoxical discovery that gain comes through loss, and to lose our life is to find it.

Young as he is, Ben intuitively knows part of the lesson. He has seen high school boys win at the wheel of fortune, and then walk away as though they had heard a dirty joke (p. 174). He knows that happiness must come through giving all that you have, not in getting. He knows that you must choose your god and worship at his shrine without expecting immediate reward. What he does not know is the name of the god who gives peace. Here the difference between his story and "Araby" is noteworthy. Joyce's boy is presented as a pilgrim of the ideal, one to whom the language of Vanity Fair is a foreign tongue. Ben is anxious to belong to Vanity Fair, to learn its songs and share its exaltation, even though he senses the treachery in its promises. It is the language of Zion that is strange to him. He is puzzled by "the queer word PEACE" (p. 176) on the man's arm. What he seeks is sweetness and light, which he

---

[11] The progressive flight from eternity as we grow older is the theme of the passage from Kafka's "A Report to an Academy" prefixed to *Pigeon Feathers.*

finds conjoined in the song of the fair, where the sugared sweetness of the song issues from white-clothed figures — the angel-choir of Vanity Fair — standing at the "core" of a light that has blotted out the "black forbidding silhouettes" of the houses of Olinger (p. 174).

Now the pursuit of sweetness and light is Matthew Arnold's definition of the pursuit of perfection. In well-known words in *Culture and Anarchy* he says that sweetness and light are the ideals of Hellenism, ideals that have been neglected in our culture because of the prevailing tradition of Hebraic moralism. Updike suggests that Hellenic sweetness and light will not satisfy the human heart, which needs to put first the Hebraic quality of *shalom* (peace). Young Ben, of course, knows nothing of Hebraism, Hellenism, or Matthew Arnold's brand of cultural humanism derived from the Enlightenment. But Updike does, and we do. Ben, in his quest for deliverance from poverty, slowness, and sadness, represents all unconsciously the course taken by Western society, since it has largely turned away from "the way that leads to peace" (Luke 19:42), the Judeo-Christian faith.

Ben is the youngest of Updike's fictional heroes, but all the rest encounter his problem — or some aspect of it — and try to cope with it according to the insights they happen to possess. Sometimes they are wiser than Ben is. But often they are less wise, for Updike does not imagine that added years or wider experience necessarily bring extra wisdom. Rather, perplexities become more far-reaching and the consequences of folly more serious. For example, Updike's latest novel, *Couples,* takes a searching look at a segment of contemporary American society and concludes that the chief preoccupation here is with more sophisticated forms of buying candy-floss and with betting on the lucky 7 — otherwise known as "tempting fate." As much as Ben, this society stands to be reminded of its position in space and time; and the reminder will certainly come, mediated through the implacable forces of history, though the cost may well be world catastrophe instead of one small dime.

One Updike story links with others, because Updike presents at all times a consistent universe where men reap what they sow and are rewarded by the god at whose shrine they serve, according to the nature of that god. The purpose of the present study is to give some account of the elements to be found in that universe, and "You'll Never Know, Dear" provides a useful preliminary glimpse of the riches of the ground to be worked. Almost any other story might have been chosen instead, but this one illustrates with particular clarity how Updike can take an incident of seemingly slight importance and invite the reader to see within it a microcosm of the human condition. "You'll Never Know, Dear" shows how in every

individual Adam eats anew the apple of the knowledge of good and
evil; how, once man has come to the point where he must leave the
innocence of Eden, he is forced to make choices having consequences
that his small stock of knowledge is inadequate to foresee, so that
experience exacts its price; and how every choice is ultimately a
decision between desolating idolatry and faith in the true God who
gives the gift of peace.

Updike is a writer, not a preacher or a moralist. But he reports
on the world as he sees it; and the real world, in his estimate, is
only fitfully perceived by the inhabitants of Vanity Fair since their
vision of "the world" is limited to that part of actuality that is ruled
by chance and fortune. The loss of innocence is inevitable for every
son of Adam who accepts the challenge of life as it opens before
him. But if he thoughtlessly rushes to embrace "the world," he will
be left with tears of bitterness; unless he has the mindful will to
walk the straight line of a paradox leading to where time and the
eternal are reconciled and the night of weeping yields to the morning of joy.

2

WRITER'S
WORLD

THE SHORT STORY CONSIDERED AT LENGTH IN THE previous chapter shows how Updike is much more than a retailer of the small change of naturalistic fiction and is better seen as a teller of parables. When a writer is concerned to bring out meaning other than the one that first meets the eye, it does not, however, follow that he is indifferent to verisimilitude in externals. Quite the contrary. In order to give his work integrity and make perfectly clear the truth he wishes to expose, he is likely to be extremely careful about constructing a framework thoroughly convincing on the literal level. Thus in *Dubliners* Joyce drew heavily on his actual memories of the Dublin in which he grew up. The home of the boy in "Araby," for example, was the Joyce family home, No. 17 North Richmond Street, exactly as described in the story.

Updike follows the same pattern, developing it to an even greater extent than Joyce did, since he has not gone on to imitate Joyce's experimentations in the extra-naturalistic use of words. Updike's readers soon become familiar with the members of his family over a couple of generations; with the two homes he knew as a boy — the first in the small town of Shillington, Pennsylvania, the second, near Plowville, a few miles away in the country; with the high school where he was a student and where his father taught; and with his subsequent career at Harvard, at Oxford, in New York City, and in a small New England town thirty miles out of Boston. They learn that he spends holidays in the West Indies, that he has been on a government-sponsored cultural visit behind the Iron Curtain, that he attends church, that he is fond of cats, and that he once wished to earn his living by drawing rather than by writing. They find that his characters tend to be exactly the same age as their creator at the time he is writing their story, that they share the same background, and that their family matches his, even to the sex and spacing in age.

It all seems so much a transcript of private experience that many of Updike's critics tend to resist the idea that his work belongs to the parabolic mode rather than the naturalistic. Only very occasionally will he depart from strict realism in his narrative. Even his poetry is largely descriptive, and seems to be whimsical rather than imaginative. So the critical applause that greeted his early work on account of his sensitive treatment of childhood scenes, his precise observation of middle-class family life with its little triumphs and disasters, and his fresh and nimble and brilliantly controlled style, grew fainter as his books appeared regularly without any obvious development in subject matter or content. And the chorus of discontent began to swell (since critics read other critics, and huddle together for warmth), suggesting that he just did not have enough to say to qualify for the title of a "serious" writer. True, the charge of being a purveyor of childhood reminiscences and slight family scenes has been modified since the recent appearance of *Couples*,[1] a novel on a strictly contemporary theme. *Time* magazine put his picture on the cover and ran a feature article on him when the novel was published and immediately became a best seller. Now the complaint has been altered to one of sensationalism, and *Couples* is described as a *Peyton Place* for the literary set. His style is admitted to be as striking as ever; but he is accused of overwriting and undercharacterization.

Updike's authorship takes on quite another aspect when it is seen from the perspective of symbol instead of naturalistic narrative. The writer Henry Bech, an Updike character who appears in three short stories, explains in "The Bulgarian Poetess" that his first novel had begun with showing people "skimming the surface of things with their lives" but that later "he had attempted to place beneath the melody of plot a countermelody of imagery."[2] We do not have to identify Bech directly with his creator to understand that Updike here is speaking about a literary device with which he himself is quite familiar. We may note in passing that Updike also introduces Bech right from the start as an author who has won immediate success with his first novel, the subsequent ones being judged disappointing and proof of a deplorable decline. Bech is pursued by all the questionable benefits of fame, including "flat-foot exegetes."

[1] New York, 1968.
[2] *The Music School* (New York, 1966), p. 228.

This is the nearest Updike gets to protesting against the way he has been received.[3]

To follow the "countermelody of imagery" will be the chief concern of the present study. But the fact that Updike believes that it makes sense to try to link meaning, through imagery, with meaning in a narrative line has to be considered too. Even if the surface of his stories gives only the lesser part of his intention, this does not mean that the surface is irrelevant, or that any melody at all would serve as the sufficient foil to the countermelody. The two levels of his fiction, the literal and the symbolic, are mutually dependent. And so we must consider Updike's view of the universe in which such a unity of different levels of meaning can be achieved by literary art.

Updike is a writer, a maker of fables, not a philosopher, psychologist, theologian or fabricator of metaphysical systems. Yet he is no devotee of spontaneous inspiration either. He does not seek to emulate Keats' nightingale and simply pour out his heart. He draws ideas from many quarters: Aristotle, Dante, Pascal, Kierkegaard, Freud, Kafka, de Rougemont, and Karl Barth. He has a high estimate of human intelligence, and a belief that every individual can use it to discover the kind of world he is living in. The givenness of an intelligible (though mystery-laden) universe, and the questioning mind of the individual who can respond to the given — these are the poles between which Updike slings his creative vision. In sharp contrast to despairing or defiant dogmatists who proclaim this terrestrial stage to be a cosmic Theater of the Absurd, he finds the world of nature and of man to be a place of intricate and marvelous patterns of meaning.

Being a writer, Updike is concerned with the individual vision, the uniquely personal report about the world which the artist, as distinct from the theoretician, feels impelled to provide. This is the root of his preoccupation with his own childhood and adolescence. He has pointed to this aspect of his writing most plainly in "The Dogwood Tree: A Boyhood," an essay first published in *Five Boyhoods*[4] and reprinted in *Assorted Prose*.[5] There he writes, "The difference between a childhood and a boyhood must be this: our child-

---

[3] He has not allowed critical opinion to deflect him from his writer's course. Asked by the interviewer in the *Paris Review* interview whether the common complaint that he had "ducked large subjects" led to his writing *Couples*, he replied: "I wrote *Couples* because the rhythm of my life and oeuvre demanded it, not to placate hallucinatory critical voices" (*Art,* pp. 100 01).

[4] Edited by Martin Levin (New York, 1962).

[5] New York, 1965.

hood is what we alone have had; our boyhood is what any boy in our environment would have had" (*AP, p. 165*).

The environment of a small town in Pennsylvania meant for this boyhood an exceptionally strong sense of security and order in the universe. Updike records in "The Dogwood Tree" how, as he grew up, he saw hardly any changes going on around him and hardly glimpsed the reasons for the seeming invulnerability of his life. "The immutability, the steadfastness, of the site of my boyhood was an exceptional effect, purchased for me at unimaginable cost by the paralyzing calamity of the Depression and the heroic external effort of the Second World War" (*AP, p. 165*). Shillington, situated between the open country and the industrial town of Reading, appears in his fiction — accurately drawn down to the details of its streets, stores, schools, and open spaces — as Olinger,[6] situated between the open country and the industrial town of Alton. Plowville carries the fictional name of Firetown. We can understand why Updike says that Olinger is for him "a state of mind, of my mind, and belongs entirely to me."[7] Growing up in Shillington created an internal vision of measured meaning:

> For the city and the woods and the ominous places were peripheral; their glamour and menace did not intrude into the sunny area where I lived, where the seasons arrived like issues of a magazine and I moved upward from grade to grade and birthday to birthday on a notched stick that itself was held perfectly steady. There was the movie house, the playground, and the schools, and the grocery stores, and our yard, and my friends, and the horse-chestnut trees. My geography went like this: in the center of the world lay our neighborhood of Shillington. Around it there was greater Shillington, and around that, Berks County. Around Berks County there was the State of Pennsylvania, the best, the least eccentric, state in the Union. Around Pennsylvania, there was the United States, with a greater weight of people on the right and a greater weight of land on the left. For clear geometric reasons, not all children could be born, like me, at the center of the nation. But that some children chose to be born in other countries and even continents seemed sad and fantastic. There was only one possible nation: mine. Above this vast, rectangular, slightly (the schoolteacher insisted) curved field of the blessed, there was the sky, and the flag, and, mixed up with both, Roosevelt. (*AP, pp. 162-63*)

---

[6] Updike insists that Olinger is to be pronounced "with a long O, a hard G, and the emphasis on the first syllable." So the town says, "Oh linger!" Updike, having lingered in his early memories through eleven short stories, said his good-bye to his youthful "state of mind" with the novel *The Centaur*, even though he wrote his final Olinger story some time after that.

[7] *Olinger Stories: A Selection*, Foreword V (New York, 1964).

In this account of his earliest convictions, Updike asks our amused tolerance for the naiveté of the vision, but also asks our serious understanding of how important it still is for him — and should be for us. Childish oversimplification of the pattern of the world can easily be corrected. Lack of any insight into the human way of understanding our existence cannot. In his work we find Updike's mature intelligence playing upon the same elements that composed his boyhood belief in a geometry inclusive of land and people, private existence and public rule. The result brings these elements into a complex unity that allows us to see our age with a clarity rarely achieved these days.

In Shillington Updike received his understanding of the unity of things within a graspable pattern not simply through his place in a physical environment. That place gained its firm contours in the first instance through the inner security he knew through his family. He was later to speak of his work having to do with "middleness," and middleness was revealed to him by the fact of his father's being a teacher at Shillington High School.

> I felt neither prosperous nor poor. We kept the food money in a little recipe box on top of the icebox, and there were nearly always a few bills and coins in it. My father's job paid him poorly but me well; it gave me a sense of, not prestige, but *place*. As a schoolteacher's son, I was assigned a role: people knew me. When I walked down the street to school, the houses called, "Chonny." I had a place to be. (*AP,* p. 166)

The sense of place was his consciousness of having a role in the community, and thus more than geographical location. Updike's geometry of existence had its inward aspect intersecting with its outward one. The houses — those social symbols planted in Shillington soil — knew him as an individual. His father was more than the nominal bearer of a social position, too, for he was "a conscientious man, a schoolteacher and a deacon, and also, somehow, a man of the streets" (*AP,* p. 152). The pattern of life flowered for Updike the schoolboy in various dimensions.

It was through his family, too, that he was introduced to the dimension of time. "The Dogwood Tree" gets its title from the tree that was planted by his parents and his mother's parents when he was born. He learned that it was exactly his age, "was, in a sense, me," and had it died, he says, "I would have felt that a blessing like the blessing of light had been withdrawn from my life" (*AP,* p. 151). An only child, he found the unchanging pattern of his home, centered around the four adults and himself, of a piece with the unchanging Shillington around him. But from the family conversation he learned of the times before he was born. He came to know that the tensions existing between his mother and her father had been duplicated many years before, by misunderstandings between his grandfather and *his* father. He also learned that his father had not always been a schoolteacher living in the same home with his mother's parents. Wesley Updike had lost his position as a cable splicer with the telephone company early in the Depression, and the move to his father-in-law's large white house in Shillington was arranged to make possible the sharing of costs. He did not gain his position at the high school until after his son's first birthday.[8]

Time means change. This Updike knew through others speaking about it. In the street where he lived there had been two violent deaths — one the result of a runaway milkcart, and the other a suicide by shooting. Yet the actuality of these and other changes did not come home to him until he was thirteen and the Updikes moved away from Shillington ten miles out into the country to the farm where his mother had been born. This is the event with which "The Dogwood Tree" ends. Parted from this other self, the boy realized that change is real. But even then, he would not allow the necessity for change to destroy his unity of vision. "I turned away before it [the tree] would have disappeared from sight; and so it is that my shadow has always remained in one place" (*AP*, p. 127).

Time for Updike manifested itself principally in continuity rather than in division. Pappy Shilling, the son of the landowner after whom Shillington had been named, was to be seen walking up and down the main street every day, "a vibrating chain of perfect-Sunday-school-attendance pins dangling from his lapel," while the trees shed and regained their leaves regularly with the passing seasons, and the view from the white house remained always the same (*AP*, p. 154). A similar continuity extended into other areas as well — into politics, for instance. The family was solidly Democratic. "My grandfather lived for ninety years, and always voted, and always voted straight Democrat. A marvelous chain of votes, as marvelous as the chain of Sunday-school-attendance pins that vibrated from

[8] Some of these details have been taken from "Flight," one of the stories in *Pigeon Feathers*. Allen Dow, his father Victor, his mother Lillian, and Grandpa and Grandma Baer in this story seem to be exact replicas of the Updikes and the Hoyers. Victor Dow, for example, is described as "the penniless younger son of a Presbyterian minister" (*PF*, p. 54). At the same time, as Updike himself points out (*OS*, Foreword, VIII-IX), the stories do not reproduce reality with full consistency in external matters of fact. In "Flight," the grandmother is dead at the time the story is told, while in "Pigeon Feathers," the grandmother is living, and the grandfather is dead. Moreover, sometimes the "Firetown" home is placed right in Olinger and other times it varies between ten miles, four miles, and one mile away from Olinger.

Pappy Shilling's lapel" (*AP*, p. 163). From his parents Updike learned how Roosevelt had changed the fortunes of America. "At the time when I was conceived and born," he says, "they felt in themselves a whole nation stunned, frightened, despairing. With Roosevelt, hope returned. This simple impression of salvation is my political inheritance. That this impression is not universally shared amazes me. It is as if there existed a class of people who deny that the sun is bright" (*AP*, p. 163). So "Roosevelt was for me the cap on a steadfast world, its emblem and crown. He was always there."[9]

It was this initiation into the reality of continuity with the past that enabled Updike, when the need to face the divisions which change brings came with the wider experience of adolescence, to integrate change also into his inner landscape.

A strong belief in the unchanging values of a stable world can lead easily to rapid disillusionment if conditions happen to change or the familiar environment suddenly disappears. That Updike never passed into either of the states such disillusionment commonly assumes — nihilistic rebellion on one hand, or frightened, conservative reaction on the other — may be attributed to the humane sanity of his home, where there was the undergirding of constant affection and understanding. But the very real clashes of temperament in that home must have played a large part also. From the first the boy was aware that life is not all of a piece, that any unity we find in it is not a seamless garment without flaws and fitting all persons alike, and that around the edges of the familiar and the safe lie areas of the unknown and the fearful.

At the beginning of "The Dogwood Tree" there is a description

---

[9] The importance of the American president in giving a definite stamp to his country during his years in office was an early impression that stayed with Updike. The image of the "crown" which he uses in connection with Roosevelt is not a casual one, for the occupant of the White House is in a very real sense the "monarch" whose "royal house" sets the moral, emotional, and intellectual tone of America during his "reign."

The *Paris Review* interviewer tells Updike, "So far as I can see, American history is normally absent from your work." This remark calls from Updike the strong rejoinder: "Not so; quite the contrary. In each of my novels, a precise year is given and a President reigns ... the social currents it traces are as specific to those years as flowers in a meadow are to their moment of summer" (*Art*, p. 105). Thus, *Rabbit, Run* is an Eisenhower book; *The Centaur* a Truman one; and *Couples* "could have taken place only under Kennedy."

One of the reasons why Updike's work has been so consistently underestimated lies in the widespread misapprehension that Updike concentrates upon the personal vision and ignores the larger context of contemporary life. In point of fact, Updike engages the social and political levels of consciousness — together with the personal — more successfully than almost any other living author in America.

of the well-kept back yard of the Shillington house, the yard ending
in a space with "an ungrateful quality" where chickens were kept
(and decapitated by the grandmother) and where an ash heap col-
ored the ground grey. A cat named Tommy, and later a squirrel
named Timmy, used to come to be fed, but neither creatures be-
longed to the household. Even Tommy, says Updike, "was too
wild to set foot in the kitchen, and only my grandmother, in a
way wild herself, could touch him" (*AP,* p. 154). From this simple
introduction to the untamed elements of nature intruding into ordered
existence, Updike seems to have grasped the truth of the world's
not being at all a simple place to be arranged tidily and bent to our
desires.

Increasingly he discovered, in addition, how human beings add
the dissonance of wills to the unruly complexities of the natural
order. Within his own family there was a notable tension between
a rural and an urban outlook. His mother's father had been raised
in the country, as had been many of their neighbors in Shillington.
His grandmother had early worked in the fields, and all her life
kept the looks and wild quality of "an Arab" (*PF,* pp. 51, 58).
Buying a big house in the fashionable part of Shillington was her
husband's choice, not hers — nor her daughter's. And when the
short time of prosperity was ended by the Depression, it was her
daughter's initiative that took them back to the Hoyer farm. Though
the move seemed to have economic advantages, Wesley Updike, a
"man of the streets," had no strong inclination for a country life.

John Updike himself knew that he had none of the instinct for
the country that his mother and his grandmother had so strongly.
Even when his parents took him for walks in the country that
bordered Shillington, he felt alien to the country sights and sounds.
"I was a small-town child," he says. "Cracked pavements and packed
dirt were my ground" (*AP,* p. 158). He felt the attraction of the
smells of the completely urban Reading. "Reading's smells were
most of what my boyhood knew of the Great World that was suspended, at a small but sufficient distance, beyond my world" (*AP,*
p. 162). Since then, he has moved through the Great World beyond Reading only to learn that, in its preoccupation with bigger
things, it ignores altogether the city he thought so wonderfully
filled with riches and power. "Reading . . . who had ever heard of
it? . . . Yet," he says, "to me Reading is the master of cities, the
one at the center that all others echo" (*AP,* p. 162).

Here we arrive at another discovery he made in his boyhood,
though this one seems to have been made gradually. It was the
discovery of the solitary nature of the individual and of the wholly
personal shape of his vision of the world. Nothing was to be more

important to him as a writer than the realization that we are, each of us, by ourselves; each of us is equipped with his own peculiar set of memories and each is stained through and through by the quality of those memories. True, the memories are social ones as well as individual (of *boyhood* as well as of *childhood,* to follow his terms), but the combination is always unique and private. As he says, speaking of his feelings as a father of children: "My own sense of the abyss of childhood doesn't come at all from being their father, it comes from having *been* a child. We're all so curiously alone. But it's important to keep making signals through the glass."[10]

No doubt being an only child contributed to Updike's sense of man's final loneliness, the loneliness that is not banished by all the bonds of family, neighborhood, and country that make one feel himself a social animal. The odd rise and decay of friendship receives due attention in "The Dogwood Tree," as do those places of social gatherings in his boyhood — the playground and the movie house. Whether because of his being in the company of adults at home or because of his imaginative temperament (or because of a combination of both), Updike never seems to have been entirely at ease among his peers. At any rate, his fictional *persona* speaks of being simultaneously accepted and rejected by the town. He was allowed to join in communal outings only in the capacity of clown, until his family's moving into the country "at last" gained him friends (*PF,* pp. 66, 236). Thus the sense of place had its limits, as had the sense of solidarity within the family that made him feel that its five members were "locked into a star that would have shattered like crystal at the admission of a sixth" (*AP,* p. 154). The limits were drawn by the stubborn apartness of each individual, whose fears and hopes and dreams could not be comfortably assimilated to the life history of those around him. The "curious aloneness" of every human existence turns for consolation and support to the company of others, yet is aware every moment of its single destiny that is turned towards death.

So we can appreciate the reason why Updike, like many other writers, turns back continually to his boyhood and his boyhood environment. The only consciousness he knows completely is his own, the being that has been formed by a peculiar set of "accidents" that could only have arisen in one particular period. The only landscape he knows thoroughly, both externally and internally, is the landscape that gave shape to his individual vision.

Nevertheless, Updike shows surprisingly little of the narcissism

---

10 Jane Howard, "Can a Nice Novelist Finish First?" *Life,* November 4, 1966, p. 74.

that has characterized the majority of "autobiographical" novelists. He is no romantic, believing that inner experience is always (just because it has bubbled up within our consciousness) "worth telling about." If an experience has *been,* then it has some value. But its serviceableness to the writer is determined by its having light to throw upon the pattern of *human existence,* the interrelatedness of different aspects of experience that can be understood by all, whatever the "accidents" shaping their individual experiences may have been. This is why for him plot and incident, which are "accidental," find their justification artistically in imagery, which is specific meaning with universal significance. It is through the use of imagery that the artist can make "signals through the glass" to reach the reader with a message that makes sense to him where he stands. The message is no mere family gossip, since it concerns the universal human situation as each man meets it in his lonely, yet shared existence.[11]

*   *   *

In "The Dogwood Tree" Updike speaks of the Three Great Secret Things — sex, religion, and art. These are mysteries with which every human being must come to terms, since they press in so demandingly upon his existence. To deny their full seriousness is to deny life. To hedge our answers to the questions they raise is to remain impotently drifting on the deep, a rudderless craft at the mercy of treacherous currents and death-bringing storms.

Sex and religion are omnipresent in Updike's writings. Because an adolescent's discovery of the range of the adult world is one that begins largely with the emergence of sexual consciousness, Updike's stories of Olinger High School are studies, in one way or another, of confrontation with the mystery of sexuality. But also, from his first short stories down to his most recent novel *Couples,* he has been concerned to focus upon one of the leading problems of our generation, namely the nature of marriage, where the social, ethical, and religious dimensions of sex demand to be (and mostly are not) faced with honesty and realism. As sex demands of us that we engage at one level with the ultimates of love and death, so religion poses the question of how these ultimates are to be

---

[11] Asked by the interviewer of the *Paris Review* if he still denies, as he did in "The Sea's Green Sameness," that characterization and psychology are primary goals of fiction, Updike states in the course of his reply: "The author's deepest pride, as I have experienced it, is not in his incidental wisdom but in his ability to keep an organized mass of images moving forward, to feel life engendering itself under his hands. But no doubt, fiction is also a mode of spying; we read it as we look in windows or listen to gossip, to learn what other people *do*" (*Art,* p. 116).

understood at every moment of our existence. For Updike, early exposure to the Christian faith in its Lutheran expression had an effect which was, as he said, surprising and permanent. "How did the patently vapid and drearily businesslike teachings to which I was lightly exposed succeed in branding me with a Cross?" he asks (*AP*, p. 181). Again, the result of his confrontation with this mystery is described all through his work. Christian imagery permeates his fiction.

Art, however, *is* his work. Thus it is a topic he very seldom discusses directly. A passage in "The Dogwood Tree" is important enough to merit quoting in full. Updike writes of his early belief that an artist was "someone who lived in a small town like Shillington and who, equipped with pencils and paper, practiced his solitary trade as methodically as the dentist practiced his. And indeed, that is how it is at present with me." He continues, referring to the boy-he-was who still directs his life's course:

> He saw art — between drawing and writing he ignorantly made no distinction — as a method of riding a thin pencil line out of Shillington, out of time altogether, into an infinity of unseen and even unborn hearts. He pictured this infinity as radiant. How innocent! But his assumption here, like his assumptions on religion and politics, is one for which I have found no certain substitute. He loved blank paper and obedience to this love led me to a difficult artistic attempt. I reasoned thus: just as the paper is the basis for the marks upon it, might not events be contingent upon a never-expressed (because featureless) ground? Is the true marvel of Sunday skaters the pattern of their pirouettes or the fact that they are silently upheld? Blankness is not emptiness; we may skate upon an intense radiance we do not see because we see nothing else. And in fact there is a color, a quiet but tireless goodness that things at rest, like a brick wall or a small stone, seem to affirm. A wordless reassurance these things are pressing to give. An hallucination? To transcribe middleness with all its grits, bumps, and anonymities, its fullness of satisfaction and mystery: is it possible or, in view of the suffering that violently colors the periphery and that at all moments threatens to move into the center, worth doing? Possibly not: but the horse-chestnut trees, the telephone poles, the porches, the green hedges recede to a calm point that in my subjective geography is still the center of the world. (*AP*, pp. 185-86)

This is the world Updike thinks worth recording through his art. It is a world of seemingly small things, a world of "middleness," a world of places where newspapers are read over breakfast rather than of places about which headlines shout. Updike knows well enough that most people would rather read headlines and live vicariously at the "periphery" of violent action than turn their eyes and their intelligence to their own exciting daily routine. He is reported as saying the following on this topic:

> There's a 'yes-but' quality about my writing that evades entirely pleasing anybody. It seems to me that critics get increasingly querulous and impatient for madder music and stronger wine, when what we need is a greater respect for reality. Too many people are studying maps and not enough are visiting places. (Howard, p. 82)

If noise and excitement are what we want, Updike will not satisfy us. He has no intention of bringing us to "where the action is," or of painting the scene in psychedelic coloring. Rather, he asks us what human action is and how we measure it, whether by its obvious and immediate quantitative effect or by its human meaning and quality. And he asks us to distinguish between the seeming and the real, between what we think we know and what there is to be known, and between the slogans we loudly proclaim to be true and the truths that commend themselves when we have patience enough to seek them for their own worth. His art may ride on a thin line, but it leads to a radiant infinity.

3

PATTERNS

UPDIKE'S FIRST AMBITION WAS TO BE A CARICATURIST,
and his beginnings as a writer showed him aspiring to be a humorist.
His early literary heroes, he tells us (*Assorted Prose,* vii), were
Thurber, Benchley, and Gibbs. He may have seen these authors as
verbal caricaturists. In any case, where humor is put on paper, word
and picture seem to be closely allied. Jokes cry out to be illustrated
and frequently literary jesters have attempted (with varying degrees
of success) to be their own illustrators. Thurber did, of course, and
many others as well: Thackeray, Lewis Carroll, Edward Lear, W. S.
Gilbert, and Evelyn Waugh — to recall some well-known examples.
Like G. K. Chesterton, Updike went to art school before taking up
writing as a full-time career, though this was for him something of
a diversion in a career already committed to literature. His youthful belief that there was no distinction between drawing and writing (*AP,* p. 185) is significant, nevertheless, in that it directs us to
note the importance in his work of the visual artist's delight in pattern.

During his first year at Harvard, Updike contributed to the *Harvard
Lampoon* (March 1951, p. 15) a five-verse poem in praise of orna-
mental alphabets. He gave it no title, but drew for it a decorated
initial letter and tailpiece. The third and fourth verses of the poem
run as follows:

> *Few centuries have dared abuse*
> *the heritage of curlicues.*
> > *The Father Adam donned the fig*
> > *when Eve got confidential;*
> > *and hence, from bra to periwig,*
> > *Man's garb is non-essential,*
> *from Dali hats to pointed shoes.*

> *The printed page of days gone by*
> *appealed to an illiterate eye;*
> *but now the slow advance of fear*
> *rolls back the line of boldness;*
> *the print is set with mien austere,*
> *the page, endowed with coldness,*
> *with few attempts to beautify.*

Updike's verse was to become more dextrous and flexible than this, but his viewpoint was to change very little. For him the wealth of pattern available to the artist means that there is always present material for giving joy, so that niggardliness in working this material indicates a failure of nerve. Later he was to document those causes of "the slow advance of fear" which resulted in a "coldness" in more than the appearance of the page. In his short story "Dear Alexandros" an American who has "adopted" a Greek boy through a charity organization writes to him: "Your nation should be very proud of producing masterpieces which the whole world can enjoy. In the United States the great writers produce works which people do not enjoy, because they are so depressing" (*Pigeon Feathers,* p. 106). The observation is certainly connected with the fact that the writer of the letter is described as *American Parent No. 10,638* and the boy is identified as *Needy Child No. 26,511.* Aesthetic and human values are bound together, being pieces of one pattern. Men turned into ciphers are deprived of spontaneous joy.

Updike's belief that pattern is enjoyable in itself can be readily seen in his poetry. *The Carpentered Hen and Other Tame Creatures* was the title he chose for his first collection of verse. The hen features in a poem called "A Wooden Darning Egg," which is an early example of the author's fascination with the skilled matching of natural and man-made patterns which carpentry demands. A carpentered hen with hinged wings is required (so Updike suggests) to account for the laying of a wooden egg; and the poem matches the patterns common to live fowls and tooled wood. In the smoothly rounded darning egg,

> *The grain of the wood*
> *embraces the shape*
> *as brown feathers do*
> *the rooster's round nape.* (p. 41)

The "other tame creatures" included in the collection are vegetable and mineral as well as animal. They are called tame, presumably, because they are brought imaginatively into relation with the pattern of the humanized world. Even a flower, as Updike points out in "Sunflower," can be seen to "wear a girl's / bonnet behind."

"A Cheerful Alphabet of Pleasant Objects" in *The Carpentered*

Hen contains several poems in which the printed words are arranged
in a pattern representing the objects described, thus adding a visual
pattern to the pattern of meaning. "Mirror" (p. 75), for example,
matches each line to its reflection on the page — words written
backwards; "Nutcracker" (p. 75) pinches the word "nut" between
two long straight lines of print; and "Pendulum" (p. 77) is made
up of lines that sway from the vertical as a pendulum does. Such
ingenuity is artificial, of course, but then Updike reminds us that
the pattern of rhyme itself is artificial. In an essay on the light verse
of Max Beerbohm entitled "Rhyming Max," he observes: "By
rhyming, language calls attention to its own mechanical nature and
relieves the represented reality of seriousness" (*AP,* p. 259).

Puns, too, relieve seriousness; for, in their own fashion, they call
attention to the mechanical nature of language, which, being forced
to use a limited number of sounds to convey many meanings, sometimes has to double up. Updike's love of puns is evident in the titles
of some of his poems — "Duet, with Muffled Brake Drums" (*CH,*
p. 1), "Shipbored" (p. 5) — and other poems are practically a
succession of puns. "Upon Learning that a Bird Exists Called The
Turnstone," in *Telephone Poles,*[1] is such a poem:

> *The Turneresque landscape*
> *She scanned for a lover;*
> *She'd heard one good turnstone*
> *Deserves another.* (p. 28)

Telephone Poles also contains a poem which is a kind of sophisticated
literary-genre pun. "The Menagerie at Versailles in 1775" (p. 26)
turns an entry from Samuel Johnson's notebook into a good imita-
tion of modern free verse simply by breaking up the prose into ir-
regular lines.

At least since the eighteenth century, puns have been regarded as
cheap wit. But the virtue of puns is that they employ shock tactics
to break down our stock responses to words. By pushing another
pattern of thought into the one we were following, puns jolt our
minds onto a new track. In this respect the pun functions as does
the poetic image; for the image also brings together two different
patterns which usually we would not think of connecting. At times,
Updike simply enjoys himself heaping pun upon pun in deliberately contrived comic effects. But this is a kind of flexing of his imaginative muscles. In the bulk of his writings puns are used continually
for image-making potentialities rather than for their own sake.

In addition to the pun, Updike employs the extended visual image
that gains its effects through building up a mental picture in the way

---

[1] *Telephone Poles and Other Poems* (New York, 1963), p. 28.

that an artist sketches a scene in successive strokes progressively defining his subject. For example, in "Ex-Basketball Player" (*The Carpentered Hen,* p. 2) we meet Flick Webb, once a high school athlete and now earning a meager living at a garage. He has some odd companions:

> *Flick stands tall among the idiot pumps —*
> *Five on a side, the old bubble-head style,*
> *Their rubber elbows hanging loose and low.*
> *One's nostrils are two S's, and his eyes*
> *An E and O. And one is squat, without*
> *A head at all — more of a football type.*

Now the pattern of the human body — limbs on a trunk and features on a face — is so familiar that we all tend to assimilate other patterns to it. Making men out of gasoline pumps is not so very original. Updike's picture of the gas-pump men is saved from banality, however, by the fact that the details are vivid and convincing. We are made to feel how much Flick is degraded by having to mingle with this team of mute, ill-matched idiots. Nevertheless, the very ingenuity of the image tends to get in the way of our receiving the full, shocking impact of Flick's predicament.

In *The Poorhouse Fair*[2] Updike tells the similar story of a man who dies of discouragement after he and his sister have failed to make a living at a country store and gas station (pp. 173-75). Here the theme of wasted existence is much more poignantly presented, because the comparison between the human and the nonhuman is obliquely suggested instead of being elaborated in detail. We are simply told that there were outside the store two gasoline pumps — "the outmoded bubble-head style" — and that, the store being on a blind corner, most cars passed by without stopping. In this account, two outmoded pumps and two lives passed by while the world rushed on are juxtaposed without comment. The reader is expected to make the connection for himself.

It seems to be Updike's method to work over his material, returning several times to themes he has experimented with, in order to develop the possibilities contained in them and not fully exploited at the first or the second attempt. His poems often seem to be seedbeds in which images sprout — to be transplanted later so that they may flower in his prose. As well as picking up the image of "the old bubble-head style" gasoline pumps in *The Poorhouse Fair,* Updike retold the story of Flick Webb twice after "Ex-Basketball Player." The predicament of the high school athlete unfitted for making a living appeared again as the short story "Ace

---

[2] New York, 1959.

in the Hole" (collected in *The Same Door*); and it was expanded, after that, into *Rabbit, Run.* Since it is clearly not a lack of inventiveness that makes Updike repeat his themes — the most sour critics of Updike's work have never accused him of lacking inventiveness — we must conclude that what he is aiming at is depth of communication. Imagery that begins by being merely fanciful is worked over until it becomes the vehicle of great imaginative power.

Imagination, though, springs from the ability to perceive pattern. Updike believes that all pattern gives delight, and therefore that purely decorative effects are not to be despised. He suggests that if we reject "the heritage of curlicues," mistakenly thinking we can do without the nonessential, then we have thrown out a large part of the joy of human existence. His poetry at its most lighthearted displays his conviction that it is good to make room in our lives for tame creatures and pleasant objects, lest we lose our true humanity. For man the imaginative creature, the nonessential is decidedly essential.

It is understandable how Updike's frank pleasure in decorative pattern and verbal juggling should have laid him open to the charge of being no more than an entertainer, a dealer in trifles who is out of touch with our age of apocalyptic terror. Yet he is by no means insensitive to the suffering of our time "that violently colors the periphery and that at all moments threatens to move into the center" (*AP*, p. 186). He just refuses to be intimidated by "the slow advance of fear" that sets the cultural mood of today, a mood alternating between bitter pessimism and hollow optimism. He has said this:

> It's true that we live on the verge of catastrophe — not worldwide annihilation, perhaps, but surely something drastic. Still, since 1945 our little dramas have generally been played out somewhat short of catastrophe. We do survive every moment, after all, except the last. (Jane Howard, "Can a Nice Novelist Finish First?" *Life,* November 4, 1966, p. 76)

His strong realism prevents him from turning his back upon the actual world we live in so as to embrace the abstract theories claiming to represent the "contemporary" vision.

The epigraph prefixed to *The Carpentered Hen* is the passage from Boethius' *De Consolatione Philosophiae* in which Lady Philosophy drives away the Muses of Poetry. By choosing this particular passage, Updike is able to give an ironic warning to those who assume his poems to be frivolous when they find them to be decorative and witty. That a poet's verse is light in texture does not mean that it is inconsequential.

Heavy seriousness in an author invariably earns Updike's anathema

— witness his parody-review of Samuel Beckett's *How It Is* under the title "How How It Is Was" (*AP,* pp. 314-18). Perhaps the completely imponderous tone of Robert Herrick's poetry has something to do with his choice of this poet when he wrote his Harvard dissertation, "Non-Horatian Elements in Herrick's Echoes of Horace." Certainly, Updike's poetic style owes much to seventeenth-century literary taste. Writers of that period were in love with pattern, using decorative effects with uninhibited boldness. The conceits of metaphysical poetry shift the reader suddenly from one pattern of meaning to another, and exploit all the potentialities of the pun. From this period also came the "shaped verse" (as it was called then), reflecting the subject visually in typographical pattern.[3] Updike uses seventeenth-century techniques without antiquarian pedantry. But chiefly he seems to have been impressed by the way in which the earlier poets, making no rigid distinction between serious and light verse, blended playful fancies and deep convictions about ultimate truths. They were not prepared to assume a necessary hostility between Lady Philosophy and the Muses of Poetry.

If an author is to wear his learning comfortably and without ostentation, he must assume his readers to be intellectually informed and alert. John Donne, for example, expected his contemporaries to see what was happening when he patterned the imagery of a poem upon the difference between the Ptolemaic and the Copernican cosmologies without mentioning either directly. Updike makes similar demands upon his readers. Not only does he expect them to recognize literary or philosophical allusions ranging all the way from Tacitus to T. S. Eliot, and from Democritus to John Dewey, but he also makes considerable use of suppressed allusions. Consider, for example, the poem "Vacuum Cleaner":

> *This humming broom, with more aplomb*
> *Than tracts by A. Camus,*
> *Refutes the ancient axiom*
> *That Nothing has no use. (CH,* p. 80)

Unlike the existentialists and their friends, Updike does not write tracts about the necessity for a creative encounter with Nothingness. Instead, he emulates the vacuum cleaner and puts negativity to work. One of his most characteristic devices for making a point is leaving out a word or phrase. For instance, there is his poem "Capacity" (*CH,* p. 24). The poem takes off from a sign in a bus reading "CA-PACITY 26 PASSENGERS." Updike makes the sign an excuse

---

[3] "... and of my own poems, 'Nutcracker,' with the word 'nut' in bold face, seems to me as good as George Herbert's angel wings" — Updike (*Art,* p. 88).

for one of his extended puns, which in this instance assimilates the pattern of twenty-six persons to the twenty-six letters of the alphabet: "Affable, bibulous,/corpulent, dull," and so on to ". . . young, zebuesque." The witticism is so engagingly carried off that probably most readers will fail to notice that the count of passengers amounts only to twenty-five. The missing letter is "u." Updike, mock-modestly, has omitted himself.

Sometimes the suppression is more obvious. A four-line verse in the *Lampoon* (October 1952, p. 19) entitled "From a Young Democrat" reads as follows:

> *Dever! Dever! burning bright,*
> *Out of earshot, out of sight,*
> *What immoral hand or eye*
> *Has framed thee?*

Here the lines follow William Blake's "Tyger! Tyger! burning bright" so closely that the fact that the expected words "fearful symmetry" do not occur — a fact spoiling the symmetry of the verse — throws into relief the pun on the word "framed." The omission of these words also sends the reader's eye back to the third line, making it impossible for him to miss another omission there, namely, the letter "t" from Blake's word "immortal." Even in such a slight, jocular effort as this one is, Updike's verbal dexterity in making omission significant is evident.

Whenever Updike quotes and leaves the quotation unfinished, we are unwise if we imagine that the ellipsis dots tell us merely that he expects us to be able to complete the quotation unaided. It is much more likely that the words he leaves out contain an essential pointer to what he is saying. Frequently, indeed, the inner meaning of a short story or a novel is given in a casually dropped reference which in itself seems hardly important, yet which has associations making it a key to a whole pattern of thought that otherwise would remain unintelligible. Not what is said but what remains unsaid is of paramount importance. Nothing has a great deal of use.

We shall be returning very often to examples of hidden allusion when we come to analyze parts of Updike's fiction. To some people, no doubt, the technique of giving information through deliberate silence will seem a perverse and unnecessary mystification. But the whole matter is really one of trust in intelligence. Updike writes for an educated and sophisticated public. Perhaps he is too optimistic. Perhaps the twentieth-century public is not prepared, as was the seventeenth-century public, to draw from the storehouse of cultural riches the currency necessary to do business in this literary market. However, Updike is willing to take the risk and to count on his readers' finding the experience of being kept on their intellectual toes an exhilarating one. Because he thinks reading ought to be an enjoyable activity, he will not compromise on the issue of the educated imagination. Why spoil the fun by making the game too easy? Convinced that dullness and pedantry are the enemies of literature (as of life itself), Updike has determined to emulate the style of life described in Horace's "Ode III, ii," which he translates in *The Carpentered Hen:*

> *Manliness, not knowing the taint of defeat,*
> *flashes forth with unsullied glory,*
> *neither lifts nor lowers the axes*
> *at a whisper from the scatterbrained mob.* (p. 68)

                                        *   *   *

Updike's mind is not a condemning one.[4] He dislikes pedantry, but his parody of T. S. Eliot's criticism shows that he thinks pedantry too can sometimes be elevated to art (*AP*, pp. 13-17). His wide sympathies, however, do not extend to complacency — and especially not to the complacency of little men who patronize greatness. He pillories this attitude in his poem "Humanities Course," which begins thus:

> *Professor Varder handles Dante*
> >*With wry respect; while one can see*
> *It's all a lie, one must admit*
> >*The "beauty" of the "imagery."* (*CH*, p. 28)

The Professor Varders of this world dismiss out of hand the notion that the original thinkers of the past may have anything to teach us, while generously admitting that "They still are 'crucial figures' in/ The 'pageantry' of 'Western thought.' "

Why Updike resents so strongly the academic smugness that sits in the condescending judgment upon "Montaigne, Tom Paine, St. Augustine" and their peers is that he is convinced ideas matter. The great men who have shaped the course of our civilization were great because they believed that what moved the mind was crucial for the happiness or the misery of humanity. Therefore to pretend that we can now look down from some detached position of superiority and place these men like counters on a board is the worst form of blindness to our own predicament. We still have to face the problems with which they grappled; and, in accepting or reject-

---

[4] "I find it hard to have opinions. Theologically, I favor Karl Barth; politically I favor the Democrats. But I treasure a remark John Cage made, that not judgingness but openness and curiosity are our proper business. To speak on matters where you're ignorant dulls the voice for speaking on matters where you do know something" — Updike (*Art,* pp. 97-98).

ing the answers they gave — so variously — to the large questions of existence, we make momentous decisions both for ourselves and for those who come after us. History is no entertaining pageant. It is solid stuff to be carved by costly decisions. Human existence is continually a choice between good and evil, truth and falsehood. It requires a faith to live by and to die for.

Another poem in which Updike displays his sense of the odiousness and meanness of detached, pretentious superiority is "Mr. High-Mind" (CH, pp. 42-43). The title refers to Bunyan's *Pilgrim's Progress,* in which Mr. High-Mind is one of the Jury at Vanity Fair condemning Faithful to death. Updike describes Mr. High-Mind's mental ascent into "the banana-colored void" of pure facticity.

> From this great height, the notion of the Good
> Is seen to be a vulgar one, and crude.

But when Mr. High-Mind "casts his well-weighted verdict with a sigh" it coincides with that of the rest of the jury his highmindedness despises.

Updike is a writer, first and last. He describes the world as he sees it, and he has the integrity of his craft too much in mind to distort his material in the interests of propaganda. At the same time, when he sees the world and gives his writer's report on it, he views it from the perspective of his personal faith, which happens to be that of historic Christianity. So he never pretends that he can stand on some neutral ground where the difference between all beliefs levels out and counts for nothing. It is simply impossible to detach the beauty of Dante's imagery from the question of the truth or falsehood of Dante's vision of reality. Similarly, the imagery of any writer cannot be isolated and held in some aesthetic test tube, sterilized to prevent any contamination from the vulgar practical world where good and evil clash. When we have risen to a height from which the notion of the Good seems vulgar, when we think we have traveled beyond good and evil, we have actually allied ourselves with the worst.

The relationship between Dante's poetry and Dante's religious beliefs is not discussed by Updike. But Updike's dissertation on Herrick considers the relationship of that poet's Christian faith to his poetic art. The "Non-Horatian Elements" he refers to in the title are, in fact, Christian ones.

Updike comments on the difference between the superficial appearance of Herrick's lyrical utterances and their actual significance. The poems look "light" and are not. The reason for this paradox, he believes, lies in the quality of the Christian faith which Herrick held most sincerely. (This sincerity has been often disputed, and critics have condescendingly remarked that Herrick does not hold "a very high place among clerical types.")[5] Updike argues that there is no innate contradiction between Herrick's spirituality and his fondness for picking his themes from trivia — and secular trivia at that. The poet, he explains, has learned the secret of genuine Christian humility. For

> ...his humility is the Christian awareness of the smallness of earthly things. His poems are short, his subjects are trivial, his effects are delicate. Yet at the same time he is willing to describe tiny phenomena with the full attention and sympathy due to a 'major' theme. ("Non-Horatian Elements," p. 40)

Updike's justification of Herrick's subjects and tone might well have been put as an explanatory foreword to either of his own volumes of poetry. No one would wish to compare the poetry of the two men all along the line; and, in particular, Updike's effects are too often too brisk and breezy to be called delicate.[6] Yet the seventeenth-century writer and the twentieth-century one at least have in common their preference for tiny phenomena lovingly described in short poems, as well as their occasional celebration of a religious theme. Quite apart from its application to Herrick, however, what Updike has to say about the Christian awareness of the smallness of earthly things goes far to explain why he is so certain that "imagery" cannot be a meaningful term when it is viewed simply as an aesthetic factor and considered in isolation from the total vision of reality entertained by an author.

Since imagery demands the recognition of pattern, and of the interweaving of pattern with pattern, a poet's view of the ultimate pattern of the universe — what it is and what it means — is absolutely crucial to determining the character of his imagery all along the line. In this regard, Updike's comments upon "the featureless ground" of art in "The Dogwood Tree: A Boyhood" are very much to the point. He asks: "Is the true marvel of Sunday skaters the pattern of their pirouettes or the fact that they are silently upheld?" (*AP,* p. 185). And then he goes on to assert that there is in fact a quiet but tireless goodness affirmed by things at rest, by a brick wall or a small stone. The conviction permitting him to make such an assertion is not drawn out of the things themselves. Rather, because he holds a particular conviction about the ground of all

---

[5] Thomas Tucker Brooke in *A Literary History of England,* edited by Albert C. Baugh (New York, 1948), p. 663.

[6] Nevertheless, in the verse Foreword to the paperback edition of his collected *Verse* (New York, 1965), Updike himself compares the "transparency" of his poems to ballerinas' skirts. And Herrick's satires are by no means delicate — in any sense of the word.

things, he sees in brick walls and small stones confirmation of the
fact of their being silently upheld. Simply by being themselves, tiny
phenomena display the "color" of goodness permeating the entire
creation. Believing that all earthly things are small, he can also
believe that nothing on earth is inconsiderable. Since the true marvel
is not the pattern made by the Sunday skaters but their skating
"upon an intense radiance we do not see because we see nothing
else," the pattern of the skaters' pirouettes is worth recording and
carries its own proper delight into our consciousness — the delight
of a reflected radiance. But to see this radiance requires a "Christian
awareness."

The specific quality of Updike's Christian awareness may be
understood best, perhaps, by taking account of the influence exerted
upon him by the Swiss theologian Karl Barth. He confesses: "Barth's
theology, at one point in my life, seemed alone to be supporting . . .
[my life]" (AP, ix). After World War I a new era in theology was
initiated by Barth's insistence that God is not a good idea that men
can think up for themselves, but that the knowledge of God comes
solely through divine self-revelation. As Barth put it, "You do
not speak of God by speaking about man in a loud voice." At this
time Barth's "theology of the Word of God" owed much to Søren
Kierkegaard. Kierkegaard spoke of the "infinite qualitative distinction between time and eternity" (i.e., between man and God). Prefixed to Updike's novel The Centaur[7] is a quotation from Barth
developing Kierkegaard's thesis:

> Heaven is the creation inconceivable to man, earth the creation con-
> ceivable to him. He himself is the creature on the boundary be-
> tween heaven and earth.

If we connect what Updike said in his dissertation about Herrick's
Christian humility and the epigraph he supplied for The Centaur,
we can see how these agree. Although man cannot rise through his
own powers to the inconceivable heaven, or cannot imagine the
eternal, the heavenly may make itself known in the earthly sphere,
which man can understand. For the individual, standing between
earth and heaven, there is always the possibility of such knowledge.
Yet it must come to him, come to him through that condescension of
heaven to earth which Christian belief knows as grace. It is only
when the patterns of earth are seen to be suffused with the radiance
of heaven's grace that they are truly seen and can be truly valued;
and, since the qualitative difference between heaven and earth wipes
out all earthly distinctions between small and great phenomena,
nothing is too small to carry the marks of infinite worth and to bring

---

[7] New York, 1963.

radiance into life. To see earth in the light of heaven is Updike's purpose in *The Centaur* and in much of his other fiction. Viewed simply as decoration, the patterns of existence give delight. But these patterns upon the surface cannot be self-sustaining or self-justifying. Even tame creatures and pleasant objects compel us to contemplate the ambiguities of flesh and the goodness of temporal things that mirror in creation the inconceivable realm of eternal glory.

4

MARRIED LOVE:
INTRODUCING THE MAPLES

AT A TIME WHEN THE ACCOUNT OF HUMAN EXISTENCE
given by Dante — and by St. Augustine, Milton, and other repre-
sentatives of the Christian tradition — is widely assumed to be "all
a lie," some alternative account must inevitably be advanced as the
true one, the completely reliable and fully believable version of the
story of man. Such an alternative cannot simply be advanced as
historically correct. It has to commend itself also as being imaginatively satisfying, that is, as an adequate *myth* explaining who man
really is and what purpose he serves in the total scheme of things.

Current mythology leads man to see himself not as a son of Adam
exiled from Paradise and endeavoring to return there, but as an
animal who has gradually evolved until he occupies his present place
of preeminence in the cosmos. Updike wittily outlines this popular
mythology in a recent poem, "The Naked Ape."[1] As Updike tells
the story, man the animal had a hard time even after becoming an
ape. There were physiological changes first, "Developing bioptic
vision and/The grasping hand." Then the naked ape adapted himself
to "glacial whim" and changed his environment and his habits.

> *This ill-cast carnivore attacked,*
> > *With weapons he invented,* in a pack.
> *The tribe was born. To set men free,*
> > *The family*
> *Evolved. Monogamy occurred.*

---

[1] *The New Republic,* February 3, 1968, p. 28. Both the title of the poem
and its factual details are derived from the popular book *The Naked Ape* by
Desmond Morris (New York, 1967).

50

> *The female — sexually alert*
> *Throughout the month, equipped to have*
> *Pronounced orgasms — perpetuated love.*
> *The married state decreed its* lex
> Privata: *sex.*

By now a social animal, the naked ape developed civilization. His efforts were successful, bringing man to where he is today.

> *. . . He suffers rashes and subdues*
> *Aggressiveness by making fists*
> *And laundry lists,*
>
> *Suspension bridges, aeroplanes,*
> *And charts that show biweekly gains*
> *And losses. Noble animal!*
> *To try to lead on this terrestrial ball,*
> *The upright life.*

This gently probing account of the human condition touches on several aspects of contemporary society which Updike has been exploring since he first started writing. In his fiction, love and the married state are on the top of the list.

*   *   *

The autobiographical content of so much of Updike's work has already been discussed. When he came to New York City to work on the staff of *The New Yorker,* he was already a husband and the father of a daughter. It is not surprising, therefore, to find some stories of this period featuring young married couples with one baby daughter and living in an apartment in New York. (Later these couples appear with a growing daughter and a baby son; and finally with four children — two daughters at the extremes and two sons in the middle — the family meanwhile having moved to a small town in New England.) The families bear different names. They also succeed in being different people, although so much alike in family background and in circumstance. For while Updike loads his fiction with autobiographical material often literally reproduced down to very small details, his stories are fiction and not autobiography in a fictional disguise. He gives a writer's account of "things" as he has seen them. He does not merely retail gossip about himself and his relatives and friends.

As a "thing" to be reported, married love does not fit easily into short-story form. Each marriage, after all, is a developing experience in the context of a particular society caught up in the stream of history. In order to depict marriage and love as partners in a marriage know it, it is necessary for the writer to show something of the history of the individual marriage; and that means recording the passage of time and the accumulation of memories giving marriage its historical destiny, its unique and living character. Updike has attempted to provide historical perspective by making his married couples, in general, age along with their creator. He draws on his past for his stories of boyhood and adolescence, but his stories of adult life are almost strictly contemporary.

However, he has also found a strategy for making the short story record marriage-history. This involves linking stories, divided in time of writing, through the expedient of having them depict successive incidents in the history of one specific marriage.

His first collection of short stories, *The Same Door,*[2] introduces Richard and Joan Maple. "Snowing in Greenwich Village" shows them as a young couple, not quite two years into marriage, who spent their first three months of married life in a YMCA camp. The Maples are absent from the pages of the next collection, *Pigeon Feathers.* But there the first story, "Walter Briggs," is about a couple who also spent the first three months of their marriage (now of five years' standing) in a YMCA camp. Jack and Clare — we are never told their last name — have a two-year-old daughter Jo and a baby boy Bobby. In the same volume, the stories "Should Wizard Hit Mommy?" and "The Crow in the Woods" give us further revelations of their family life. Updike's third book of short stories, *The Music School,* drops Jack and Clare, but brings back the Maples in two stories: "Giving Blood" and "Twin Beds in Rome." In the first of these, Richard and Joan have completed nine years together and are the parents of four children — Judith, Richard, Jr., John, and a baby daughter Bean. The second tells how the tensions of their marriage, very evident in "Giving Blood," have led the pair to the brink of separation. They are still together, though, in the four recent stories "Marching Through Boston," "Your Lover Just Called," "The Taste of Metal," and "Eros Rampant."[3] The tensions have, if anything, intensified; yet the marriage bond has held, to the present, in spite of recurring crises.

The fact that marriage involves intense conflicts finding no permanent resolution has been a theme of Updike's fiction from the first. The Jack and Clare stories, among others, illustrate Updike's conviction that the essential difference of vision in man and in woman makes such continuing conflicts inevitable. Yet, another theme has

2 New York, 1959.

3 "Marching Through Boston," *The New Yorker,* January 22, 1966; "Your Lover Just Called," *Harper's Magazine,* January 1967; "The Taste of Metal," *The New Yorker,* March 11, 1967; "Eros Rampant," *Harper's Magazine,* June 1968.

become dominant in Updike's writings. This is the intolerable strain put upon marriage by the values current in North American society. In the sterile artificiality of our culture the male and female aspects of human nature, which should be complementary patterns, are turned to mutual destruction.

Updike's first novel, *The Poorhouse Fair* (1959), touches upon this theme; and *The Same Door* (1959) contains two stories, in addition to "Snowing in Greenwich Village," "Sunday Teasing," and "Incest," that describe the hazards to married happiness introduced by city living. But the earliest direct indictment of the American way of life in the area of sex and marriage is "Dear Alexandros," a story first published in 1959, and collected in *Pigeon Feathers* (1962). Updike's second novel, *Rabbit, Run* (1960), continues the attack, and his fourth, *Of the Farm* (1965), intensifies it. More than half the stories in *The Music School* (1966) deal with infidelity and broken relationships. Updike's most recent novel, *Couples* (1968), is a long and detailed account of multiple adulteries ending with the remarriage of the two principal characters at the cost of divorcing their respective partners and abandoning their families. *Couples* has gained some notoriety as a sex novel. It certainly focuses upon the *"lex privata:* sex." Nevertheless, it is essentially a commentary upon the contemporary effort of man the Noble Animal to live the virtuous life, asking whether the relationship of marriage can be understood by those who have ceased to know themselves as sons of Adam.

Updike leaves the reader in no doubt about his conviction that the decay of loyalty in marriage is disintegrating the fabric of our whole civilization. Where a permanent human relationship can be surrendered lightly, there is a fundamental retreat from personal integrity and from social responsibility. The result must be a forgetfulness of all humane standards and the evaporation of any sense of transcendent meaning in life. In *Couples* marriage is stated to have a double foundation, admiration and trust (p. 43). In the religious sphere, this is the reason why man turns to worship his Creator. In the human sphere, this is the condition making possible kindness and selflessness, both in private and public life.

Updike's third novel, *The Centaur* (1962), is his celebration of the virtuous life actually achieved, through a fully human life that has remained open to God, society, and family. This book, incidentally, is Updike's tribute to his father as the teacher of a wisdom which is a pattern of living rather than merely an intellectual construction. George Caldwell of *The Centaur,* who is a teacher at Olinger High School and is also Chiron, the teacher of the children of Mount Olympus, is that rarity in our age of the anti-hero, an individual genuinely heroic. The book contains a definition of a hero: "a king sacrificed to Hera" (p. 298). Hera, it should be remembered, is the goddess-patroness of sacred marriage. It requires more than a hairless ape to make the heroic sacrifice.

Evidently it was his growing concern over the decay of American family life that caused Updike to turn again to the Maples, who had been passed over after their first appearance in "Snowing in Greenwich Village." Jack and Clare, although quite similar to the other couple in some respects, demonstrate how marriage can bring a unique joy in moments of fulfilled trust. The marriage of Joan and Richard, on the other hand, is unstable.

In "Snowing in Greenwich Village" Updike goes out of his way to stress, in particular, Richard's immaturity and vanity. Thus the Maple household provides an obvious setting for exhibiting the insecurity of conjugal love under the pressures of modern living. Taken together, the six Maple stories to date bring us into the heart of Updike's diagnosis of the sickness infecting American marriage — and of the signs of health still persisting.

The names of the Maple couple may well have had something to do with the decision to bring them back into circulation. Updike is very careful in his choice of names. He usually starts from a name having a personal association with people or places he has known. (Few of his names are purely fanciful inventions, and most of them are quite ordinary names, suiting an individual's ethnic or regional background.) He then exploits the general associations of the name, in two directions. There are first the associations of the name itself (e.g., Fox) or of its sound (e.g., Merritt); and there are, second, the associations of the name that are derived from history and literature. The associations gathering round the names of Richard and Joan Maple are very specifically American ones.

To begin with, the *maple* tree is a North American tree holding an intense attraction for Updike. "Home," a story included in *Pigeon Feathers,* spells this out clearly. In this story two young Americans return from England with their baby daughter. (The circumstances are similar to the Updikes' return after their year in Oxford.) Robert, the husband, recalls how when his wife Joanne had just given birth to Corinne in an English hospital, he went to a Doris Day movie. Set in a Hollywood-created "mythical Midwestern town," the movie made him homesick. "The houses were white, the porches deep, the lawns green, the sidewalks swept, the maples dark against the streetlights" (*PF,* p. 153). Maples, then, stand for the small-town existence at the center of the America Updike loves.[4] Here is the American "family tree," a living emblem of American home life.

.*Richard* and *Joan* are first names linked permanently with America as a nation, and with Pennsylvania in particular. Benjamin Franklin created the legendary figure of Poor Richard — "A Famous PENN- SYLVANIA Conjurer, and Almanack-Maker," as he is described on the title page of Franklin's *Father Abraham's Speech* (1758).[5] Poor Richard's wife and faithful companion was Joan, described (in verse rather less polished than Updike's) by her admiring husband:

> *Of their* Chloes *and* Phyllises *Poets may prate,*
> *I will sing my plain COUNTRY JOAN;*
> *Twice twelve years my Wife, still the Joy of my Life:*
> *Bless'd Day that I made her my own.*

In the Maples, Poor Richard and his Joan live again. Modern America has once more its prototype of married bliss. But whether Joan will still be the joy of Richard's life at the end of twice twelve years is an open question. Certainly, he did not choose her originally because she was a plain country type. In the context of the modern city the ideals of rural simplicity set forth by Franklin seem comically antiquated. But then the issue arises as to what *is* the contemporary ideal of marriage, and whether anyone either knows or cares.

Conditions obtaining in the era of the American Revolution clearly can give little guidance for the shaping of the mores of the Great Society of today. Clearly also, Updike has no thought of holding up Franklin as a beacon to light our path in the present. He would not endorse, in any case, the latter's evolutionary optimism or deistic religion. Yet it was the intellectual coherence of the thinking of Franklin, and of others whose estimate of the universe ran along similar lines, that molded a democratic America and launched "a nation so conceived" into history. Franklin was, above all, a moralist of the practical life, deeply concerned to foster a *virtuous* and *harmonious* American community, one based on industry, thrift, and the sense of a divinely ordained destiny for the nation. *Poor Richard Improved* of 1755 gives this advice: "Think of three Things, whence you came, where you are going, and to whom you must account." Changed times, far from making this

---

[4] He mentions the maple seeds on the streets as one of his memories of Reading (*AP*, p. 162). His wooden darning egg in the poem of that name is maple wood too.

[5] A facsimile edition (G. K. Hall & Co., 1963) issued by the Massachusetts Historical Society carries a note saying that this work — later entitled *The Way to Wealth* — has been printed and translated oftener than "any other work from an American pen."

particular piece of advice superfluous, lay upon Americans more urgently than ever the duty of responsible self-knowledge. Updike's fiction raises some searching questions about the present neglect of this duty.

Updike does not call his Poor Richard the Pennsylvania Conjurer. Indeed he gives him an origin in West Virginia — perhaps pushing him over the border of his own state in order to indicate that this Richard has a national rather than a regional significance. A conjurer, in the old meaning of the word, is an unusually sagacious person, an oracle. Richard hardly seems to be that. Yet in Richard's family chronicle America may have an almanac of its fortunes. The first Maple story gives some indication of such a possibility.

Superficially, "Snowing in Greenwich Village" seems a slight domestic sketch, deftly drawn, though overcrowded with casual detail. Richard is in the advertising business in New York, and he and Joan have just moved into a new apartment on West Thirteenth Street. Rebecca Cune, a friend of Joan from student days at Cambridge, has her apartment on the other side of the street, less than a block away. So they have her in as their first guest. She charms them with her lively, if rather fantastic, anecdotes about herself; but Joan has a slight cold, and Rebecca insists on leaving early. It has started to snow, and on Joan's suggestion Richard walks their guest home. He is invited up to see her apartment, which is shabby and unattractive. When Rebecca steps up to him and offers her face to be kissed, he excuses himself awkwardly and runs downstairs.

The story begins by saying Rebecca was invited to the Maples' "because they were now so close." It ends with the words: "Oh, but they were so close."

By thus enclosing this story within a pun, Updike alerts the reader to his method of telling his story through wordplay. The narrative is crowded throughout with puns and punning allusions. The double meanings bring to light, to begin with, how Rebecca is more than the amusing friend the Maples imagine her to be. Here the first indication is their guest's name. In literary terms *Rebecca* suggests Thackeray's Becky Sharp, who is described, in Victorian parlance, as an adventuress. Updike provides his Rebecca with a more explicit second name, one which would have been unacceptable to Thackeray's public. "Cune" is a four-letter word. It fits Rebecca "to a T" — a letter which Updike characteristically omits, substituting instead a silent "e."

Punning references in abundance support the name. Laying Rebecca's "weightless" coat on the bed in the Maples' one bedroom, Richard feels himself elated by the smooth way she had managed the "business" of allowing him to slip it off her. The business of this "light" woman seems to be undressing to please. Rebecca explains that she was taught her present (unnamed) job by a girl friend, and learned it in one day. Immediately, she left her room in a "hotel for ladies" — an awful place, she said. She now starts out each day (not each morning) for work at ten.

In the Maples' apartment Rebecca sits on the floor with her arm resting on a Hide-a-Bed. In her own one-room apartment the scene is dominated by a large double bed, looking like "a permanently-installed, blanketed platform" rather than a piece of furniture. At all times an accompished actress, she is a professional, and this is her stage. The sloping walls in this apartment under the room, so Richard notices, make her few meager pieces of furniture seem to lose their verticality; and soon she moves toward him, tilting her face beneath his. Nothing here proclaims the "upright" life. When Rebecca first comes into her room she announces that it is "hot as hell"; yet she keeps her coat on. Then she draws Richard's attention to the stove, which sits most strangely on top of the refrigerator. Frigid herself, she seeks to heat the passions.

All these details — and there are many more — might be excessive to prove the point of Rebecca's concealed nature, were Updike's only concern to suggest that she is another Becky Sharp. But Rebecca is also a symbol, taking the reader through to the archetypal figure of the female-destroyer-temptress. In classical mythology one can think of Circe, Echnida (mother of the Chimaera and the Harpies), and the Sirens. A connection with the habits of the Harpies is suggested by Rebecca's conversation about flesh-eating. She never ate turkey at Thanksgiving until she was thirteen (puberty). A school for young mothers is opposite her apartment. And her talk of the young butchers coming out "all bloody and laughing" reminds Richard of how he has heard that a former occupant of their own apartment was a wholesale meat salesman, calling himself a Purveyor of Elegant Foods, who kept a woman there. In these instances sex and killing are combined, as in the classical prototypes.

However, the name Rebecca points most strongly to the Old Testament, where (as with Thackeray's Becky) Isaac's wife features as the type of the deceiving woman. Updike seldom stays with the obvious, as we have seen; and, having directed the reader to this source, he points him to another woman in the Old Testament — the cunning prostitute of the Book of Proverbs (Chs. 2, 5, 7, 9). Early in the story we are told of Rebecca that "She had a gift for odd things" (p. 73). There is a punning reference here to the "strange woman," as the King James Version calls her. The correspondence between the Old Testament character and the modern one is worked out in detail, against the background supplied by the Book of Proverbs. As their guest charms both the Maples with her fascinating conversation, she proves herself to have a mouth which is "smoother than oil" (Prov. 5:3). She is a meat-eater consuming "the flesh and body" of her victims (Prov. 5:11). When Richard is invited to come to her apartment, he forgets the warning of Proverbs, "Come not nigh the door of her house." In the Book of Proverbs the Wise Teacher *looks out of his window* and sees "the young man void of understanding" coming in the evening through the streets to the strange woman's house, "in the twilight, in the evening, at the time of night and darkness" (Prov. 7:6-10). This is the time when Richard escorts Rebecca through the streets. Once upstairs, Richard comments on the large lighted window opposite Rebecca's room. Previously she had told him there was always someone there, and that she did not know what he did for a living (p. 79). Yet tonight is an exception, for the room across the street seems deserted. For once the watcher is not at his window, because for once the woman who ensnares "the simple ones" through "much fair speech" (Prov. 7:21) and kisses "with an impudent face" (7:13) is not to succeed in catching her prey.

That Rebecca's impudence in offering herself to be kissed that causes Richard to recoil. (He "decided in retrospect, that her conduct was quite inexcusable" [p. 81].) And he answers her disappointed "Good night" with the single word "Night." Thus he leaves behind him the night of infidelity, "that black and dark night" (Prov. 7:9) in which, according to Proverbs, the strange woman entices youths to "the way of hell" (7:27). Richard was surprised when Rebecca remarked that her room was "hot as hell"; for he had never heard her swear before. Actually, she was not swearing. She was stating the fact explained by the Wise Teacher in Proverbs. Hell is where the strange woman has "decked her bed" (Prov. 7:16).

That Updike should use the background of the Book of Proverbs for his first Maple story will not seem surprising if we remember that proverbs represent the stock-in-trade of Franklin's Poor Richard. "Snowing in Greenwich Village," after all, is a story about Richard and his Joan. Rebecca Cune has importance solely in relation to the Maple marriage, and the issue hangs on whether Richard will allow her to come between Joan and him.

In conversation, Rebecca reveals that *coming between* is her principal role. The first anecdote she tells about herself is how she formerly lived with a girl friend and the friend's lover, her name appearing on the mailbox written *between* theirs (p. 70). Later, she explains, the lover married another girl. Rebecca had parted them.

At first, Rebecca's professional technique of making herself the enigmatic charmer, the still center around which others orbit, suc-

ceeds completely. Richard, who usually lolled with the attitude of
a spoiled child expecting to be waited on, is all activity this evening,
pressing on Rebecca gifts of a plainly sexual character: costly wine
and nuts served in a silver bowl. The wine was stolen for him (p.
71); and "stolen waters are sweet" is the invitation of the "wanton"
woman in Proverbs to the "simple youth" (Prov. 9:17). It looks
as though Rebecca will part this pair of lovers also.

Then they look out of the window to discover that it is snowing.
The Maples embrace spontaneously, leaving Rebecca looking on detached. From that moment on, Richard knows intuitively that Rebecca belongs on the other side of the street, and the strange woman's
spell is broken.

The Maples' drawing together in affection and isolating Rebecca
is the act of separating two worlds, the worlds of sacred and profane
love, the worlds of heaven and hell. Earlier the Maples had felt
that the only stories about themselves they could think of — how
they had spent their honeymoon at a YMCA camp, and the like —
were so much less amusing than Rebecca's stories. Their memories,
in fact, all involved the sacred. Rebecca's stories demonstrate that
the sacred is the sphere from which she is excluded. She tells about
her boy friend who used to pretend he was the Devil. One night the
two of them went to a big nightclub "on the roof of somewhere."
Her escort sat down and played the piano unasked, until a woman
playing the harp told him to stop. When she and the Maples look
out of the apartment window at the falling snow, they see the unusual
sight of six mounted policemen galloping, two abreast, down the
street. Rebecca is not surprised. "They do it every night at this time,"
she remarks (p. 74). The guardians of the law, two for each person
in the room, are alert at the time when the sacred law of marriage
is in danger.[6] Rebecca knows all about that. Not only had she and

---

[6] The Book of Isaiah contains the following report from the "watchman"
set at his post by God's command:

> "... and at my post I am stationed
>   whole nights.
> And, behold, here come riders,
>   horsemen in pairs!"
> And he answered,
>   "Fallen, fallen is Babylon;
> and all the images of her gods,
>   he has shattered to the ground" (21:8-9).

The linking of the horsemen riding in pairs with the defeat of Babylon is
made relevant in the present context because of the identification (in the Book
of Revelation) of Babylon with the "mother of harlots." The coming of the
riders announces Rebecca's defeat in her attempt to divide the Maples. Updike
draws on this same chapter from Isaiah in a later Maple story. See below,
pp. 213-14.

her boy friend been ordered to leave the big place on the roof;
they had also come out of the subway and were looking up at
Manhattan Bridge when two policemen directed them back into the
subway. In this universe, the boundaries between the sacred and
the profane are guarded by angels. Each individual is directed to
the sphere where he or she belongs.

It is only when the snow falls that the true division between the
sacred and the profane is understood by the inhabitants of earth.
Updike's use of the image of snow as a message from heaven is so
important that it requires separate examination.[7] Here it is only
necessary to notice that falling snow (emphasized in the title of this
story) is the medium whereby the Maples are brought to an unconscious understanding of their true relationship and of Rebecca
as an alien presence. Because the snow keeps falling, Richard later
learns enough to make him run from Rebecca's apartment.

The snow is coming down hard as Richard and Rebecca step outside. At the traffic light, Richard notices how Rebecca hesitates to
cross on the green light, and is impelled to ask whether she does
live on the other side. Although green is not her color, Rebecca
has to agree. They pass a church, and Richard tries to make conversation:

> "Poor church," he said. "It's hard in this city for a steeple to be
> the tallest thing." Rebecca said nothing, not even her habitual
> "Yes." He felt rebuked for being preachy. (p. 78)

Rebecca would not normally have refused to say "Yes" to a man,
but this subject is taboo.

Here Updike, indifferent to the charge of being thought preachy,
states the problem of marriage in contemporary society. A wife with
a cold cannot compete in attractiveness with a poised and witty girl.
What meaning can the laws of the Christian Church have today,
when the Church is so patently a thing to be pitied, so ineffective
an institution, overtopped as it is by the big concerns of the Secular
City? Our answer to that question depends upon whether we find
relevant to our century the words of the Wise Teacher in Proverbs,
and whether we admit the possibility of receiving supernatural mail
at an apartment in New York City.

Updike, however, is primarily a writer, not a preacher. His concern is to present "things" as they are. In "Snowing in Greenwich
Village" he suggests that "things" are much more complex and belong
to a far more intricate pattern than the popular philosophy of the
ordinary city dweller today allows for. Whether or not the Maples
have eyes to see it, the messengers of God ride without fail down

---

7 See Chapter 7.

Thirteenth Street to enforce the eternal law of Things as They Are. Men are free, of course, to break the laws of the universe; and they are free to ignore them, or stupidly to remain ignorant of them. Human freedom ends only at that point where people wish to avoid the consequence of their actions. Then, whether they know it or not, and whether they like it or not, they are put in their place.

It is an uncompromising view that Updike presents, and an unpopular one. For it assumes that freedom is not an absolute, but something that is known solely when the limits upon freedom are first recognized and respected. The free man is supremely the man who has learned that self-will is slavery, since it is the desire to *create* the real rather than to respond to it. Dante is one of the influences found throughout Updike's work; and Dante's "In His will is our peace" might be written as the epigraph to a number of the stories.

Freedom is a theme to which Updike returns continually. Ken Whitman, one of the characters in *Couples,* remembers what it was like to be a child who, "after a long hide in the weeds shouts *Free!* and touches the home maple" (p. 98). This discovery of joy in freedom recurs in many different forms throughout Updike's fiction. In the Maple stories, the goal of married love is presented precisely as the winning of freedom to break loose from an alien environment in order to reach "the home maple."

Richard Maple in "Snowing in Greenwich Village" finds that freedom in the falling snow, and hurries down the stairs from the "strange" environment of Rebecca's apartment back to his own home and his own Maple. Yet, as Updike suggests time and again in his stories, the common experience we have is of having to spend most of our time hiding in the weeds. Only occasionally do we find the liberating moment when we can shout *Free!* and dash home in triumphant style. The later experiences of the Maples, described to us in the stories that follow this one, make the point very plain.

5

THE SOVEREIGN
STATE OF MARRIAGE:
MORE ABOUT THE MAPLES

"SNOWING IN GREENWICH VILLAGE" SHOWS THE Maples' marriage coming through an early time of testing, a crisis that threatens yet never develops. Updike allows seven years to elapse before he writes another Maple story. The return to this particular family not only coincides with Updike's specific concentration upon the problem of marriage in modern North American society; it also comes at a time when he is probing ever more deeply into the phenomenon of contemporary life that is generally given the title of alienation.

The malaise of alienation is one which Updike seems to attribute to the inability of twentieth-century man to recognize the universe of things surrounding him. All desperate attempts at self-knowledge through introspection — including the concentration upon private history urged as a therapeutic technique by the practitioners of psychoanalysis — remain, he thinks, ineffective so long as the individual remains ignorant of the nature of the world in which, as an individual, he has to live. The more an individual tries to know himself in isolation from his environment, the greater becomes his capacity for self-deception and the wider becomes the gulf that separates him from his fellows and leaves him in frightening loneliness. Marriage, in which two individuals must either share a common existence or destroy each other's happiness, becomes a test case for the ability of contemporary man to understand his world — and, by natural sequence, himself.

In the later Maple stories, Richard's immaturity and lack of self-knowledge (the traits accented in "Snowing in Greenwich Village") become central; for what is partly excusable in the inexperienced young adult becomes increasingly less so as experiences multiply and demand the capacity to take responsibility for other lives. Updike's treatment of the tensions in the Maple marriage brings to the fore his growing interest in presenting "the ambiguities of flesh" in terms of the internal pattern of the human psyche *seen as an objective pattern mirroring the universe at large.*

Already in his first novel, *The Poorhouse Fair* (published three years after the first appearance of "Snowing in Greenwich Village"), we find Updike turning to examine the constituents of the soul or *anima*.[1] The approach he adopts is largely unfamiliar to our present way of thinking, though it was employed almost universally by the great minds in our Western culture from the time of Socrates to the Enlightenment, until Romanticism destroyed its prestige. The tradition which Updike revives is one seeing the constituents of the *anima* as a pattern of degrees of worth. According to this view, the health of the soul depends upon a right balance between its various elements. It is a kingdom to be ruled through a preservation of due degree, the lesser powers serving the greater, and the greater powers exercising their authority for the good of the whole, thereby excluding the opposite and interconnected evils of tyranny and anarchy. This pattern of just order is one extending from man, the microcosm, to the universe, the macrocosm. Freedom for the individual, the family, and the state is therefore a product of justice. The existence of freedom anywhere is contingent upon the existence of order everywhere. It is a delicate balance. The sovereign must be wise and magnanimous. His subjects must be loyal and diligent.

* * *

The second and third Maple stories are collected in *The Music School*. They tell of the disastrous consequences in the Maple household of a failure to preserve a just balance. Through Richard's inability to rule wisely, the kingdom of his marriage has fallen into disorder. And the roots of this disorder lie in the imbalance within Richard's own soul. "Giving Blood," the first of these two stories, opens with these dispiriting words: "The Maples had been married now nine years, which is almost too long" (p. 18). The Maples have left New York City and are living in New England, thirty miles out of Boston. They have four children: Judith, Richard, Jr., John, and Bean. The story tells how Richard drives unwillingly into Boston on a Saturday morning, so that he and Joan can donate blood to a "sort of cousin" who is lying dangerously ill in a large Boston

---

[1] See below, Chapter 8.

hospital. Richard is angry with Joan, mainly because he feels guilty about flirting with a neighbor, Marlene Brossman, at a dance the night before. Moreover, he has previously avoided giving blood, and is frightened at the prospect. But while they are in the hospital, lying on separate beds but giving blood simultaneously, his love for Joan is renewed.

The theme of kingship is introduced when the Maples enter the hospital room. Richard remembers how he once had worked with teletype machines in a room much this size. At this hour in the morning, the work of pasting the tapes together would have been done. "It came back to him, how pleasant and secure those hours had been when, king of his own corner, he was young and newly responsible" (p. 25). The memory returns because in this room the tapes of the scattered items of his life with Joan can be spliced into a meaningful record; and once again he can be a king renewing his youth in taking up the responsibilities he has lately ignored.

In this Boston hospital there is also said to be the King of Arabia, who has come, attended by his four wives, to be treated for glaucoma. Richard too is a sick king, with eye trouble. But he sees himself not as a king, but as a slave to a demanding and ungrateful family making unreasonable demands upon his time and energy, draining him even of his life's blood and putting him (as he says accusingly to Joan) upon the rack. The act of giving blood, reluctantly entered into, changes his mood. He tells Joan he loves her, he praises her for her courage, and he feels assured of his manhood when she tells him *he* was brave. Irritability returns, all the same, as they stop for coffee and pancakes before driving home and he discovers he has not enough money to pay. All his resentment against the demands made upon him by his family boils over when he finds that he has only one worn dollar in his wallet. Joan ends the story with the response, "We'll both pay."

Richard's decline from king to slave results from his inability to see that marriage depends upon two lives being united in giving and paying. After he gives his blood, Richard gropes after this truth, uncertainly. "I don't really understand this business of giving something away and still somehow having it" (p. 33). Like Ben Franklin's Poor Richard, this latter-day Poor Richard knows the law of hard cash: a penny saved is a penny earned; but he does not really grasp the law of spiritual wealth: you gain only what you spend. Staring angrily at his single dollar, he remains confused between the laws of the physical and the spiritual realm. In the hospital his blood will not at first flow for a blood sample to be taken. He has no will to give, and resents the fact that Joan has laid this obligation upon him for the benefit of someone who is not even a near relative. Then, lying on the hospital bed, which is at *right* angles to the bed where his wife is giving blood, his vein empties more quickly than Joan's. It is normal for a man to flow faster, the attendant comments; and it is playing the man's role that restores Richard's self-confidence and makes his *husbandly love* overflow. In spite of the experience that giving is gaining, however, he fails to *see* clearly the meaning of what has taken place. His visit to the hospital is not an unqualified success. He is still a king with eye trouble.

The introduction of the King of Arabia, his eye disease, and his four devoted wives, seems rather odd in an otherwise ordinary account of a New England family going through the routine experience of giving blood in modern hospital. Once again, we find Updike expecting the reader to be well-informed enough to fill in the background knowledge needed. Through the Middle Ages the Arabs were famous for their medical knowledge, derived partly from the manuscripts of Greek medical works preserved in the East. Arab medicine was founded on the tradition of Galen, who based his system on the four humors; and it produced many famous physicians, notably Ali Ibn Isa, who identified a hundred and thirty diseases of the eye. Today, so Updike suggests, the East has to come to the Western world to benefit from its scientific methods of medicine. But the West has forgotten the wisdom of Galen, whose theory of the humors is applicable to the human *anima*. As a reminder of this truth, the King of Arabia comes with his four wives. And the Maples wonder whether they will *see* him.

Following his normal pattern of wordplay, Updike multiplies references to humor in its various senses. Richard clowns through nervousness, and his attempt at *humor* is not appreciated by the intern. (It is interesting that Richard should think this young man resembles "an apprentice barber," thus recalling the barber-surgeons of the eighteenth century who did bloodletting.) Today the earlier sense of the word "humor" lives on solely in the name for the fluids of the eye. This fact finds indirect expression in talk which Richard overhears in the hospital room about a certain Iris who is angry (inflamed). Then Richard and Joan privately discuss the classical four humors, recalling them imperfectly.

Had Richard and Joan been able to recall the theory of the classical humors, which placed health in the right balance between the four vital fluids of blood, phlegm, yellow bile (choler), and black bile, they would have understood the reason for the tensions in their marriage. Joan comes near to doing so. (Richard calls her "educated," though he manages to turn the compliment into a jibe.) She wonders whether the splenetic man and the sanguine man are

the same (p. 33). Blood and spleen are the humors predominating
in her husband, who annoys her by his sanguine temperament —
always *putting on a show,* as she says — and whose choler (spleen)
is usually concentrated on herself. In his turn Richard cannot understand Joan's detached (phlegmatic) disposition,[2] believing it to be
smugness, or her tendency to melancholy (black bile) as evidenced
in her spiritless refusal to fight back when she is attacked. As a
result he needles her for being "sexless." Then, momentarily reconciled, Richard loses his bluster and becomes tender, finding Joan
responsive. They visit the Pancake House before returning home,
exchanging their former acidity for sweetness over a simple meal
(pancakes — and maple syrup?) with coffee, which Richard connects with the days he was "king of his own corner." Yet Richard
is soon back at his old ways, wanting to show off and angered by
his wife's refusal to fight back.

Ignorant of the humors, Richard is deprived of the education
necessary for kingly rule. It is said that when Aristotle instructed
Alexander the Great, he taught him first the four elements, the
four "complexions" of man, the principal divisions of the earth, and
then the fifth element, *Orbis,* containing the whole.[3] Without understanding the parts, Richard cannot comprehend that which would
give his kingdom of marriage wholeness. At the hospital he is told
that a man's blood flows more quickly than a woman's because man
has the stronger heart. He is flattered by the knowledge, yet he
never applies the lesson to himself, or recognizes that he has the
major responsibility for keeping the marriage in good heart through
his affection. Instead of seeing Joan as the complement to himself,
he blames her for possessing exactly those qualities needed to balance
his own. Most of all, he neglects to consider how a king rules not
for his own benefit, but for the good of the whole. Only in the
room at the hospital, as man and wife lie "at right angles together,"
does Richard have a glimpse of the cosmic dimension of the kingdom
of marriage: "His blood and Joan's merged on the floor, and together their spirits glided from crack to crack, from star to star on
the ceiling" (p. 27). *Orbis,* the whole, which the true king must
know, reaches from the floor where physical life belongs to the ceil-

---

[2] That Joan has to reckon with excess of *phlegm* is indicated by her long-
continuing cold, mentioned in "Snowing in Greenwich Village."

[3] See John Gower, *Confessio Amantis,* Bk. VII, ll. 203-632. Bk. VII treats
of kingship, and is followed immediately in Bk. VIII by an exposition of the
laws of marriage. The *Confessio Amantis* was immensely popular until the
17th century, and Gower's teaching was echoed in many works now better remembered than his.

ing of the stars to which the spirit can ascend. Because man and woman are different, they can rise together to the highest bliss.

* * *

"Giving Blood" begins with Richard's complaining that he is exhausted. Tension has made the Maples' nine years of marriage seem "almost too long." Glaucoma, the disease bringing the King of Arabia to Boston, is caused by a tension of the humors of the eye; and it is a deadly disease, leading often to permanent blindness. In "Twin Beds in Rome" the marriage of Joan and Richard has come almost to a breakdown through the acute stage of tension at which they have arrived. Their conversation has become an intolerable strain of opposed wills, and only physical love-making keeps them together: ". . . when their tongues at last fell silent, their bodies collapsed together as two mute armies might gratefully mingle, released from the absurd hostilities decreed by two mad kings" (p. 76).

Thus the kingdom of their marriage has fallen from disorder to suicidal civil war. There cannot be two kings in one kingdom; nor can a state survive when the king regards only private ends and forsakes the common good. By way of a kill-or-cure treatment, Richard and Joan leave home and go off by themselves on a holiday to Rome.

Although they make no plans, they find that on their arrival they are treated like royalty. Even the hotel they are taken to, though described as second-class, is tiled with rose marble and draped in imperial purple. There is only one thing that bothers Richard: their room is furnished with twin beds.

Richard is the one who objects to the arrangement. Yet he sleeps soundly. When Joan puts out her arm to keep him from feeling lonely, he shouts out in his sleep that he wants to be left alone. However, when they first go out sightseeing, he develops unaccustomed pains in his feet. Then, after easing his feet by buying new shoes, he gets a severe stomach ache. An hour's rest banishes the trouble (which he recognizes as nervousness), and they explore Rome together. From then on, it is taken for granted between them that they have at last been parted. They change in their behavior, becoming "with each other, as in the days of courtship, courteous, gay, and quiet" (p. 86). But now Richard, seeing Joan happy within herself, becomes jealously reluctant to leave her. With this indication that the visit to Rome has not proved a clear-cut kill or cure, "Twin Beds in Rome" closes.

While Rome does not solve their marriage problems once and for all, the city in its ancient wisdom does teach them much about their marriage. Its buildings and monuments speak silently and tellingly. As they enter the city, they see the Colosseum looking like a ruined wedding cake. They gaze at the Victor Emmanuel Monument, "a titanic flight of stairs leading nowhere" (p. 81). Richard wonders whether this was the king who unified Italy. Joan ("she is so intelligent") connects him with the funny little king in Hemingway's *Farewell to Arms*. They walk over floors which are graves adorned with rounded figures worn flat by passing feet. Among these "sleeping people" they find, behind a pillar, one face seeming "a vivid soul trying to rise from the all but erased body" (p. 82).

The Maples have come to Rome less in the hope of saving their marriage than of ending the conflict that has left the marriage "bleeding, mangled, reverently laid in the tomb a dozen times" — yet unable to die (p. 76). On their arrival at the hotel Joan says: "You're supposed to relax. This isn't a honeymoon or anything, it's just a little rest we're trying to give each other" (p. 79). Yet Richard will neither relax himself nor let his wife relax. He follows his old tactics of trying to pick a fight by mingling compliments with jibes, until Joan, "sickened by simultaneous doses of honey and gall," is driven either to tears or to retreat into herself. The architecture of Rome makes them face the ruin of their early married hopes, the steps they have taken leading nowhere. If Richard is not to be the king who unifies his warring kingdom, he may nevertheless feature in "a farewell to arms." Out of the sleep which Rome will give as its gift to the Maples, the soul of the marriage may be able to rise from the tomb where its bleeding, mangled body has been laid so often.

Rome has housed a thousand princes, and it will not allow Richard to forget that he is one. Hence his discomfort from the time he arrives at the purple-draped hotel room until he accepts the welcome Rome has prepared for him on its terms ('When in Rome, do as the Romans do'). His feet hurt him because he has to walk on marble; his stomach ache is most acute when he refuses to go into the Basilica of Constantine. He associates his internal pains, incidentally, with having to hand out large tips. Medieval tradition made Largess the second point of Policy in Kingship (the first being Truth),[4] so that Richard's unwillingness to give gladly is an unkingly quality aristocratic Rome will not tolerate. Obviously, he is still unable to answer the question he himself raised in "Giving Blood" — how one can give and, through giving, possess also.

Most of the princes of Rome are dead, belonging to the past. This seems to explain why the chief gift Rome can offer the Maples is to wipe out the recent, unhappy days and to return them to their

---

[4] See Gower, ll. 1985-2794.

past. Here in Rome they find a local anaesthetic to deaden present pain. Richard's feet cease to trouble him after he has exchanged his "vital" American shoes for a pair of "dead" Italian ones (p. 81). Rome's kindly attentiveness to their needs permits them to lose their agonizing tensions, to return to the relaxed condition of earlier days. Nevertheless, because the Eternal City contains within it so many reminders of how a civilization makes order out of chaos, it offers them some specific, positive guidance for keeping the peace as well as a chance to say farewell to arms. During their stay Richard comes to see Joan "as if freshly," in the same light as when they first met (p. 85); and he becomes resigned to the fact that she is "separate" from him. She, from the knowledge gained through studying the buildings around her, explains to Richard that she is classic, and he baroque (p. 84).

In Rome these two styles certainly manage to exist harmoniously side by side, different though they are. Richard's behavior when asleep proves that he, as much as Joan, wants to be a person in his own right. It is his jealous possessiveness that is making a shared life impossible. The twin beds — beds in which they both sleep and are refreshed — provide the basic setting for the lesson to be learned; for they show that instead of two kings locked in insane warfare, there should be one king and his consort, each giving a separate and distinct contribution to the order of a united kingdom.

The lesson of separation is, in fact, beginning to be followed. Courtesy — the civilized and aristocratic virtue — has succeeded rudeness; gaiety has sprung up with the lessening of tension; and quiet has come at the cessation of fighting. The question left unresolved at the end of the story is whether Richard's "jealous" reluctance to leave Joan can be any foundation for a rebuilding of the kingdom. For it is seeing her happy, and not any thought that he may give her happiness out of his own resources, that leads him to want to remain with her.

* * *

Since the two Maple stories collected in *The Music School,* four more have appeared. In the new stories, Richard's irresponsibility and immaturity are brought out more forcibly than ever. In addition, the Maple marriage is shown to be undergoing strain from without as well as within, as though it were headed inevitably for some showdown, some "moment of truth." The four stories do, in fact, focus on the issue of truth and falsehood. We may remember that Truth is the first point in the Policy of Kingship; so it may prove that Richard is being brought to the place where he must either decide to rule his kingdom responsibly or be forced to abdicate. To date, though,

Richard's capacity for out-Hamleting Hamlet in postponing action, while waiting to see how events will develop by themselves, seems boundless.

The first of these stories, "Marching Through Boston,"[5] tells how Joan, now twelve years married, becomes involved in the civil-rights movement and persuades Richard to accompany her in a march being held in Boston. She has already taken part in the freedom march in Alabama. While her activities have given her an unusual bloom of health and beauty, Richard has grown "jealous and irritable" (p. 34). On the April day they set off for Boston, Richard feels a fever coming on but continues in spite of Joan's offer to go alone. As they drive home, the march and speeches by Martin Luther King and other black leaders over, he upbraids her for making him "stay to hear every damn speech" (p. 37); and, at home, he insists on talking like a stage Uncle Tom. Asked to stop it, he finds that he cannot. He is put to bed, and Joan leaves him still compulsively babbling.

"Marching Through Boston" is a repetition of "Giving Blood," without any breakthrough into temporary union of spirit. As in the earlier story Richard resents Joan's social conscience and covers up his own guilty feelings with insults and clowning, so now the comic coon accent he effects is adopted to ridicule her altruism and concern. When he first begins his parody of the Negro voice Joan says, "Aren't you mean" (p. 34). His meanness is really his unwillingness to give her his cooperation.

Formerly, Marlene Brossman had been on his mind, giving the edge to his bitter banter. Here his memories of Carol, a sixteen-year-old student beside whom he walked after being separated from Joan on the march, are obscurely driving him to humiliate his wife. He keeps blaming Joan for keeping him through the speeches, demanding her sympathy for his fever in front of the children. Joan tells their daughter Bean, "Daddy has a tiny cold." But the child, sensitive to the spiritual temperature beyond the physical, wonders whether he will die (p. 38). There is indeed cause for anxiety, and Joan has already warned Richard that he is a very sick man. His sickness, however, lies in the condition that causes the voice he has assumed to take control of him against his will, becoming a cry "from the depths of oppression for attention" (p. 38). Richard has heard a King speaking, and has transformed the kingly tones into the whine of a slave.

Richard realizes that he is incapable temperamentally of sharing his wife's enthusiasm. But, because he insists upon punishing her for

---

[5] *The New Yorker,* January 22, 1966.

the differences between them (as he learns from Joan's former psychiatrist whom they meet on the march), what might be creative tensions become destructive divisions. While this situation continues, Joan's health means Richard's sickness. Freedom marches for the wife spell slavery for the husband. Having warned him of the seriousness of his condition, Joan can only leave him alone. For his sickness is self-induced; and the way to health lies in his having the courage to face the truth about his marriage and the determination to conduct himself as a king instead of a slave.

The three Maple stories that follow "Marching Through Boston" form a distinct group. The early pair of the group are placed near together in time: "Your Lover Just Called"[6] in the transition from late summer to early fall, and "The Taste of Metal"[7] a few months later, when winter has begun. But although "The Taste of Metal" is the second in sequence, it may be considered first, since "Your Lover Just Called" links in theme with the third story, "Eros Rampant."[8]

Common to the first two stories is the Maples' friendship with a municipal bond salesman Mack Dennis and his wife Eleanor. In "Your Lover Just Called," the Dennises are in the process of being divorced, and in "The Taste of Metal" they are legally separated. "The Taste of Metal" finds Richard at a party where, after rather too many drinks, he concentrates his attentions upon Eleanor. Mack, of course, is not there; but his absence is noticeable since the separation was recent.

The Maples agree to drive Eleanor home, and so she slips into the front seat of Richard's new Mustang, while Joan sits in the rear. It is beginning to snow. Richard knows he is too drunk to be driving, but will trust no one else to drive his beautiful new car. He finds himself on this perfect night in a perfectly ordered world: "Eleanor was beside him, Joan behind him, God above him, the road beneath him" (p. 49). Then suddenly, on a dangerous bend, he loses control of the car and it slides "as if magnetized, to a telephone pole that rigidly insisted on its position in the center of the windshield" (p. 50). The collision wraps the Mustang's bumper around the pole, so that the car cannot be backed onto the road again. A passing car takes Joan away to find help. Richard stays with Eleanor, who has seemingly lost the use of her legs — her handsome, vivid, long legs Richard so much admired at the party, when she hitched up her miniskirt and kicked the lintel of a doorframe. He is kissing her when the police car arrives.

---

[6] *Harper's Magazine*, January, 1967.
[7] *The New Yorker*, March 11, 1967.
[8] *Harper's Magazine*, January, 1968.

A number of interesting links connect this story with "Snowing in Greenwich Village." Once again we find it snowing; only this time it is no more than a flurry, "an illusion conjured to administer this one rebuke" (p. 51);[9] it passes, and so does Richard's control of the situation. Once again there is a woman who is an amusing conversationalist. Eleanor entertains the Maples with fantastic anecdotes of Mack's conduct toward her — anecdotes calculated to reflect indirect credit upon herself. As Rebecca Cune told of not having eaten meat at Thanksgiving when she was a child, so Eleanor tells of having tuna sandwiches instead of turkey at Thanksgiving after her husband left her. As Rebecca made her advances in a hot apartment, so Eleanor takes the initiative in kissing Richard after he has turned on the heater in his car. The police, who in "Snowing in Greenwich Village" were seen passing, here close in upon the guilty pair whose transgression of the law of marriage is illuminated by their car lights. Thus the catastrophe averted in the first Maple story is not averted in the fifth. In Rebecca's apartment the verticality of the furniture seemed *threatened*. In the accident with Eleanor the telephone pole *asserts* the vertical. It divides the windshield precisely between Richard and Eleanor, refusing to withdraw its upright judgment.

The fresh elements introduced into "The Taste of Metal" emphasize two aspects of Richard's situation belonging to the fact that he is no longer a young husband whose mistakes may be excused by inexperience. The story title is based on the gold cappings a dentist has put on his worn teeth. The metal in his mouth seems to him "as disciplinary, as a *No,* spoken to other tastes" (p. 49). He senses that this prohibition, which he now carries with him always, refers also to his "taste" for Eleanor. But he disregards it, just as he disregards the "rebuke" of the snow and his wife's pointed references to the "slippery" road he is taking "too fast." There is another side of Richard's present position to which our attention is directed, and of which he himself is conscious: the irreversibility of time. Once the car's bumper is locked around the telephone pole, Richard, knowing that he is too drunk to face the police, nevertheless has no choice but to wait for them to arrive. Sitting beside Eleanor, he reflects how "never again, never again, would his car be new, would he chew on his own enamel, would she kick so high with vivid long legs" (p. 51). On the car radio a Handel oboe sonata is being played. He imagines that if only the music would reverse, they

---

[9] The *rebuke,* here attributed to the snow, is "a flat whack surprisingly unambiguous" at the moment of hitting the pole. Richard feels "the sudden refusal of motion, the *No*" as a decisive event carrying consequences for himself (p. 50).

could pull back onto the road. But time will not reverse, and we all have to go into the future bearing our guilt.

"The Taste of Metal" is a wry commentary on the widespread belief of our generation that no law should interfere with our ideas of what we want for ourselves. After the accident Eleanor remarks, "This pole is hit so often it's just a nuisance to the neighborhood" (p. 51). She speaks for all who see the permanence of marriage vows (among other fixed rules) as an unnecessary restriction on the individual's freedom to live by his own standards. Updike draws the picture of a society where fidelity is just a nuisance, where order is disregarded (Joan relegated to the back seat), and where the *No* of reality is ignored by people whose minds, like that of Richard at the time of hitting the pole, are "deeply cushioned in a cottony indifference" (p. 50).

Indifference to the *No* of reality means that truth itself has become a matter of indifference. In a world that absolutizes pleasure, deceit is not simply permitted — it is made into an essential feature of social life. When we play life the way we want it, inventing the rules as we go along, then keeping others in the dark about the game we are playing, the outcome must always be to our advantage. In *Couples* Updike gives his extended comment on a way of life in which gameplaying and playing with lies have come to be the two principal pursuits of existence.[10] In "The Taste of Metal" the driver of the passing car who takes Joan to get the police is a boy, looking sexually drained and offering an unnecessary and unintentionally revealing lie about being on his way back from a poker game (p. 51).

"Your Lover Just Called" exhibits one of the games that can be played in preference to the arduous business of seeking truth. It is the dangerous game of playing with reality in such a way that the distinction between fact and fantasy disappears.

* * *

In this story Richard is shown at home one Friday with a cold. Unlike Joan's persistent cold in "Snowing in Greenwich Village," Richard's cold was slight, and it did not inhibit his verbal duelling with his wife. When the telephone rang and went dead immediately after he answered, he affected to believe that it was Joan's lover expecting him to be at work. He suggested various possible names, including that of Mack Dennis, who was coming to dinner that evening (Eleanor being in Wyoming suing for divorce). He allowed himself finally to be packed off to bed; but as he settled under the blankets, the phone rang again. Joan told him it was someone trying to sell them the *World Book Encyclopedia*. " 'A very likely

---

[10] See below, pp. 219, 224, 239.

story,' he said, with self-pleasing irony, leaning back onto the pillows confident that he was being unjust, that there was no lover" (p. 49).

Before dinner that evening, Richard went out to buy cigarettes. On his return he saw Mack and Joan kissing in the kitchen. He said nothing until after the third round of martinis, when he began to attack them with bitter jokes about what he had seen, producing embarrassed apologies from Mack and curt words of rebuke from Joan. Next day, as Joan prepared to go out for her usual Saturday morning tennis, she and Richard continued to bicker over the incident. The phone rang, and this time it was Joan who answered only to be cut off. Now it was her turn to say the caller must have expected her to be out of the house. While Joan went to her game, Richard took the children to the playground and the stores. In the afternoon the Maples, both tired, decided to take a nap. Richard soon turned from discussing Joan's possible lover to making love. Once again the phone began to ring. They allowed it to go on ringing until the "lover" hung up.

Clearly, there is an urgent question of truth at the heart of this story. At Richard's initial suggestion that it was his wife's lover at the other end of the phone, Joan says sarcastically that if he will go out to buy cigarettes, she will call her lover back and explain what has happened (p. 48). It is while he is out getting cigarettes that Joan and Mack take the opportunity to kiss. Richard sees they are perfectly free with each other. Yet he treats the incident wholly as an opportunity to display his wit. After the first phone call, Joan had been incensed because he looked so happy while he was accusing her. While taunting Joan and Mack with what he has seen, he is triumphant. "A profound happiness was stretching him from within; the reach of his tongue and wit felt immense, and the other two seemed dolls, homunculi, in his playful grasp" (p. 50). But the grasp in which Mack held Joan in the kitchen looked more than playful, although Joan afterwards tries to pass it off as only that. Richard has to deal with real people in a real situation, not with dolls. Wives do take lovers, especially wives whose husbands give them continual disparagement instead of affection.

If there is an actual triangle here, then it is Richard who is the doll, manipulated by the other two. If there is not, then the course Richard is following is the one most surely calculated to create what he imagines. Either way, Joan is justified in her question: "What I'd like to know is, why are you so pleased?" (p. 51).

It is Richard Jr. who lets us know what the whole story is about. He has a collection of Batman cards, and he recites to his father "a boundless plot" detailing his hero's battle against assorted villains (p. 51). His father does not pay attention, but anyone having some small acquaintance with the super-hero dedicated to human dignity and the pursuit of happiness knows that in stately Wayne Manor there is a hot-line phone that summons Batman whenever there is a wrong to be righted. If Batman is not at home, Aunt Harriet complains, "There it goes again — that same mysterious call with nobody ever at the other end of the line."

Joan is the only one who gets an answer — once — when their domestic hot-line phone rings. She is offered the resources of all the world's wisdom (the *World Book Encyclopedia*); and Richard does not believe her. The powers of justice might be called to set things right. Richard Jr. says, "Then, see Dad . . ." (p. 51; ellipses in the story). But Richard does not see. He is too busy feeling pleased with himself over being unjust to Joan to realize that he is faced with a situation requiring action by a champion of justice.

At the end of the story he is as much out of touch with reality as ever. Turning from accusations to love-making, and letting the phone ring on unanswered, do nothing but postpone a day of reckoning. In "Twin Beds in Rome" the bodies of Richard and Joan joined in love are compared with exhausted armies temporarily released from an insane war. Such respites cannot halt the war, because it is not the troops but their leaders who decide affairs of state. When Richard rises from the marriage bed, he is still answerable for allowing the war to continue, and for encouraging the forces inimical to truth and justice to take over the city of his marriage.

* * *

Self-satisfaction is Richard's dominant mood in "Your Lover Just Called." Futile regret (tuned to the grating note of an oboe) is his final mood in "The Taste of Metal." When truth is put aside for play and when right order is flouted, then self-induced euphoria cannot last. In "Eros Rampant" the question of truth presents itself in a way that cannot be avoided any longer. For Joan, after getting Richard to admit that he has made an unsuccessful *play* for one of the secretaries at his office, tells him that she has been sleeping for some months with an assistant director in the museum where she works part-time, and further confesses that in the past she had other lovers, including Mack.

"Eros Rampant" is a story embodying several of the themes Updike has introduced prominently in his later writings — particularly in *Of the Farm* and *Couples*. On that account, it will be considered in detail later.[11] At this point we need only touch on the elements connecting it with the theme of kingship.

Richard begs his wife to tell him the names of all her men, feeling that "each name is a burden of treasure she lays upon his bowed serf's shoulders" (p. 63). The fall from kingship to serfdom is a catastrophic one; but perhaps even more catastrophic is Richard's acceptance of his status as a serf without any thought of rebelling against it. As in "The Taste of Metal" he had gloried in a state of disorder flattering his ego ("Eleanor was beside him, his wife behind him," etc.), so now he glories perversely in another state of disorder that humiliates him. Having become accustomed to justifying his conduct romantically in the name of "love," without facing the actuality of the world in which each act carries with it inevitable consequences, he finds it easier to persist in his dreams than to take any active steps to deal with the unwelcome situation in which he suddenly finds himself.

Among the truths Richard would never face squarely is the one stressed in the two Maple stories collected in *The Music School* and also in "Marching Through Boston": the truth of the difference between Joan and himself, a difference both of temperament and of sex. Now he is compelled to recognize that difference, although he cannot readily come to terms with it. Plaintively, he comments on the (to him) inexplicable contrast between his philandering and hers:

> "Tell me all your men."
> "I've told you. It's a pretty austere list. You know *why* I told you? So you wouldn't feel guilty about this Vogel person."
> "But nothing happened. When you do it, it happens."
> "Sweetie, I'm a woman," she explains, and they do seem, in this darkening room above the muted hubbub of the television, to have reverted to the bases of their marriage, to the elemental constituents. Woman. Man. House.

In being thus recalled from the world of fantasy to the world of fact, Richard is given the chance to climb out of the morass of romantic unreality in which he has been trapped.[12] The unreal

---

[11] See below, Chapter 12.

[12] Richard's position recalls the part of the Batman adventure which Richard Jr. details to his father in "Your Lover Just Called" (*Harper's*, January 1967, p. 15). Richard Jr. describes how a bank was being filled with water by the Penguin and his masked accomplices — "I don't know why, to make it bust or something, and Robin was climbing up these slippery stacks of like half-dollars to get away from the water, and then see Dad . . ."

Half dollars would seem to indicate that there was a fifty-fifty chance of escaping from the flooded bank. Since the Penguin is short and stout, and Mack Dennis has such a figure, the application here may be that Mack is

world of love with which he has been preoccupied is symbolized by the television downstairs, where "a woman neglected and alone, locked in a box, sings about *amore*" (p. 63). The scene of Joan's confession, the darkening bedroom, reflects the darkening of Richard's marriage, and at the same time holds the hope that Richard will now be roused to action bringing him to the light. Stripped of the pretenses it has accumulated through his blind self-confidence, his marriage at this moment has been reduced to *what it is:* man, woman, and house.

The question of truth raised in "Eros Rampant" is a question of how the three basic elements of marriage can be related in a just order. *House,* we should remember, is here not primarily the physical structure — Corbusier's "machine for living in" — but the family complex created by the union of one man and one woman. The archetype of the house is the dynasty or Royal House. At one time Richard and Joan had the opportunity for being matched together as king and queen, founders of a royal house. It seems that they have thrown away that opportunity, having become mad rulers bent on destroying their kingdom. And human existence, like oboe sonatas, cannot be played backwards; their past mistakes, and the consequences of those mistakes, remain to plague the two Maples. Nevertheless, the bases of their marriage are still there. If Truth is allowed once more to become the first principle of the Policy of Kingship, Largess may again become practiced and order be restored to the sovereign state of marriage.

This possibility is held out as a live option in "Eros Rampant" (which has much to say about *balance*), and so it reads as a hopeful rather than as a depressing story. But Richard's resistance to truth and reality, his Hamlet-like capacity for intellectualizing a situation instead of facing it, is also stressed. The Maples have not yet solved the North American problem, namely how kingship can be made possible for everyone. Their troubles are bound up with those of the society of which they are part. Twentieth-century Poor Richard and his Joan are not out of the weeds. They still have to shout *"Free!"* and touch the home Maple.

---

threatening the Maple marriage — making it "bust." Batman himself does not appear in the account, because his escape would be certain. But Robin the apprentice, like Richard, is often overconfident; and, when Batman is not present, his good intentions are not always successful.

6

THE
QUALITATIVE
DISTINCTION

KIERKEGAARD'S NAME KEEPS CROPPING UP ON UPDIKE'S
pages. Walter, the narrator of "The Astronomer" in *Pigeon Feathers,*
explains that he "discovered" Kierkegaard when he was twenty-four
and living in a building on Riverside Drive overlooking the Hudson.
Every week Walter brought back to the apartment one or more of
Kierkegaard's books, whose "typographically exhilarating" pages
loaded with the vehement and contorted outpourings of the author's
mind, provided him with a fascinating spectacle and gave him "much
comfort" (pp. 179-80). So we are probably safe in concluding
that it was during his time in New York City that Updike familiar-
ized himself thoroughly with Kierkegaard's ideas. The tone of most
of his references to Kierkegaard is abrasive yet sympathetic, and the
fact that those works of Karl Barth which appealed to him were
written when Barth was strongly influenced by Kierkegaard suggests
that at least some of Kierkegaard's beliefs must have made a permanent impression on him.[1] One of these, certainly, was Kierkegaard's

---

[1] The poem "Die Neuen Heiligen" (*Telephone Poles,* p. 69) links Kierkegaard with Kafka and Karl Barth. Updike's most extended statement on Kierkegaard is an essay "The Fork" in *The New Yorker* (February 26, 1966, pp.
115-136). The essay is a review of a selection of Kierkegaard's journals, *The
Last Years,* edited by R. Gregor Smith (New York, 1965), and it concentrates
upon Kierkegaard's life and the final phase of his thought. Thus it is not in
any sense an estimate of the worth of Kierkegaard's writings as a whole. "The
Fork" has been reprinted in *Toward a New Christianity: Readings in the
Death of God Theology,* edited by Thomas J. J. Altizer (New York, 1967),
pp. 59-71.

insistence upon "the absolute qualitative distinction between time and eternity."

Another seems to have been Kierkegaard's urgent anouncement to his reader: "Only the truth which edifies is truth for thee." Kierkegaard believed that the spectator attitude to existence is basically a selfish and immature one that must be exchanged for an involved and (he invented the term) *existential* one. The attitude to life that is uninvolved and estimates everything in terms of the enjoyment we can get out of it he called the *aesthetic.* There are three spheres of existence: the *aesthetic,* the *moral,* and the *religious.* In order to come to maturity, he insisted, we must transcend the aesthetic and discover the moral and religious spheres, where, leaving behind the pleasure-pain calculus, we expose ourselves to reality by seeking that which has absolute worth. And that we can only do by putting our very lives behind our convictions.

Updike's writings are continually concerned with "the truth which edifies." Writing of the ambiguities of flesh, with all its ironical, funny, and tragic involvements, he sees human life in the light of the infinite. And like Kierkegaard he seems to think that the infinite first reveals itself to us in the absolute demands of the moral. Even if man is called a naked ape, he still cannot avoid the challenge of moral imperatives:

> *Noble animal:*
> *To try to lead on this terrestrial ball*
> *With grasping hand and saucy wife*
> *The upright life.*

Transcending the aesthetic values of covetousness and lust, man aspires to the nobility of moral kingship.

To be human, then, is to know that uprightness is not just a physical state but primarily a moral one. Once the moral vision has been achieved, said Kierkegaard, the religious one is unavoidable. Updike's noble animal stands and looks up to heaven. His sphere is the terrestrial one. Yet to speak of the *terrestrial* implies awareness of the *celestial.* As Updike put it in his poem "The High-Hearts" (*TP,* p. 25), man hears the whisper, "The universe wants men." And he cannot help responding.

> *So still he strains to keep his heart aloft,*
> *Too high and low at once, too hard and soft.*

Man, in Barth's phrase, is the creature on the boundary between heaven and earth.

Because human life belongs on this boundary, Updike finds heaven is always accessible on earth. The most commonplace objects can provide parables of trans-temporal realities. Indeed, he has learned

from Herrick that trivial subjects may keep the heart aloft with
less strain than impressive ones. For instance, there is the poem
which opens *Telephone Poles,* a poem on the mundane subject of
a washing machine:

BENDIX

This porthole overlooks a sea
Forever falling from the sky,
The water inextricably
Involved with buttons, suds, and dye.

Like bits of shrapnel, shards of foam
Fly heavenward; a bedsheet heaves,
A stocking wrestles with a comb,
And cotton angels wave their sleeves.

The boiling purgatorial tide
Revolves our dreary shorts and slips,
While Mother coolly bakes beside
Her little jugged apocalypse.

Here the poet's initial observation of how the washing machine
reverses the course of nature (the sea falling from the sky) prompts
him to recall the account in the Book of Revelation of the end of
the world, with the angels waging war in heaven. Judgment follows,
where the sins of men (our dreary shorts and slips) are purged.
Only, of course, this apocalyptic scene carries no terror, because
it is contained within the Bendix in the kitchen. The world's work,
personified by Mother's baking, carries on as usual.

A moralistic writer would have tried to improve the occasion
by suggesting that even a Bendix can teach us all to be prepared
for the end of the world. Updike's art avoids this kind of solemn
absurdity. Instead of using the Bendix as an excuse for delivering
an "edifying" lecture, Updike goes in for another type of edification,
one which does not exploit the subject in the interests of moral
uplift "to point a moral or adorn a tale," but rather allows it to
be more fully itself. He never lets us forget the kitchen. The angels
he shows us are plain cotton ones. Nevertheless, the smallness of
earthly things is made explicit by balancing them over against events
described in the Book of Revelation. The wrestling between the
stockings and a comb becomes the distant echo, in another dimension, of the binding of the Beast of Chaos. Thus the washing machine that we had taken previously to be simply another ingenious
product of modern technology is seen now to be *also* a "little jugged
apocalypse."

One of the principal functions of poetry is to break down our
stock responses to the world around us. This Updike does superla-

tively well, with a sure touch and a wit that is dry and yet does not exclude tenderness. He reminds us that our eyesight is myopic unless it can see earth in the light of heaven.

* * *

A reminder of how much we miss by narrowing our vision to immediately available sensation is given in the pair of quotations providing the epigraph for *The Same Door*. The first of these is taken from Bergson's *Laughter*. It asserts that the quality of our present emotions is largely supplied by memories of our past. The second, from T. S. Eliot's poem "The Elder Statesman," speaks of the enveloping, invisible love within a family allowing all other loves to be understood. Several of the stories in *The Same Door* have to do with the way in which contemporary life tends both to restrict and to distort our genuinely human power of sight by occupying our attention and concentrating it exclusively upon the commonplace and depressing present. One in particular deals with this theme. Entitled "Toward Evening," it portrays the darkness that can descend upon the human spirit in a large city.

There is even less plot in "Toward Evening" than in most of the companion stories in this early collection. Rafe, coming home from the office by bus, carries a box containing a mobile for his baby daughter Elizabeth. He delivers his present, has dinner with his wife Alice, and afterwards sits at the apartment window overlooking the Hudson.[2] Night descends, blotting out the view. Over the rooftops a flashing neon sign dominates the night sky, and Rafe speculates about how it got there.

Making few demands on our attention, the slight plot allows the imagery to carry the story. Four distinct clusters of images stand out.

The first is the modern city dweller's position in time and space. From the bus, Rafe sees the numbers on the houses as they pass, and begins to connect each with a date in history:

> 1832, 1836, 1846, 1850 (Wordsworth dies), 1880 (great Nihilistic trial in St. Petersburg), 1900 (Rafe's father born in Trenton), 1902 (Braque leaves le Havre to study painting in Paris), 1914 (Joyce begins *Ulysses;* war begins in Europe), 1926 (Rafe's parents marry in Ithaca), 1936 (Rafe is four years old). Where the present should have stood, a block was being torn down, and the numbering began again with 2000, a boring progressive edifice. (*SD,* pp. 65-66)

---

[2] This is evidently the same apartment which is home for Walter in "The Astronomer." "The Astronomer" tells us that the apartment is on the sixth floor, and it also contains a description of night descending over the Hudson.

Here is the setting for Rafe's existence (which coincides with Updike's).

His commentary on the house numbers begins with the death of Wordsworth, the poet who wrote, "The world is too much with us; late and soon, / Getting and spending, we lay waste our powers." After this, world events center around nihilism and war. Braque and Joyce are artists whose works attempt to unify the broken experiences of the modern world. The present is completely blank, and the future promises nothing except boredom.

The broken world is further exemplified in a second set of images: the advertisements in New York City. Rafe looks up from reading the street numbers and sees a cellulose poster in the bus. This is an "ingenious" affair meant to show a coffee drinker in two stages of enjoying his drink. But the angle of Rafe's vision shows him both pictures at once, spoiling the illusion and making him feel bus-sick. At home, the descending darkness leaves nothing visible of the city except the endless three-stage sequence of the neon sign raised above the rooftops and announcing "Spry, Spry FOR BAKING, Spry FOR FRYING."

The third cluster of images concerns bird life. Rafe's gift to his daughter is a mobile of seven celluloid winged birds hanging from a coarse wire. Carrying it, Rafe notices three women on the bus. Each in turn suggests a different bird-image, and even the bus doors are seen as flapping pterodactyl wings. What birds in the city mean to Updike is described in one of his pieces for "The Talk of the Town" in *The New Yorker,* where he writes: "No matter how long we live among rectangular stones, we still listen, in the pauses of a rain, for the sounds of birds chirping as they shake themselves" (*AP,* p. 104). So birds stand for natural life stirring in the midst of dead forms.

When taken out of its rectangular box, the bird mobile fails to please, because it carries no promise of life. Rafe's wife Alice has expected "a genuine Calder, made of beautiful polished woods," and the baby takes no interest in "the abstract swinging, quite unlike the rapt infant shown on the box" (*SD,* p. 66). Lacking the natural beauty of wood, the rubber birds with their celluloid wings are of a piece with the cellulose sign. In his poem "Mobile of Birds" (*TP,* pp. 67-68) Updike indicates what such a mobile *can* suggest. The poem begins, "There is something / in their planetary weave that is comforting," and goes on to say that their motion is "random as nature" yet "calculable," recalling

> *those old Ptolemaic heavens small*
> *enough for the Byzantine Trinity,*

> *Plato's Ideals,*
> *formal devotion,*
> *seven levels of bliss, and numberless wheels*
> *of omen, balanced occultly.*

In New York City, however, there is no memory of these complex and meaningful patterns. The perfect number of seven, strung on a coarse wire and lacking Calder's carpentered artistry, conveys nothing. The only trinity the city-heavens hold is "Spry, Spry FOR BAKING, Spry FOR FRYING."

So far, the story details the eclipse of history, the destruction of human values, and the coming of a new Dark Age in which the heavens hold no comforting vision and man is broken by the products of his mechanical ingenuity. Yet there is another cluster of images relieving this depressing recital. These are images of nourishment.

In any age, nature sees to it that we eat and drink. Even cellulose posters advertise coffee, and flashing neon signs urge us to cook. Unconcerned with the abstract qualities of the mobile, Elizabeth tries to stuff it in her mouth. And while man continues to seek nourishment, he is not totally ignorant of the presence of goodness in the world. Seen in this perspective, the title "Toward Evening" not only predicts the falling of darkness. It also recalls the biblical story of the walk to Emmaus. "Abide with us: for it is toward evening, and the day is far spent," say Cleopas and his companion (Luke 24:29), and the Risen Lord breaks bread with them.

Within the home, at least, the hope persists that life will be renewed. As Rafe approaches his home, he senses that the warm air guarantees Spring. In the apartment, the baby has just been fed, and his wife is relaxing "flushed and sleepy." "That invisible gas goodness, stung his eyes and made him laugh, strut, talk nonsense" (p. 66). Rafe's dinner is a near sacrament, "his favorite everything," the gift of his wife's care for him. And at the table a triangular piece of bread, "falling to her lap through a width of light, twirled and made a star" (p. 67). Although Spry signs are the only legible words written in the contemporary sky, the erratic human wills that set them there are not wholly at variance with the good order of nature. The day of coherent human purpose in harmony with cosmic wholeness is far spent. But the night of deepening ennui has not put out all the stars. Before the year 2000 arrives the gap in history may have been filled with more than emptiness.

* * *

"Dentistry and Doubt," another story in *The Same Door,* deals with another aspect of preserving a vision of goodness in the con-

temporary world. The central character in this story is an American
Episcopal priest whose probing of the weakness of his faith coincides
with an English dentist's probing of the decay in his teeth. Vision
is palpably the theme. "We'll do the eyetooth," the dentist comments
(p. 44).

Burton, the American priest, is in Oxford writing a thesis on
Richard Hooker, the sixteenth-century defender of the Church of
England. In this context, his name suggests Burton the author of
The Anatomy of Melancholy — also a cleric and an author whose
subject was man's dissatisfaction with the world. The modern Burton
has been obsessed all morning by feelings of doubt. When the dentist
asks him to quote something Hooker wrote, he cannot remember a
single passage. But after the dentist finishes the work required by
one of his teeth — Burton finds him unusually kind, with a sweet
and spicy breath — he does finally remember a passage (p. 50):

> I grant we are apt, prone, and ready to forsake God; but is God
> as ready to forsake us? Our minds are changeable; is His so
> likewise?

At the same moment the dentist tells him his name (which Burton
has also forgotten). It is Merritt.

In keeping with its talk about theologians, "Dentistry and Doubt"
treats of a theological theme: the tension between faith and works.
Burton, we are told, "thought of the world as being, like all music,
founded on tension" (p. 49). His temptation is to want to "do
something" all the time. But he overcomes this temptation as Dr.
Merritt fills his tooth; he looks at the objects in the room and
outside it "as things in which an unlimited excitement inhered" —
a sensation which he "had frequently enjoyed in his childhood and
more rarely as he aged" (p. 48). Thus he comes to understand
that vision, not effort, is primary. We must become receptive to
wonder like little children if we are to enter the Kingdom of Heaven.
In theological terms, we must learn that faith is the gift of divine
grace and is not to be earned through striving to do good works,
that is, through our own *merits*.

Dr. Merritt fitly puts him to the test. At the beginning of the visit
Burton, trying to ingratiate himself with the dentist, boasts that his
native Pennsylvania produces more than ninety per cent of the
world's anthracite. Dr. Merritt, he senses, does not believe him. At
the end of his ordeal, in answer to the question of why his teeth
are "so, ah, indifferent," Burton confesses that Pennsylvania has
one of the worst dental records of any state. It is then that he remembers the quotation from Hooker and also learns the dentist's

name. Only when we cease to justify ourselves and confess our short-comings and our need of help, can we stand justified.

This last theological statement is put by Updike into concrete terms. As Burton walks into the surgery the dentist seems unwilling to place any confidence in him. He looks quizzically at Burton's clerical collar, seeing a stranger from another land and certain only of the "rather heavy tartar on the incisors" (pp. 41-42). By the end of the story their relationship has changed:

> Dr. Merritt smiled. The two men stood in the same position they had hesitated in when Burton entered the room. Burton smiled.

Doubt has gone, and tension is resolved both within and without.

In "Dentistry and Doubt" bird imagery supplements the imagery of *eye*teeth that are decayed and need to be restored to soundness. Dr. Merritt has a feeding station for birds in his back yard. Burton asks him about certain black birds outside, and is told they are starlings. "A greedy bird. They take everything they can away from the wren" (p. 48). Shortly before, brooding upon the unexplained evil in the world, Burton thought about the Devil, and immediately his eyes rested on these *black* birds. "They kept falling out of the sky and the tree-tops, but he noticed few ascending" (p. 47). When overwhelmed by doubt, his internal and external vision dwells exclusively upon blackness — exemplified in decayed teeth, anthracite, the Devil, and starlings — and so upon falling downwards from brightness.[3] The story ends by describing how his eyes, now that his eyetooth is restored by the disciplinary action of the dentist's drill and brightened by a silver filling, look differently upon the birds: "Outside the window, the wrens and the starlings, mixed indistinguishably, engaged in maneuvers that seemed essentially playful" (p. 50). The presence of evil along with good is no longer a problem when God's grace is seen to rule in the cosmos.

* * *

Birds and the testing of faith reappear together in "Pigeon Feathers." The hero of the story is David Kern, fourteen years old

[3] Blackness also is exemplified in Burton's mood of doubt. Doubt — *acedia* or spiritual sloth — is, incidentally, the traditional besetting sin of the cleric. Burton's name, as we noted, associates him with Burton's *Anatomy of Melancholy;* and in terms of the humors, which feature prominently in that book, melancholy is excess of *black* bile.

Ascent and descent are symbols of hope and despair constantly used by Updike. In "Toward Evening," when the mobile fails to please Rafe's daughter, his wife goes to make dinner "in an atmosphere of let-down" (*SD*, p. 66). And it is because his wife is irritated by his failure to answer some well-meant question about the office that the bread falls, like a star of brightness, from her hand (p. 67).

and having a home background duplicating more or less that of Updike after his family moved from Shillington to the farm near Plowville.

The Kern family has just moved to Firetown, and David has started to read some of his mother's books that are still piled on the floor. He comes across Volume II of H. G. Wells' *The Outline of History,* and is appalled by the description given there of Jesus as an obscure political agitator. All the Christian teaching that he has until now accepted unquestioningly looks like a lie, opening up in his consciousness an overwhelming fear of death. In the hope of finding assurance that there really is a God who has made men to share his eternity, David begins to ask questions about the afterlife. He asks the Lutheran minister, who tells him that heaven is like Lincoln's goodness living on after him; he asks his mother, who talks of the wonder of being alive, and wants him to read Plato; he asks his father, who treats the matter with a savage irony which is somehow reassuring. He seeks an answer in prayer, but cannot tell whether he has been given an answer or not. He even tries the dictionary, and there he at least finds a judicious definition of the soul. But all alike fail to give him "the hint, the nod, he needed to begin to build his fortress against death" (*PF,* p. 139). Around him, his parents' talk suddenly seems to be of nothing but death.

Assurance comes later and quite unexpectedly. Asked by his grandmother to get rid of some pigeons which are becoming a nuisance in the barn, he takes the gun recently given him for his fifteenth birthday and shoots six birds. Before burying them, he sees the intricacy of their plumage, where "each filament was shaped with the shape of the feather, and the feathers in turn were trimmed to fit a pattern that flowed without error across the bird's body" (p. 149). The pigeons, bred in the million and exterminated as pests, were miracles of form and color, no two alike. Joy hangs in the air, and then "he was robed in this certainty: that the God who had lavished such craft upon these worthless birds would not destroy His whole creation by refusing to let David live forever" (p. 150).

At first glance, David seems to have stumbled upon the old and (for most people today) discredited Argument from Design. Actually, the story has little to do with any such argument. What David finds is not the visible pattern but the radiance which silently upholds all pattern as its transcendent ground. In the story David was waiting for the *hint,* the *nod,* to build again the fortress against death which H. G. Wells' "engines of knowledge" had knocked down. The fortress was not any abstract belief in a theistic hypothesis; it was the child's faith in the reliability of the Christian teaching he had received. In particular, what hung in the balance was belief in Jesus as the authoritative revealer of the Father in Heaven. So David felt utterly betrayed when his mother — of all people — seemed anxious to turn aside his frantic questions about God and the afterlife and expected him simply to accept the loveliness of the world he could see here and now.

Handling the dead pigeons, David receives "the hint, the nod," he has been waiting for. When he had prayed in bed, holding up his hands in the dark and begging Christ to touch them, he had felt nothing. Yet he had wondered whether, after all, he *had* been touched. "For would not Christ's touch *be* infinitely gentle?" (p. 128). Now at last the gentle touch is unmistakable. The iridescent feathers of the birds convey to him much more than an ingenious pattern requiring a designer. They tell him not just of any Almighty Creator, but precisely of the Father in Heaven who cares for his creation just as Jesus taught. David's joy comes through realizing that the dead "worthless birds" have spoken to him, silently, the actual words of Jesus: "Fear not, therefore; you are of more value than many sparrows" (Matt. 10:31). When he had read H. G. Wells, David had tried "to supply out of his ignorance objections that would defeat the complacent march of these black words" (p. 119); yet he had known that anything he might think of would bear the mark of wishful thinking. The answer comes in the end not from the wishful world of the living, but from the truthful world beyond death.

Updike's poem "Deities and Beasts" (*TP,* p. 12) refers to "the sparrow, whose fall / Is never mentioned in the press at all." Neither does he himself mention the sparrow's fall in "Pigeon Feathers," but that is because he expects his readers to make the connection for themselves.

Once again we are given an example of his way of using a single image as the focus of different levels of meaning. On the one hand, the dove is seen as a common bird, and, as such, a handy contemporary equivalent of the New Testament sparrow. But in addition, pigeons have a special significance for Updike on the personal level. In a *New Yorker* "Talk of the Town" essay entitled "No Dodo," he dwells upon the ancient association of the dove with man. He gives an Arabian version of the dove's return to the Ark, and notes "a Filipino legend that, of all birds, only the dove understands the human tongue" (*AP,* p. 54). It is likely that in Updike's mind this bird so near to humankind is well suited to carry the message of hope that men must have.

"Pigeon Feathers" also exhibits, in striking fashion, Updike's technique of deliberate omission. When David is desperate to know whether God and the afterlife are not lies, his mother wants him

simply to accept the goodness of the world about him as self-justifying: "But, David, you have the *evidence*. Look out the window at
the sun; at the fields" (p. 137).

David, however, will not be comforted by her words, even though
he knows that they issue out of her love for him: "He would not
be wooed away from the truth. *I am the Way, the Truth. . ."* (p. 138;
ellipses in the text). Here David quotes only two of the claims Jesus
makes about himself in the Gospel of John (John 14:6), breaking
off before the third. Yet the claim *I am the Life* is precisely the
assurance he needs before he can begin rebuilding his fortress against
death. At the catechetical class in the Firetown church, David is asked
to fill in the blanks in the sentence, "I am the . . . , the . . . , and the
. . . , saith the Lord" (p. 132). If this claim is the truth, then Jesus
is the Word of Life that takes away the fear of death. So long as
the claim remains unsubstantiated, the "black words" of H. G.
Wells darken the universe, and death blots out the sun and the
fields. However, once David feels certain that Jesus himself has
touched him through the dead birds, addressing him personally and
saying, "Fear not," everything is changed. H. G. Wells has been
refuted. The Word of Life has spoken directly from heaven.

There are other noteworthy images in "Pigeon Feathers." David's
"fortress against death," for example, surely recalls Luther's hymn
"A mighty fortress is our God." In "The Dogwood Tree" Updike
refers to the "grave" effect this hymn still has upon him (*AP*, p. 181).
Then there is the effect of H. G. Wells' "black words." As in "Toward
Evening," the blackness that descends over the human spirit is
equated with the blotting out of the stars. Sitting in the outhouse,
David is "visited by an exact vision of death," a vision ending thus:
"And the earth tumbles on, and the sun expires, and unaltering
darkness reigns where once there were stars" (p. 123). Perhaps most
intriguing of all, though, are the evident references to Kierkegaard's
"absolute qualitative distinction between time and eternity."

After David experiences his vision of death, he reflects that this
kind of extinction is not just another threat, another pain — "it
was qualitatively different" (p. 124). Again, arguing with his mother,
he refuses to believe that God is simply a part of the mystery of
existence, or is brought into being by man's thinking about him.
He insists: "No. God has to be different" (p. 137). At that moment
"all her grace, her gentleness, her love of beauty gathered into a pas-
sive intensity that made him intensely hate her." The reference here is
to the words of Jesus: "If any one comes to me and does not hate
his own father and mother . . . he cannot be my disciple" (Luke
14:26). That love and hatred can coexist is only possible on Kierkegaard's premise that the earthly and the heavenly are qualitatively

different dimensions. Neither David's love for his mother nor his understanding of her love for him is ever in doubt. Yet he sees with complete clarity — and sees that she, illogically, does not see — the importance of priorities. Because God *has to be different,* nothing temporal can stand in the way of loyalty to the truth that is eternal.

Earthly affection, indeed, can stand between us and our spiritual peace, which is qualitatively different because it involves our direct relationship with heaven. After telling his mother to leave him alone, David is distressed by the thought that he has hurt her. Nevertheless, this "immediate worry" is "smaller" than the deep ache he carries within him over the horror of death that reigns in the absence of faith (p. 138).

* * *

The inability to recognize priorities is the theme of another story in *Pigeon Feathers.* "Lifeguard" is a monologue spoken by a student of divinity who spends his summers perched on a lifeguard's chair above a resort beach. He meditates upon the peculiarities of various theological writings he studies in the seminary — including "the terrifying attempts of Kierkegaard, Berdyaev, and Barth to scourge God into being" (*PF*, p. 212). His final comments in this area are of the "diverting productions of literary flirts like Chesterton, Eliot, Auden, and Greene" who "in the end all infallibly strike, despite the comic variety of gongs and mallets, the note of the rich young man on the coast of Judea who refused in dismay to sell all that he had" (*ibid.*).

So "Lifeguard" takes up the thought, introduced in "Toward Evening," that our contemporary problem is that the world is too much with us. For one thing, there are so many people around! Though personally and professionally concerned with the afterlife, the lifeguard finds it hard to envisage the "breeding swarm" that "blackens" the beach as having any kind of immortality other than the physical immortality of the beehive. This crowd, which has lost the habit of church-going, is a "sea of others" that exasperates and fatigues him (p. 218).

Then the fact that the actual sea, with its mysteries and terrors, "no longer comfortably serves as a divine metaphor indicates how severely humanism has corrupted the apples of our creed." We seek God, says the lifeguard, in "flowers and good deeds" (p. 213). That is, we find meaning in temporal beauty and goodness, but have allowed ourselves to be wooed away from eternal truth.[4] Faced with

---

[4] The poem "Seven Stanzas at Easter" (*TP*, pp. 72-73) emphasizes that Christ rose in human reality: "It was not as the flowers/each soft spring recurrent."

such a limited consciousness, the lifeguard can only offer the directive, "be joyful." "Stretch your skins like pegged hides curing in the miracle of the sun's moment," he says (p. 219). And he adds, "be children." Where there is ignorance of the eternal and its raging storms, no mature vision can arise. The only advice that seems likely to be heard today is Horace's *carpe diem,* advice echoed (with a non-Horatian difference) by Herrick in the seventeenth century.

There is a strong seventeenth-century flavor in the lifeguard's meditation, which is sprinkled with antique words and phrases: "politicking," "unguents," "fudging commentary," "stony chambers," *"momento mori."* The rhythms of Sir Thomas Browne's balanced prose are pervasive. For example: "I myself can hardly bear the thought of stars, or begin to count the mortalities of coral" (p. 213). Yet, if the style is from that quarter, the thought is from quite another. For the leading images strongly suggest Kierkegaard.

The image of the *crowd* recalls one of Kierkegaard's most significant notions, namely that the modern age is an age dominated by the crowd. For Kierkegaard "the crowd is untruth." By leveling everything to a common denominator, the influence of the crowd-mind takes away the very idea of quality and turns everything into quantity. But religion, says Kierkegaard, can be understood only by the individual who remains apart from the crowd in its collective anonymity. Because of his elevation on his lifeguard's chair above the beach *blackened* by the crowd, the lifeguard has the quality of an individual. Because of this he can connect the earthly scene he contemplates with the heavenly truths he is in contact with through his theological studies. The chair he sits in is a chair marked with a cross that signifies temporal realities ("bandages, splints, spirits of ammonia, and sunburn unguents"); but he sees it as another cross, with trans-temporal significance, and climbs his chair as if "into an immense rigid, loosely fitting vestment" (p. 213). He understands the world as a parable of what lies beyond it.

The lifeguard knows, too, what the crowd has forgotten: that the sea *is* a divine metaphor. And it was this metaphor that Kierkegaard used when, speaking of faith as existential risk, he said we

---

And: "Let us not seek to make it less monstrous,/for our own convenience, our own sense of beauty."

In the *Paris Review* interview Updike speaks of how "God" can appear in two different senses: "the more or less watered down Puritan god" and the god who "means ultimate power." He adds, "I've never really understood theologies which would absolve God of earthquakes and typhoons, of children starving. A god who is not God the Creator is not very real to me..." (*Art,* p. 101). The context of this remark is a discussion about God in *Couples,* but the distinction Updike makes is relevant throughout his work.

must "venture far out to remain out upon the deep, over seventy thousand fathoms of water."

Watching the bathers — a full sample of humanity from the very old to the very young — the lifeguard sees them keeping to the shallow water. He warns them: "The tides of time have treacherous undercurrents. You are borne continually toward the horizon" (pp. 219-220). One day he expects to hear a call for help, and it is for this that he has prepared himself. (Of course, he has. He is a student of *divinity*.) So far the call has not come; for the crowd is ignorant of anything that lies on the horizon, being as nearsighted as Kierkegaard said it is.

Kierkegaard always insisted that he wrote, not for an audience (a crowd), but for that *individual* who would know that the words had been written just for him. The lifeguard also waits for that individual who will detach himself from the crowd and venture far out, taking the profound risk of faith. In that existential moment, the cry for help will be assurance of salvation.

*   *   *

One of Updike's recent poems, published separately (1968), plays a deft variation on the theme of the contrast between deep and shallow waters. "Bath after Sailing" describes the sensations of relief at lying "at ease in a saltless sea my size" after seven hours on a sloop on the open sea. It ends:

> . . . *how much I prefer*
> *the microcosmic version*
> *of flirting with immersion.*

"Lifeguard" speaks of the "literary flirts" who avoid the full rigor of Christ's call. "Bath after Sailing" wryly admits that flirting is much more comfortable when it involves no risk. But Updike has faced the venturing far out "over seventy thousand fathoms of water"; and so his comment is, as Kierkegaard would say, existential and not merely aesthetic. "I was afraid," he says in the poem, "I did not want, / I had not wanted / to die. I saw death's face." Later in the poem he says:

> *I thank you, God of trees and air,*
> *whose steeples testify*
> *to something steady slipped by chance*
> *upon Your tar-green sliding face,*
> *For this my mock survival.*

It is one thing to stay in the shallows, and quite another thing to return to ease after knowing the terror of remaining out upon the deep. The difference between the dimensions of time and eternity, in the second instance, remains an indelible experience. The "mock survival" of the bath has the humor which Kierkegaard says is to be allied with the religious dimension. In "Bath after Sailing" the humor chimes without discord with a hymn of praise to the God who is like the sea, "deep and opaque and not me."

When we trust ourselves to an encounter with this God, an encounter which is more than a safe flirting, there is death to be faced. The qualitative distinction between time and eternity is one we can contemplate only, in Kierkegaard's phrase, with "fear and trembling." The truth is that the tides of time have treacherous undercurrents. We cannot bask forever in the miracle of the sun's moment, or bathe childishly in protected shallows. Yet launched out into the deep, we can know also that in the terrifying flux around us are things that testify to "something steady." Even where death faces us, deep and opaque and alien, there is a goodness by which we are silently upheld.

7

SUPERNATURAL
MAIL

UPDIKE'S CARE IN CHOOSING NAMES TO FIT BOTH A naturalistic and a symbolic context is well illustrated in "Pigeon Feathers." David is the name the Updikes gave their first son, and *David Copperfield* is the best known of autobiographical novels. So, in this most personal of all the Olinger stories, the boy is called David. Then, too, since the biblical King David is described as a man whose heart was wholly true to his God (I Kings 11:4), the name David (the Hebrew means *beloved*) is a suitable one for a story describing a crisis in faith issuing in a renewed belief in the everlasting love of God.

The German name Kern is natural enough in view of the Pennsylvanian setting of the story. But furthermore, *kern* literally means in German "kernel" (and therefore metaphorically "heart of the matter"). And in suggesting kernel, the name also echoes St. Paul's words about resurrection and death, about what is sown in the earth not coming to life unless it dies (I Cor. 15:36-38). St. Paul says that a "bare kernel" (RSV) is put in the ground and then God gives it a new body. In "Pigeon Feathers," David Kern's faith dies and is resurrected.

Another "heart-of-the-matter" story is "Packed Dirt, Churchgoing, A Dying Cat, A Traded Car." It comes at the end of *Pigeon Feathers*. In this story we learn that David Kern, now grown up, married, and turned writer, has again lost his faith. For some, the moral is that Christianity may appeal to children but is not a viable faith for modern adults in a world that (to use Dietrich Bonhoeffer's phrase) has "come of age." But the second story about David Kern is too complex to support any such naive conclusion. It complements the first one rather than cancelling it; and it ends *Pigeon Feathers* on a note of affirmation rather than on skepticism, though its note of joy is less obvious than that of "Pigeon Feathers."

Unlike "Pigeon Feathers," "Packed Dirt, Churchgoing, A Dying Cat, A Traded Car" is told in the first person. Its drawn-out title suggests that it is a necklace of reminiscences loosely strung together. Nevertheless, it proves to be a very closely-woven fabric of images. It takes up the central theme of "Pigeon Feathers," placing it in the context of contemporary North American life. Once again, we are shown the collapse of the personal fortress against death. This time, however, Updike demonstrates that the "dense fear" of death that David Kern felt as a boy is not simply one that rises destructively in the growing mind exposed to adult values. Death can envelop in an aura of horror the experienced as well as the innocent; and it can also cast its shadow over a whole culture, whether its presence is felt consciously or only unconsciously.

David Kern the boy was pulled back from death into life. But whereas for innocence trembling on the edge of experience one overwhelming intuition of a sustaining goodness is sufficient, adult consciousness requires more than a single moment of ecstasy. Faith can die and be reborn in an individual many times. So David Kern the man looks back, in the course of his four-part narrative, to certain memorable seasons of his life. In the last sentence of the story, David addresses his readers in the persona of a hitchhiking sailor. The sailor has been puzzled by David's inability to explain exactly what he writes about. "Oh — whatever comes into my head" is the only answer David can think of; and then the sailor asks "What's the point?" — and is told "I don't know. I wish I did" (*PF*, p. 264). But, at the very end, David has found his answer: "We in America need ceremonies, is I suppose, sailor, the point of what I have written."

In order to see the point, we shall have to follow the four sections of David's almost plotless story.

* * *

The opening section, "Packed Dirt," describes how a new road is being constructed near David's house. David sees in the earth piled up by bulldozers the marks of children's feet making little paths. Roadmaking in America, says David, has attacked the "enormity of nature we have been given" as a hostile force to be subdued. "We have explored on behalf of all mankind this paradox: the more matter is outwardly mastered, the more it overwhelms us in our hearts" (p. 248). Packed-dirt paths made "accidentally" by children are, on the other hand, "human" and comforting. They revive childhood memories of similar paths we ourselves made in our past, and they possess "that repose of grace that is beyond willing."

"Churchgoing" takes up the theme of the first section, but puts it in a religious context. Although church services may be boring, unintelligible, or out of place in the modern scene, they provide "paths worn smooth in the raw terrain of our hearts" (p. 249). These paths are vertical ones, not horizontal.

Here the implication is that man cannot live by patterns of his own devising, and that to attempt to do so is to find desolation of heart. If the evidence supporting this truth is writ large over the face of modern America, the reasons for its being true lie buried deep in the nature of things. The mystery of why *grace* and not our *willing* must shape our patterns for us is probed in two gnomic sentences opening the third section, "A Dying Cat": "Matter has its radiance and its darkness; it lifts and buries. Things compete; a life demands a life."

David Kern then goes on to tell of an incident from the time when he and his wife were in England and their first child was born. As his wife lay in labor at the hospital, he found a cat dying in the street. It had been hit by a car and would not recover, but he saw it was plump and wore a collar. "Some one had loved it" (p. 255). So he lifted it and left it in the dirt behind a hedge. It was the size of a baby, and he thought it was female. After reaching his house, he wrote a note for the cat's owners and returned to place the paper under its body. "It suggested I was making too much fuss, and seemed to say to me, *Run on home*" (p. 256). That night he slept peacefully, to be awakened at three in the morning by the phone ringing to tell him that his baby daughter had been born. His own birthday was in March. It was by now the first day of April, but still March in the States.

This incident of the cat is described by David as "supernatural mail." He adds that it "had the signature: decisive but illegible" (p. 253).

In "Toward Evening" the stars that share the sky with the extremely readable Spry sign are described as "illegible" — and also as "uncreated" (*SD,* p. 68). Supernatural mail cannot be read in the way that we read neon signs or newspapers, because it comes from the inconceivable realm of heaven. All that we need to do, however, is to recognize that the signature it carries is authentic. Earth is the place of patterns we can decipher in our human way. Heaven is the source of radiance keeping all earthly patterns in being. When we receive supernatural mail, its message is always the same one, *Run on home*.[1] How to obey the message is something we have to discover for ourselves, since its illegible script cannot be deciphered by worldly wisdom.[2] We have to find the path by keeping our hearts open to grace.

Because all earthly patterns rest upon the radiance of heaven, every truly human path leads back home. Thus the dirt paths made by children's feet look random and unplanned. Yet they exemplify "that repose of grace that is beyond willing," for they always lead the children back home. What is true of horizontal paths is equally true of vertical ones. They are visible patterns that rest upon an invisible radiance, and they are made by love. These patterns are what we call ceremony.

* * *

That ceremonies are the human way of keeping alive beauty and innocence is the theme of W. B. Yeats' well-known poem, "A Prayer for My Daughter." Consider these lines:

> *Ceremony's a name for the rich horn,*
> *And custom for the spreading laurel tree.*

Updike's exploration of the same theme brings in another dimension; for he believes, as Yeats did not, that there is a supernatural God to answer our prayers for our daughters. Ceremony for him, therefore, finds its most complete expression in the Christian liturgy, which is the vertical path by means of which all children of the

---

[1] The image of supernatural mail, like so many of Updike's images, starts from the level of actuality. In "Pigeon Feathers" the notion of mail sent from heaven arises from the delivery of mail at David's house. David has prayed that two war-effort posters he has sent for would arrive the next day, "and though they did not, they did arrive, some days later, together, popping through the clacking letter slot like a rebuke from God's mouth: *I answer your prayers in My way, in My time*" (*PF*, p. 120).

In this instance, the supernatural mail administers a rebuke and does not seem to say anything about home. But, in fact, anything that keeps open the paths of the heart directs us to the way home. The destruction of David's "fortress against death" is so terrible an event because it leaves David homeless. His first full realization of the horror of death, we should note, occurs in the *out*house. This is a place of darkness. Here David realizes that he is shut out of the Father's "house," in outer darkness.

The image of *Run on home* also occurs, of course, though without being placed in the context of supernatural mail, in the passage in *Couples* where an adult remembers how, as a child, he was able to shout *Free!* and touch the home maple.

[2] Legibility seems always to be linked with misleading superficiality. Thus in "Toward Evening" the Spry sign is described as dominating the "night view" by virtue of brightness and readability (*SD*, p. 67). In "Pigeon Feathers" the print of *The Outline of History* is "determinedly legible and smug, like a lesson book" (*PF*, p. 118). The readable sign suits the *night* view, and H. G. Wells' *black* words are most legible, a lesson easily read by the children of this world.

Father in Heaven can find their way home. So, when churchgoing has become an unfamiliar pattern in the lives of people today, all ceremonies tend to lose their meaning and to become disregarded.[3] Unless "the raw terrain of our hearts" has paths worn on it by religious customs that delight "purely as a human recreation" (*PF,* p. 249), matter, though outwardly subdued, will inevitably overwhelm us and leave us homeless orphans.

By the ceremony of lifting a dying cat out of the road and leaving it on the earth where it seemed "at home" (p. 256), David Kern found a way to see meaning in the dual aspects of matter, its radiance and its darkness, its meting out of life and death. Before he slept that night, he read a book: "I remember the title, it was Chesterton's *The Everlasting Man*" (p. 256). Updike tells us nothing except the title of G. K. Chesterton's book; yet the book's subject would have a special meaning for David Kern, for it was written as a Christian answer to H. G. Wells' *The Outline of History*. Whether the adult David found its argument convincing we cannot know, but reading it brought peaceful sleep that night. It opened a vertical path to the everlasting, the qualitatively different, dimension.

How hard it is today to keep our confidence in anything everlasting is the motif of the fourth section in David Kern's story, "A Traded Car." Like "Pigeon Feathers," this section describes the destruction and rebuilding of David's fortress against death. Desolation comes to the adult David through his guilty feelings over a casual but intense encounter at a party with "a woman not my wife." The words of Jesus about committing adultery in one's heart (Matt. 5:28) are what unnerve him. Like King David, he cannot maintain kingly rule over his own sensuality. Immediately, he imagines that the universe is hurtling downward toward death. In such a universe, "to touch the brink was to be on the floor of the chasm" (p. 260). Life is erring, senseless, destructive. Again, as when he was faced as a boy with the horror of death, he prays and asks for a sign to show him that his despairing vision is mistaken. "Each second my agony went unanswered justified it more certainly; the God who permitted me this fear was unworthy of existence" (p. 261).

The next day is his birthday. Just as in his earlier experience of dense fear his parents' talk had seemed to be all about death, so now the newspaper seems full of accounts of atrocities. Later in the day his mother phones from Pennsylvania. He thinks it is for his birthday, but finds that it is to tell him that his father has been

---

[3] This point is touched upon in Michael Novak's sensitive study of the two David Kern stories, "Updike's Search for Liturgy," in *Commonweal,* May 10, 1963.

taken to the hospital with heart trouble. The news comes to him as a great relief. Death is no longer "like a wide army invisibly advancing." "My father had engaged the enemy and it would be defeated" (p. 262). This evening, a Saturday, he has a small birthday party. The next morning he goes to church, after bringing his two older children to Sunday School. After midday dinner he drives off to Pennsylvania in his old car, due to be traded in a few days. He has heard the message, *Run on home.* It is on this journey that he gives a lift to the young sailor.

Entering his home state, he feels renewed in spirit. Even the old car seems to respond. But before accompanying his mother to the Alton hospital, he learns from her that his father has lost his faith. George Kern does not, however, let his loss of faith show, and sends a timid girl from the Lutheran Home Missions on her way transfigured. ("As a star shines in our heaven though it has vanished from the universe, so my father continued to shed faith upon others" [p. 276].) David finds it impossible to say to his father what is in his heart, for "there were no words, no form of words available in our tradition" (p. 274). When, however, he says he must leave for home, he is alerted by his father's clasping his hand and telling him he is a good son and a good father.

On the "endless" return drive, David's old car seems to take over with a will of its own, "though its soul the driver had died." His safe homecoming is described in these words: "Above my back yard the stars were frozen in place, and the shapes of my neighbors' houses wore the wonder that children induce by whirling" (pp. 278-79). The story ends with David's regretful reflection about how the car that carried him home so faithfully will soon be turned in, like so many others before, "dismissed without a blessing, a kiss, a testament, or any ceremony of farewell" (p. 279). Then follows the final apostrophe to the sailor concerning the need for ceremony in America.

David Kern's four-section story does not culminate, as "Pigeon Feathers" does, in an ecstasy of revelation. Maturity is not childhood, and it has different needs. Comprehensiveness of vision is demanded by adult responsibilities, while intense feeling marks childhood experience.

David Kern the man gains the sustaining vision allowing him to accept the fact that matter has both radiance and darkness. His birthday comes at the "dull season" of the year "during which Spring is gathering the mineral energy to make the resurrection that the church calendar seizes upon as conveniently emblematic" (p. 250). He has known this season as the bringer of birth and death: once when his daughter was born and a cat died on an

English street, and now again when his birthday brings word of his father's possibly fatal illness. On both occasions supernatural mail has arrived making possible "that repose of grace that is beyond willing," bringing peaceful sleep, release from the fear of death, and a safe return to his own back yard, illumined by wonder. Supernatural mail always says, *Run on home*. But where is home? Things compete, and earthly affection is divided. Those we love die. Life moves on, and time will not wait for us. Ultimately, we are sustained only by that radiance which can take us through death to resurrection.

David trusts his father's faith to defeat the enemy death. It is true that his father, apparently, has lost his faith. Yet Hooker's words quoted in "Dentistry and Doubt" hold good. "I grant we are apt, prone, and ready, to forsake God; but is God as ready to forsake us?" In Alton, the doctor, explaining George Kern's illness to David, points out that the obstruction affecting the heart is "in one of these little vessels on the outside, luckily for your dad" (p. 268). The "heart," then, is not fatally "obstructed" in its relation to God, and loss of faith is external only. David knows that his father still communicates the radiance of faith that has power to defeat death. So when he receives his farewell blessing and handclasp, David comments, "I felt I would ascend straight north from his touch" (p. 277). The background to this reference is the biblical association of God's dwelling-place with the north, as described in the Psalms:

> *Mount Zion, in the far north,*
> > *the city of the great King.*
> *Within her citadel God*
> > *has shown himself a sure defense.* (Ps. 48:2-3)

Receiving his father's blessing, David realizes that his father is one of those who can "ascend the hill of the Lord" and there "receive blessing" (Ps. 24:3, 5).[4]

---

[4] In "Dentistry and Doubt" Burton's melancholy doubts engender images of *descent*. He thinks of the Devil, and "with the Devil the whole cosmos became confused, and Burton's attention by default, rested on the black birds. They kept falling out of the sky and the tree-tops, but he noticed few ascending" (*SD*, p. 47).

This juxtaposition of images — the Devil and black birds falling out of the sky — is a clear echo of the fall of Lucifer as described in the Book of Isaiah:

> *"How you are fallen from heaven,*
> > *O Day Star, son of Dawn!*
> *How you are cut down to the ground,*
> > *you who laid the nations low!*
> *You said in your heart,*

A lifetime of churchgoing makes George Kern a star continuing
to light the path of others to the north where God dwells, even
when he feels his own faith extinguished. But there are not so many
today who keep the paths of the heart open to heaven. The disregard
for ceremony that characterizes America is one of the reasons why
we so readily lose heart and fall a prey to the fear of death. Before
David sets out for Alton, his wife cooks him a lamb dinner (p. 263).
But this residual symbol of Christ's death and resurrection has lost
its significance. It is just a meal. Without the support of living traditions — so David realizes in the hospital — we cannot even speak
of the things most in our hearts. How then can we keep our hearts
unobstructed or hope to rise from our beds of fear with hope of
renewed life? How can we live through the "dull season" to experience a resurrection?

Cars are one of our most familiar modern symbols. So George
Kern expresses his concern for his wife by saying that he hopes
she will not smash up his car. The pity is that these symbols are
not fully accepted as such, being dismissed without ceremony after
they have served us well. If we disregard the material body of the
car, we will not value at the proper worth "its soul the driver" either.

David, having shared his car with the hitchhiking sailor, watches
the sailor turn and go without the parting ceremony of a wave of
the hand. He is "just one more sailor, anonymous, at sea" (p. 265).
The sailor is young and healthy, he has been all over America. "He
had that instinctive optimism of the young animal that in America
is the only generatrix we have allowed ourselves; until recently, it
seemed enough" (p. 263). Updike seems to be saying through
David Kern that we are all anonymous sailors on the sea of American culture, traveling perpetually, yet without real hope of arriving
anywhere. In this same environment, David has discovered that,

----

> 'I will ascend to heaven;
> above the stars of God
> I will set my throne on high;
> I will sit on the mount of assembly
> in the far north;
> I will ascend above the heights of
> the clouds,
> I will make myself like the Most
> High.'
> But you are brought down to Sheol,
> to the depths of the Pit." (14:12-15)

David's thought of ascending north is thus the exact reverse of Burton's. The
black birds, if attempting to ascend to heaven (the north), fall from the sky
as did Lucifer, the greedy starling who tried to take the universe away from
God. Faith ascends. Doubt descends.

having exhausted his own resources, he is brought safely home by his car through an act of grace beyond his willing. When the optimism of being self-sufficient by virtue of physical health fails, we can still learn that "things" retain their goodness and their strength. But we shall not be able to learn this lesson unless we keep vertical paths worn by ceremony and custom — we shall simply be overwhelmed by the futility of our horizontal ones.

When his car has brought him home, David sees the stars "frozen in place." It is a vision of the unchanging heaven set over earthly mutability. The true north does not shift. The sailor need not, ever, be "at sea" while he has the Pole Star to steer by. So long as the vertical holds, it does not matter where we are at any particular time. We have a place to be, which may be now the place of the joy of birth, and now the place of darkness where death has to be faced. Anywhere, anytime, supernatural mail bearing a decisive signature can reach us. *Run on home.*

* * *

The place of death is the theme of a story in *The Music School* called "The Dark."

The story opens with these words: "The dark, he discovered, was mottled" (p. 203). These words recall the young David Kern's thoughts in "Pigeon Feathers" of "his own dying in a specific room, specific walls mottled with wallpaper . . ." (p. 128). The unnamed "he" of "The Dark" is also in a specific bed in a specific room, and he knows he is to die within a few months. But the mottling has been taken off the wallpaper and now is attributed to the dark within the room. The meeting of radiance and darkness dominates the imagery of this story.

In "The Dark" there is another echo of the thoughts of David Kern, but of the adult David, not of the child. In "The Traded Car," David finds his horror of death rising during a spell of insomnia. He tries futilely to soothe himself "with the caress of headlights as they evolved from bright slits on the wall into parabolically accelerating fans on the ceiling that then vanished: this phenomenon, with its intimations of a life beyond me, had," he says, "comforted wakeful nights in my earliest childhood" (*PF,* p. 260). "The Dark" is a detailed record of what David Kern describes as "the wrinkled, azoic territory of insomnia," and the man in the bed, lying like David beside his sleeping wife, finds a similar comfort in watching for the shifting intrusions of light made by passing automobile headlights. He regards these as "his only companions, guards, and redeemers" (*MS,* p. 204), each "an angel of light stolen from another world" (p. 205).

As the hours pass and the cars cease to come by, the sleepless man comforts himself in the darkness by imagining himself upheld by "a giant hand" which he supposes to be "an echo from Sunday School, some old-fashioned print" (p. 208). He is troubled by fearful, "unwanted images" such as being given spiders to eat, but the thought of being held up "at some height" yet without any fear of falling is one that banishes these terrors. When it becomes at last too hard for him to continue imagining the hand, the morning light begins to return, outlining objects in the room. Then all fear passes away in the knowledge that "in a finite time, he would trickle through the fingers of the hand" and "slip blissfully into oblivion" (p. 210).

If the giant hand is an echo from Sunday School, the patches of light coming in the guise of redeemers have, of course, a similar source in Christian imagery. Christ the Redeemer in the Gospel of John is he who comes into the world as the light of men. "The light shines in the darkness, and the darkness does not overcome it" (John 1:5). The waking man is puzzled because not all the lights can be those of automobiles, for some "seemed to be projected from a much higher angle than that of the street" (p. 204). In the Gospel of John it is the mark of Christ as the unique agent of God that he is *from above* (John 3:31; 8:23).

The pattern for one of the reveries of the man lying in the dark is also taken from the Gospel of John. This is his picture of himself walking through a mansion of many rooms, each airy and painted white, until finally he finds himself trapped in one of them without a key to fit the lock on the door. He knows that there must be a way of opening the door, and doctors agree but cannot help him. He knows that there are many more rooms in this "mansion without visible end," but now the door has become a solid, blank wall; and his only hope lies in proving the solidity to be an illusion (pp. 205-6). "In my Father's house are many rooms" ("mansions," King James Version), says Jesus (John 14:2), calling forth the question from one of the disciples, "How can we know the way?" Jesus' answer is the declaration, so prominent in "Pigeon Feathers," that he himself is the Way, the Truth, and the Life. That the dark is not solid but mottled indicates that there is hope of finding the way through the blank wall. Looking at the reflection of his face in "time," the man on the bed is shocked to discover that his face is black (p. 206). But trust in the "giant hand" dissipates thoughts of blackness (spiders). Eternity can supply the key which time has taken away, bringing light into darkness.[5]

---

[5] In "Pigeon Feathers," at the time when David thinks of his death in the room with mottled wallpaper — "the murmuring doctors" and nervous rela-

The image of the hand of God belongs to the Old Testament rather than to the New, and there it is sometimes called the "good hand" because it saves men from destruction. It is linked frequently with the assurance of life that follows a time of trial, as in the following passage from the Book of Psalms:

I bless the Lord who gives me
counsel;
in the night also my heart instructs me.
....
Therefore my heart is glad, and my
soul rejoices;
my body also dwells secure.
For thou dost not give me up to
Sheol
or let thy godly one see the Pit.
Thou dost show me the path of life;
in thy presence there is fullness
of joy,
in thy right hand are pleasures
for evermore. (Ps. 16:7, 9-11)

The experience of the waking man seems very close to that of the Psalmist, and he too can testify, "Weeping may tarry for the night / but joy comes with the morning" (Ps. 30:5).

There is no indication in the story that the man in bed has any conscious faith in the God of the Bible. Indeed, the reference to "an echo from Sunday School" might suggest that his contact with biblical thinking was purely a childhood one. What we can be certain of is that supernatural mail is delivered here. The "glowing rectangles" of the patterns of light are seen by the man on the bed to be "delivered like letters through the slots in his room" (p. 204).

In Updike's stories, the supernatural breaks into the earthly sphere whether or not it is received with belief. The truth of revelation not only comes from the eternity of heaven but it also makes itself known in time and space, without waiting for us to ask for it. David, recalling his early experiences of churchgoing, with the generally "oppressive futility" of the worship services, adds this: "Even to usher at a church mixes us with the angels, and is a dangerous thing" (*PF,* p. 251).

---

tives going in and out, "but for him no way out" — he sees the light in his parents' room and imagines that there will be "a crack of light, showing the door from the dark room to another, full of light" (*PF,* p. 128). Here the reference to the "many rooms," spelled out directly in "The Dark," is obliquely suggested.

Angels appear with some regularity in Updike's works. As we have seen, he finds nothing strange about finding one in a washing machine. His angels, though, are not cute choirboys or vapid females in nightgowns. They are, as in the Bible, the awesome and reassuring messengers of the Most High God. In *Pigeon Feathers* there is a story called "Archangel" which is a monologue by this mighty visitor from another world in which he promises free gifts of rare beauty and complete perfection: "Onyx and split cedar and bronze vessels lowered into still water: these things I offer. Porphyry, teakwood, jasmine, and myrrh: these gifts I bring" (p. 169).

According to the tradition current in the Middle Ages, the lesser orders of angels are guardians of individual souls, while archangels are set over the whole world. Updike's archangel declares that heavenly grace bends continually to the earth, offering "pleasures as specific as they are everlasting" (p. 170). In every joy of temporal existence the perfection of heaven appears in "glimmers." Casual sights and sounds and smells we experience can carry a quality of goodness that has eternal validity and need never be lost. In the masterpieces of art, in cherished family memories, in games well played, in intellectual precision, and in each moment of "White" radiance, appears some note of the heavenly song which is "a stream of balm" (p. 171). The promise of the archangel echoes the Epistle of James in the New Testament:

> Every good endowment and every perfect gift is from above, coming down from the Father of lights in whom there is no variation or shadow due to change. Of his own will he brought us forth by the word of truth that we should be a kind of first fruits of his creatures. (James 1:17-18)

The heavenly gifts described by the archangel are specific as well as everlasting. Once more we find Updike speaking of the radiant blankness which is not emptiness. For mankind, perfection is expressed in *patterned* workmanship — bronze vessels of intricately chased design, and tapered beams each fashioned by one continuous swipe of the plane (pp. 169-170). Updike's special affection for the carpenter's art is evident. In the hands of a skilled craftsman, woodwork is firm and enduring and carries a personal signature. The carpenter leaves the mark of his own integrity upon his handiwork.

"Embrace me; come, touch my side, where honey flows. Do not be afraid," says the archangel. He adds, "Why do you turn away?" (p. 171). This invitation recalls Christ's invitation to Thomas to touch his side and "not be faithless, but believing" (John 20:27). The archangel offers no proof that he can give what he promises, and he does not try to compel belief. He simply asks us to trust him: "Stay. Praise me. Your praise of me is praise of yourself; wait. Listen. I will begin again" (p. 171).

Updike's stories are all, in one way or another, narratives of individuals who listen to the archangel, or who turn away in obstinate refusal to trust him. Yet the patience of heaven is never exhausted. The offer of grace is always there, however often it is refused. The word of truth, which formed us and gave us free choice, speaks to us continually through the patterns of the world around us. If we turn away, missing the radiance, the loss is ours. Our inability to trust the word that speaks from heaven robs us of our own proper worth. Unbelief, in the end, springs from the faithlessness of fear. The voice of the archangel is the voice David Kern heard speaking silently in the patterned pigeon feathers, the voice of Christ saying "Do not be afraid."

8

SHELTER
AND THE
WEATHERS

WE HAVE SEEN HOW PROMINENT IN UPDIKE'S WRITINGS
are two pairs of opposites, namely, *up/down (ascent/descent)* and
light/dark (day/night; white or, more often, *radiant/black).* Another
basic contrasting pair, *inside/outside,* is less frequent but is important
also.

The first two pairs of opposites furnish images of the divine and
the human spheres, because they suggest opposing qualities. Thus
they can be used to establish the qualitative distinction between the
inconceivable and the conceivable, between heaven and earth, between eternity and time. They make a vertical axis, with the light
resplendent above and the dark cowering below. *Inside/outside,* however, is a horizontal contrast. Neither side is intrinsically superior
to the other, and which we ought to choose depends entirely upon
our situation. A perverse will alone would choose to be left permanently outside heaven or inside hell; but, on earth, to be always inside
or always outside is equally impossible and undesirable. We carry
about with us our external features and our interior qualities. As out-
siders we know independence, and as insiders we know community.
At one moment we want inside information, and at another outside
help. To be human is to go in and out freely for our own purposes
and at our own choice. Nothing attacks our human dignity more
than to be either shut out or locked in without our consent.

Updike assumes that man's verticality means one thing only:
humanity must try to lead the upright life. Horizontally, man's ability
to go both outside and inside gives him scope for his varied enter-

106

prises. On the physical plane, he goes inside to find shelter from the rigors of weather that make the Great Outdoors, at times, his enemy. Inside he can make his own little world out of human elements, insulated from the elements of nature outside.

The story "Archangel" tells how the first gift that heaven offers is food, and the second shelter. "Though the windows are open, the eaves of the roof are so wide that nothing of the rain comes into the rooms but its scent" (*PF*, p. 170). Updike has put on record his wish to be a turtle, long-lived, able to retreat immediately, and living close to the grass. "I also like the sound of rain on a roof, which a turtle must get quite a lot of."[1] Rain heard from inside the house is the theme of his poem "The Blessing" (*TP*, p. 81). It is a love poem, telling how love rushed with unique intensity when the rain began:

> then the rain came bursting,
> and we were sheltered, blessed,
> upheld in a world of elements
> that held us justified.

The blessedness of shelter is a peculiarly human joy given by heaven in its generosity, a grace given in acknowledgment of man's need to know a corner of existence that he can call his own.

Surrounded by human elements, man discovers his capacity for kingship. For example, in "Giving Blood" Richard Maple remembers how, "young and newly responsible," he had felt that the completion of his office duties made him "king of his own corner" (*MS*, p. 25). As God is King of Heaven, so every man is given kingly rule over that little part of earth for which he is responsible. But each earthly king rules only *inside* the boundaries of his realm. His kingship is real, yet limited.

Updike insists that nothing is more necessary for us earthlings to know than the exact limits of things. We cannot know earth itself without knowing that it is distinct from heaven, and that we ourselves stand on the boundary. Recognizing our limits, we are certain of our responsibilities and of the riches we possess. This is why the sound of rain outside makes us assured of blessedness within. The roof above us is the dividing line between the elements of nature and the elements of the human world we have constructed for ourselves in the home; and our consciousness that this line holds (that is, that nothing of the rain comes into our rooms but the scent) tells us that we are kings of the whole sheltered space beneath the roof and within the walls.

---

[1] Jane Howard, "Can a Nice Novelist Finish First?" *Life*, November 4, 1966, p. 74.

What is inside, then, is valued only when we contrast it with what is outside. Moreover, a completely sheltered life would hardly be life at all. There can be no substitute for firsthand encounter with the natural elements; for, unless we are aware of what we are being sheltered from, shelter loses its power to comfort and bless. Modern urban man, living in an almost wholly man-made environment, tends to find that environment boring and oppressive rather than joyous. The reason for this, Updike suggests, is that any sense of a clear boundary line between outside and inside has been lost.

This point is illustrated in his description of New York City in his essay in *The New Yorker* on "Spring Rain." The essay opens with the remark that, as the sky is pushed farther and farther away by the upward thrust of buildings, "we sometimes wonder if what is reaching us is really weather at all" (*AP,* p. 102). Hardly any-one bothers to look up at that "semi-opacity old-fashionedly termed the Firmament" (p. 103). Nevertheless, when the rain really begins to fall, it has "the effect of exquisitely pressing the city down into itself" and of conveying "a sharp impression of shelter" (p. 104); and this brings joy. It proves that the ceilings of the corridor-streets along which crowds hurry are "indisputably sky" (p. 105).

Another "Talk of the Town" tells us what we learn by going outside into the weather. In "Central Park" Updike lists thirty-four things he saw in the park on the first day of spring. The list looks like a random throwing together of chance impressions, but it presents a coherent account of how the springtime renewal of life affects mankind centrally.

To begin with, a park is a place within the city where the build-ings do not push away the sky until it is barely recognizable. Here the *outside* really is recognized as such. But also, Updike presents Central Park and its weather at a boundary line where the quality of the weather makes itself felt in a decisive way. Not only is the day the first day of spring, but there has been fresh snow which is still piled high in the gutters and is just starting to melt. In yet another "Talk," entitled "Our Own Baedeker," Updike tells us what snow that does not melt means. He writes there about Antarctica, a frozen world without rain, disease, and "in a sense" without time (*AP,* p. 62). So "Central Park" shows us what is, in effect, time beginning again. The list of sights he records is more than a com-monplace roster of happy signs of warmer days ahead. New York City's park visitors appear as though they were the first inhabitants of earth, engaged in discovering the different dimensions of existence, and in probing earth's resources for providing joy and sorrow to the human heart.

The list begins with the earth heaving itself out of frozen snow, as though primeval life, halted long ago, were just beginning again: "Great black rocks emerging from the melting drifts, their craggy skins glistening like the backs of resurrected brontosaurs" (*AP*, p. 51). This image seems to recall the reemergence of the earth after the Flood, for the next one is: "A pigeon on the half-frozen pond strutting to the edge of the ice and looking a duck in the face." Here the picture suggests the dispatching of the dove to find out whether the waters have returned to their place, and the division between sea and dry land is once more clearly defined. The third picture is of human society establishing itself by recognizing the need for law and the penalty for breaking it: "A policeman getting his shoe wet testing the ice." The fourth picture is of three elderly relatives coaxing a small boy to ride downhill on a sled with his father; the sled spills, and everybody laughs (except the boy, who sniffles). Man the son of Adam discovers in every generation how prone he is to fall.

Thus, in this time of the division of two weathers, "Central Park" directs mankind to find out for himself where the place of division lies between danger and safety, between tears and laughter. The rest of the items on Updike's list of what he saw there describe the environment in which the human comedy is played out. Animals in the zoo turn their backs on man and busy themselves with their own affairs. Birds, those symbols of the natural order, proclaim the unchanging cycle of life. The cafeteria is almost full, while the Merry-Go-Round overflows with music but few children are there to hear it; for the children of men have little appetite for enjoyment of the harmony of existence. But the forbidden always attracts them. There are footprints around a KEEP OFF sign. And sex — like food — never loses its ancient power; it causes solitary men to throw snowballs at tree trunks (unconsciously wishing to violate the dryads), while a pretty girl in *black* pants falls backwards on the slippery ice.

Man in Central Park knows transcendent stirrings, too. Idealism attracts the young; for the green head of Giuseppe Mazzini (founder of Young Italy) stares forward, unblinking, although the sun is in his eyes. Kindness is present in nature — exemplified by two pigeons feeding each other — and it is not absent in mankind. Unfortunately, human generosity is all too often condescending, arbitrary, and inadequate. In the park there is a plump old man feeding *peanuts* to the squirrels. The list of things seen ends with an affirmation that man is meant, ultimately, for heaven: "An airplane, very bright and distant, slowly moving through the branches of a sycamore" (p. 53). The vision is of no naked ape hanging from the branches with grasping hand, but of a bright flyer seeking to climb into the skies.

"Spring Rain" explains "how all water is in passage from purity to purity" (*AP,* p. 103). Coming from heaven and returning there, water is not contaminated by its contact with the blackness of earth. "Puddles, gutters, sewers are incidental disguises." The transparency of rain and the whiteness of snow serve to remind us that our lives are always open to visitations from another dimension.

Light, of course, is the most familiar messenger of heaven. Yet — although in his poem "Trees Eat Sunshine" (*TP,* p. 70) Updike asks us to observe that leaves lap up sunshine like milk and therefore all creatures are nourished (directly or indirectly) on light — we may feel that the light of heaven merely touches the earth. Rain and snow, on the other hand, make extended visits and actually share our world with us. So these gifts from above provide images in the Bible of how heaven communicates with men, as in this familiar passage from the Book of Isaiah:

> *For as the rain and the snow*
> *come down from heaven*
> *and return not thither but water*
> *the earth,*
> *making it bring forth and sprout,*
> *giving seed to the sower and*
> *bread to the eater,*
> *so shall my word be that goes forth*
> *from my mouth;*
> *it shall not return to me empty,*
> *but it shall accomplish that which*
> *I purpose,*
> *and prosper in the thing for*
> *which I sent it.* (55:10-11)

"Snowing in Greenwich Village" and "The Taste of Metal" are stories in which snow carries a decisive message from heaven, as we have already seen. What is instructive in these two stories is that snow becomes a vehicle of the heavenly Word when it is near to turning into rain, or when it is intermittent. In "Snowing in Greenwich Village" we are told that the snow "was not taking on the wet street" (*SD,* p. 75); and in "The Taste of Metal" that the snowstorm comes and goes, delivering its message at the critical moment, and immediately departing. We understand the significance of the weather, Updike suggests, when we grasp the quality of one kind of weather by observing it as it is on the point of giving way to another kind of weather. *Then* we hear what it has to say to us. Otherwise, we are apt to take it for granted. In "Snowing in Greenwich Village" Joan Maple is the first to react to the fact that it is snowing. "She was pathetic about snow, she loved it so much, and in these last years had seen so little" (pp. 74-75). Unless we are conscious of a boundary line eliciting the shock of surprise, the *pathos* that could open to us the lesson heaven wishes to teach is lacking, and our senses remain closed.

Hard frost is inhuman weather. In its grip even time seems suspended, and life is immobilized in a way that seems to us hard to distinguish from death. This truth is stated by Updike not only in his essay on Antarctica, but even more clearly in his review of Conrad Aiken's collected short stories, which carries the title "Snow from a Dead Sky." Updike ends the review in this way: "Aiken is impressive when he snows, but nutritious when he rains; I wish that somehow the climate had permitted him to rain more" (*AP*, p. 234). This judgment is closely connected with his observation that Aiken was obsessed by "cosmic vacuity" and "the great white light of annihilation" (p. 232). Believing that heaven is empty, that the universe is shapeless, and that we skate upon an emptiness that is white but not radiant, Aiken finds snow (as in his story "Silent Snow, Secret Snow") to be a symbol of death. But the pathos of human love alone shows that some melting into the warmth of life is possible (as in "Your Obituary, Well Written," where the characters exchange childhood memories about the rain). But, though Updike *does* believe — unlike Aiken — that snow is a form of lifegiving water, he equally notices that we recognize this truth best when snow falls wetly and melts upon contact with the earth. Thus snow without moisture is suited for administering a rebuke ("The Taste of Metal"), but wet snow brings with its soft fall an evident blessing from heaven.

* * *

Wet snow provides the setting for "A Sense of Shelter," one of the stories in *Pigeon Feathers*. It falls against the high school where William Young, a senior with his gaze set on a brilliant college career, finds the gloom inside the school creating an atmosphere of joyous security. He decides to declare his love to Mary Landis, who was his mother's early choice for him, though now she is a girl about whom wild stories circulate. But Mary, telling him he has never loved anybody, goes out into the snow to meet someone from the big world outside the school. William is humiliated, yet relieved. As he shuts his books in his locker in the school basement, "his self seemed to crawl into the long dark space" (p. 100). He has nothing to do now except wait for his assured future of academic success.

"The temperature must be exactly 32°" (p. 83). So thinks William Young as he watches the snow fall. This boundary line awakens him to the boundary line in his own life. Up to the present he has been a teacher's pet, "a puppet king" (p. 84); but now he feels a king in his own right. He is looking out over the school parking lot, noticing how each school bus, after backing out, has left on the white ground the mark of its tires, "an autocratic signature of two V's" (p. 83). Seeing these imprints of his own initial on the earth, William no doubt recalls how the autocratic monogram of another King William was also two V's — but combined with two more V's inverted to make the initial "M" of Mary his wife and co-ruler. Young King William decides that today he will choose his Queen Mary. He will tell Mary Landis he loves her (p. 85).

Updike does not tell us the process of William's thoughts. He just presents the single elements and allows us to put them together for ourselves. And he does not tell us, either, that the imagery of this story is to be read in connection with Don Marquis' book of poems, *the lives and times of archy and mehitabel*.[2] He just refers to the book obliquely when William, hearing his juniors discuss a history of reincarnation going back to ancient Egypt, asks, "Wuh-well, was he ever a c-c-cockroach, like Archy?" (p. 88).

Mehitabel, the promiscuous alley cat, had once been a queen in Egypt. Mary has always seemed a queen to William, and it is as such he addresses her (*PF*, p. 97). Mary's eyes are green (pp. 85-86), and her face, when he speaks to her, reminds him of a cat's (p. 95). She has had a succession of boy friends as continuous and varied as Mehitabel's; and William, asked by her to say what he knows about her, finds nothing to reply except, "That you're not a virgin" (p. 99). William notices that she laughs less now that her interests lie outside the school and its warmth. Similarly, Mehitabel's "unsheltered life sometimes / makes her a little sad" (*archy and mehitabel*, p. 49).

William has something in common with Archy the poet-cockroach — imagination. He is also like a cockroach in seeking gloom and basements. He goes to the low-roofed study room in the basement to read about Aeneas in the Underworld (*PF*, p. 91). Afterwards, meeting Mary on the second floor, he goes downstairs with her. (Archy writes: "it takes all sorts of / people to make an / underworld" [*archy and mehitabel*, p. 200].) But his definite identification is with the kings described by Don Marquis. These are museum-housed Egyptian kings reclining in dry sarcophagi. William finds maximum satisfaction in two sarcophagi-shaped spaces: "a strange, narrow boy's lavatory that no one ever seemed to use" (*PF*, p. 95), and his locker in the annex basement into which "his self seemed to

---

[2] Garden City, New York, 1935.

crowd." At the end of the story he has the same outlook as the Egyptian king in Archy's lines: "time time said old king tut / is something i aint / got anything but" (*archy and mehitabel,* p. 51).

The sharpening of William's sense of shelter comes when he is sharpening pencils, standing close enough to the school window to feel outdoor air on his face (p. 83). It is the cold outside meeting the warmth inside that stirs his imagination to thoughts of kingship. But he is unwilling to go outside into the cold. He prefers the coziness of the basement study room where he prepares for his future as an academic. This future he imagines as "the lining of a long tube," roofed with "acoustic tiling," walled with "acoustical books," and ending with "the last transition from silence to silence," which would be his dying, like Tennyson, with a copy of *Cymbeline* beside him (pp. 91-2).

Thus his future is to be one insulated from outside troubles, quiet and enclosed. His dream of a scholar's painless death picks out Tennyson's example as the ideal one. Why? The reference to *Cymbeline* would seem to provide the answer, since it is in this play that there is found the dirge commending a quiet rest in the assurance of fame:

> *Fear no more the heat o' the sun,*
> *Nor the furious winter's rages;*
>
> . . . .
>
> *Quiet consummation have;*
> *And renowned be thy grave.*

The same song emphasizes the transience of love:

> *All lovers young, all lovers must*
> *Consign to thee, and come to dust.*

William Young decides that the path of the lover is not for him, since it leads out into the sun and the storms. Safety is remaining in the dim underworld.

"The Sense of Shelter" is a story of the denial of vision, a refusal to accept the truth that the blessing of shelter comes only to those who know the outside as well as the inside of existence, cold as well as warmth. After Mary rejects William's advances, she exclaims in one breath that it is too hot inside and that she has to wait for someone outside. He follows her "into the weather," and the snow which clings to her eyelashes melts on his back, making him shiver (pp. 98-9). She tells him that he has never loved anybody: "You don't know what it is" (p. 100). The path Mary chooses, in the world exposed to extremes of weather, where the joy of love entails exposure and vulnerability, is one that William has turned his back on.

His choice means abandoning the vision of being a king reigning with his queen. Even at the moment of asking Mary to marry him his vision falters. He wonders whether his love for her is perhaps not his own idea but rather his mother's (p. 97). The song he has been humming earlier, *"Eef* I were king, dilly dilly / You would: be queen" (p. 87) is unsuited to his acoustically muted tube. Mary goes out into the snow appearing to him, instead of a queen, "a peasant woman in a movie of Europe" (p. 98).

Yet Mary could have been his guide to the life of love he knows nothing of, the dangerous life making us either king or peasant. From early days in school she had always been able to outrun him because of her lean, athletic legs (pp. 85, 87). But the vanity assuring him that he can outpace others intellectually prevents him from trying to keep up with her. In the classroom she stands confident in her beauty, "a Monitor badge pinned to her belly" (p. 86). He will not allow her to be his monitor in the sphere of the emotions. By insulating himself from animal passion he has cut himself off also from human compassion. He waits for renown, not for *someone*.

When William says she is not a virgin, Mary, "returning good for evil," tells him that she knows he is "basically very nice" (p. 99). And, as she leaves him, she is not merely any tired peasant woman. Her head scarf is "like a broad plaid halo around her head," and she "cradles" her books in her arms "her back bent humbly" (p. 98). Another Mary, whose virginity also was questioned, spoke of how God, showing favor to the humble, "has put down the mighty from their thrones, and has exalted those of low degree" (Luke 1:52).

*   *   *

The sense of shelter brings a sense of possession. William Young saw his "autocratic signature" inscribed upon the ground outside. "The Crow in the Woods," also in *Pigeon Feathers,* emphasizes this aspect of shelter. Jack and Clare (a couple appearing in other stories in this volume) have rented a small house in the country. They dine with their elderly, wealthy landlord and his wife. The brilliant, artificial, yet uniformly harmonious evening has its climax when the guests leave; for, outside, the world is thinly draped in snow. "The universal descent of snow restricted the area of their vision; outdoors had a domed intimacy" (p. 222). Their host is delighted. Everything, including the snow, pleases and seems to be *his*. By closing in the physical world, this weather makes the ego seem monarch of all it surveys. Such happiness is without jealousy. On their return, Jack and Clare see their rented home as belonging both to their landlord and to them. Bound together in love, late as it is, they make love.

In the morning the world is beautifully clothed in unbroken white. Jack rises early when their daughter cries. Changing a diaper is an unusual act for him, but impelled by gratitude and the memory of a night of love, he leaves his wife sleeping, gives his daughter comfort, and starts to get breakfast. Every sight and sound is clear, precise, and joyous. As Jack hesitates over preparing food, Clare joins him and deftly prepares all that is needed. Nothing is lacking on this blissful morning. "Like her sister the earth, the woman puts forth easy flowers of abundance" (p. 225).

Thus the snow, making the vast universe contract into a peaceful dwelling place for man, takes the world out of time also. For the moment, Adamic innocence is restored. The world that comes from God's hand is good, and Adam is placed in this enclosed space with Eve ("the woman") as his helpmeet. The story "Leaves" (in *The Music School*) contains the remark that Nature is that which exists without guilt (p. 52). When Nature is covered by the purity of snow, we glimpse what human existence could be without the presence of human guilt. Here Jack rises in the freshness of the morning and puts on a *purple* bathrobe, the garb of a true king. In "Leaves" Updike describes the "casual precision" and the "effortless abundance" that is the hallmark of Nature (p. 52). Jack sees the fullness of pattern all around him in the snowy landscape. Then "a huge black bird" enters the scene (*PF*, p. 225). There seems to be no room for him, and Jack is alarmed. But the crow settles effortlessly on a high branch. In relief, Jack cries out, "Clare!" She, not seeing the bird but snow only, looks at him with "pragmatic blue eyes." She calls him back to his forgotten breakfast, to the boiled egg she has smashed for him, which is running out onto a piece of toast. "Eat your egg" (p. 226).

In a pure world, blackness appears. Man's intellect cannot solve the problem of how God can allow evil to fit into the pattern of a good creation. Nevertheless, against all reasoning, it can be fitted. What intelligence rejects, intuition accepts by having its focus of concern in a different area. The sacramental dimension of life, where heavenly goodness flows into the common things of our world, holds the solution to our questionings. The answer to the existence of evil, the crow in the woods, comes through accepting the abundance of divine love, to which human love points us. *The woman*, who does not concern herself about birds as abstract entities, seeing them pragmatically as providers of eggs, gives the answer that takes away fear. And, beyond the voice of quiet reassurance at the family table, there is another voice saying, "Take, eat..." (Matt. 26:26).

There are echoes in this story of others we have already con-

sidered. The black crow recalls the black starlings which so disturbed Burton in "Dentistry and Doubt." Burton came to accept
the vision of starlings and wrens existing together without conflict.
In "The Crow in the Woods" it is noteworthy that the black intruder
finally settles peacefully on a *high* branch. While his mood of doubt
lasted, Burton always saw the starlings flying downwards.

The family meal as the symbol of goodness (and as a type of
the meal over which Christ presides) has been introduced in
"Toward Evening." There, because of the threatening darkness of
city-life boredom, the love feast was imperfect. The star of toast
fell from Alice's hand. Here, the egg Clare has cooked runs out
over the toast in fulfilment of the biblical saying, "good measure,
pressed down, shaken together, running over, will be put into your
lap" (Luke 6:38). In keeping with the imagery of this passage,
Clare has not merely cracked Jack's egg — she has *smashed* it. No
half measures! And the egg is steaming between Jack's hands, a
bounty defying all limits. A moment before, when he called out to
Clare, *his heart overflowed* (p. 226).

The difference between man and woman, spiritually as well as
physically, is a theme to which Updike constantly returns. Richard's
inability to recognize this difference is stressed in the Maple stories
as one reason for his failure to remain a king. Jack's secure kingship within the rented house leads naturally to seeing Clare as *the
woman*. The intuitive vision of *the woman* is exhibited as the necessary complement to the intellectual vision of *the man,* correcting an
overly theoretical approach to existence with a pragmatism that is
more than mere worldly wisdom because it is imaginative ("blue-
eyed"). In "Pigeon Feathers" David and his father also recognize
that the absence of masculine intellectualism is a virtue in *the woman,*
although in this story there is lacking the atmosphere of mutual
trust that permeates "The Crow in the Woods." George Kern tells his
son, speaking with his usual self-mocking irony: "You can't argue
with a femme. Your mother's a real femme. That's why I married
her, and now I'm suffering for it" (*PF,* p. 121). And when David
has his furious argument with his mother over God's existence, he
reflects: "She was so simple, so illogical; such a femme" (p. 137).
This difference between man and woman leads often to storms.
But it provides the climate in which the vision of kingship can be
glimpsed. It is because she is *a real femme* that a woman can be
a queen in a royal marriage.

In the Maple stories, a royal marriage fails to flourish because
of Richard's unwillingness to give kingly largess. William Young
in "The Sense of Shelter" loses his queen and becomes a dead king
because he hugs to himself his selfish ambitions and loses the op-

portunity to respond to Mary's returning good for evil. The self that he leaves in the long, dark space of his locker is "the humiliated, ugly, educable self" (*PF*, p. 100); it is the self that should have understood Christ's words that the condition of receiving good measure running over is that you do not judge or condemn, but that you forgive and give (Luke 6:37). "The Crow in the Woods" illustrates the mutuality of giving and receiving that maintains royal rule. Jack "in a reflex of gratitude" does not wait for Clare to attend to their daughter when she cries. *Noblesse oblige:* "the man arose instead of his wife, and administered comfort" (*PF*, pp. 222-23).

* * *

The immediate consequence of the falling of the snow in Updike's stories is a sharpening of our physical senses, followed by a sense of ownership. But snow comes from heaven, and its message is ultimately not about earth and its delights. It is about the heavenly origin of all goodness.

The passage from Isaiah identifying the sending of God's word to man with the coming of rain and snow has already been noted. There is a passage from the Book of Job that is also relevant:

> God thunders wondrously with his
> voice;
> he does great things which we
> cannot comprehend.
> For to the snow' he says, "Fall on
> the earth";
> and to the shower and the rain,
> "Be strong."
> He seals up the hand of every man,
> that all men may know his work.
> Then the beasts go into their lairs,
> and remain in their dens.
> . . . .
> Whether for correction, or for his
> land,
> or for love, he causes it to happen. (37:5-8, 13)

Man as well as beast is forced to take shelter when rain or snow comes from heaven. Thus man's hand is sealed up; that is, he is forced to stop all outside work. At such times he has leisure to look at the weather and to learn about the elements that go to make up his life.

In "Central Park" Updike shows the snow preceding the coming of spring which is given to God's land to awaken it from its frozen sleep, but which is also given for man, who responds to the awakening in ways displaying his wayward, yet educable, nature. In "Snowing in Greenwich Village" — and especially in "The Taste of Metal," where the snow comes "to administer a rebuke" — the snow is for correction. And in "The Crow in the Woods" the snow brings a message of divine love that comes to bless human love. Looking at the snow in the morning light and wondering whether he has ever seen anything so beautiful, Jack notices that every twig in the woods around him supports "a tall slice of white, an upward projection" (*PF,* p. 221). The snow which comes from heaven also points upward to heaven. The beauty it spreads outside reflects, inside, the light of joy. Earth below discovers that every good and perfect gift comes down from the Father above.

o

9

THE
POORHOUSE
FAIR

UPDIKE'S USUAL STARTING POINT IS A PERSONAL REC-
ollection, and this is certainly the origin of his first novel, *The Poorhouse Fair.* From "The Dogwod Tree" we learn that "an immense
yellow poorhouse" (the County Home) surrounded by a sandstone
wall stood at the end of the street in Shillington where he was
born (*AP,* p. 156). His father, almost convinced that he would
end his days inside it, used to joke that it was a comfort to know
that he could walk there when his time came. Once a year, it seems,
the townspeople could come inside the poorhouse wall for the
customary fair, meeting their neighbors and buying the simple
handicrafts made by the old folk.

Shillington's County Home has been pulled down, but its fair,
having become a part of Updike's "state of mind," endures. In
re-creating this well-remembered day, Updike puts it deliberately in
the future instead of the past. Whenever novelists project us forward
in time, we may be sure that they are assuming the role of social
critic and telling us what to expect after the good or evil tendencies
in our society have had time to develop to their logical conclusion.
With *The Poorhouse Fair* Updike joins the company of Huxley and
Orwell in predicting the hell, the Utopia of horror, we are headed
for. This particular hell is near enough to the world we know now
not to look particularly horrific. But the motto prefixed to the book
gives a warning from the New Testament: "If they do this when the
wood is green, what will happen when the wood is dry?" (Luke
23:31; E. V. Rieu translation).

119

Updike has put on record that he does not wish his fiction to appear less ambiguous than life. *The Poorhouse Fair,* with its social "message," might seem to be an exception. Yet there is much more to it than the lecturing voice of a tract, as the critics who have termed it a poetic novel testify. The blurb on the bookjacket concludes:

> While *The Poorhouse Fair,* insofar as it regrets the decline of patriotism, handcraft, and religion, carries a conservative message, its technique is unorthodox; without much regard for fictional conventions, the author attempts to locate, in the ambiguous area between farce and melodrama, reality's own tone.

In other words, the novel shows us Updike doing much the same thing that he does throughout his writings. *The Poorhouse Fair* is typical rather than exceptional.

Plot, as usual, is slight — no more than we might find in one of his short stories, though the list of characters is slightly longer.

Having nudged the years on into the 1970's, Updike describes an America freed from the Cold War and from internal tensions and engaged in planning for unlimited prosperity. To the people in the Diamond County Home for the Aged in New Jersey (Shillington's poorhouse has been moved slightly East), the shape of things to come is evident mainly in the increase of the power of bureaucracy. This is typified in the persons of Conner, the poorhouse "prefect," and Buddy, his assistant, who is expert at typing complicated reports. Although in his three years of running the poorhouse Conner has made many overdue improvements, he has failed to win the confidence of the inmates. On the day of their annual fair (an institution he wishes to discontinue) they at last find an expression for their corporate disapproval of him. He asks them to carry away the debris from the poorhouse wall after a truck bringing soft drinks to the fair has knocked down a section by the gateway. They stone him on impulse, not hard enough to break bones but sufficiently hard to convince him of their acute antagonism, which he interprets as moronic ingratitude. Yet the fair goes on; and the day ends with the annual ritual taking its customary course in spite of the passing threats of weather and imposed authority.

Among the crowd of three-dimensional characters in this novel, Conner emerges as oddly two-dimensional. He certainly is drawn without one lovable feature or amiable eccentricity. He is even denied preeminence in his faults, and walks the road to hell that is paved with good intentions. "Young for the importance of his position, devout in the service of humanity, Conner was unprepossessing" (p. 14).

He is a humanist without knowledge of humanity except as a sentimental ideal, an altruist whose visions of serving mankind dissolve into pictures of himself being congratulated in committee rooms, and a believer in progress with eyes fixed upon advancement in the bureaucratic hierarchy. Uncomprehending before the mystery and awesomeness of the universe, he "cons" the external face of nature with the conviction that it can be molded to fit his insipid dreams. He cannot conceive that the way things are is more important than the way he sees them, or that there is more in heaven and earth than his philosophy allows. Consequently it seems to him that he is always being thwarted by "unfortunate" circumstances and "unreliable" people. His ignorance of nature and of man is compounded in his utter lack of self-knowledge. Convinced of his goodwill towards the old folk in his charge and the injustice of their hostility towards him, he looks down from his office window and says, "Damn these people" (p. 22).

His malediction falls principally upon John F. Hook, ex-schoolteacher and, at ninety-four, the oldest of the pensioners. Basically, Conner's dislike of Hook is born of mediocrity's desire to destroy excellence. Hook, for his part, sees Conner as weak and in need of help. While his companions rage against the latest affront to their dignity imposed by the official mind, Hook tries to restrain them by explaining, "A child like Conner must tinker endless-ly" (p. 10). Yet Conner is sure that Hook is continually plotting against him. The fact that Hook happens to be nearby when the stoning begins, he sees as clear proof that it is a planned operation — so carefully planned, indeed, that he has failed to notice the old man give the signal for battle. Having explained to the stonethrowers that they are forgiven, he vindictively deprives Hook of his cigar on the pretext that it is a danger to health and safety. Earlier in the day, too, this man he takes for a cunning enemy has withstood his cogent argument that belief in God is an absurdity, turning aside each thrust, and ending with the comment: "There is no goodness, without belief. There is nothing but busy-ness" (p. 116). Who could forgive that?

Conner's mind is dominated by an abstract idea of progress. His vision is "of Man living healthy and unafraid beneath blank skies" (p. 65). His creed is a simple one: "Man was good. There was a destination. Health could be bought" (p. 124). He is the human equivalent of the "boring progressive edifice" that Rafe in "Toward Evening" saw announcing the year 2,000. If the edifice proclaiming the progressive future was boring, Conner is bored. Automatic promotion awaits him in two years' time. Meanwhile, he is hard put even to keep up a show of the "busy-ness" which Hook has ascribed to him. Such idleness is galling, because the idealistic reformer in him is impatient to begin sweeping away the clutter of the present:

> He wanted things *clean;* the world needed renewal, and this was a time of history when there were no cleansing wars or sweeping purges, when reform was slow, and decayed things were allowed to stand and rot themselves away. (p. 64)

Among the "decayed things" are, of course, the old people; and he knows that his new world of cleanness will not arrive until after they are gone. Although he is eager for their gratitude, he feels this to be a weakness. Moreover, "he had heard the older men whose disciple he was, discuss not entirely in joking, mass murder as the ultimate kindness the enlightened could perform for others" (p. 16).

Conner himself shrinks from being an executioner, for the sight or thought of suffering upsets him. Yet the particular context of his meditation about wanting things "clean" is an order of execution. A cat, hit by a car and badly hurt, has been seen in the poorhouse grounds. Conner has told Buddy to shoot it — which Buddy does with zest, and with the same efficiency that characterizes his typed reports. (Actually, the *report* on this occasion disappoints him by seeming trivial and local [p. 61].) In the sense of being another embodiment of humanistic idealism, he is, indeed, Conner's twin. Lacking his chief's squeamishness, he reacts with the callousness of youth and health to age and infirmity. Thus he shows the other face of humanism to be one of cruelty.

The situation of the pensioners is like that of the cat. Within the poorhouse walls those who have been mortally wounded by the wheels of technological progress are left defenseless. Hook remarks that if a group of children were to find the dying animal, "they would make uncommon sport of him" (p. 52). Earlier, Conner had imagined the cat appealing to him with "a request, polite, for mercy" (p. 45). But in the group to which the *child* Conner and his twin belong there is no room, ultimately, for either courtesy or mercy.[1] So Conner denies the cat's request, and Buddy enjoys his sport. In spite of the humanitarian principles their prefect professes, the pensioners see him as "the tyrant of the place" (p. 52). Says Amy Mortis, one of them, "I have no delusions as to whose mercy we're dependent on" (p. 43).

---

[1] Whereas David Kern in "A Dying Cat" will not leave the cat he finds on the road to die without ceremony, Buddy has no time to stop and bury the cat he shoots. Later he returns to dispose of the carcass, since decayed things cannot be left lying around. The cat was shot in the first place because Conner thought it might spread disease.

Hook is the perfect foil to Conner in that he respects reality, while the latter deals in arid abstractions. Conner thinks of Man in the abstract. When he tries to visualize the human ideal, this abstract Man turns out to be Conner himself playing blissfully in a "world which worships him" (p. 125). Hook sees each face he meets in terms of the students he recalls, by name, from his past. He sees men, not Man. In place of Conner's blank skies, his vision is linked to the years when he lived beside the Delaware and watched the changing colors of that historic water as it reflected the weather of the varied seasons. The patterns of life, he has discovered, are painfully traced and yet give permanent joy and wisdom.

Thus Hook, the teacher whose work it has been to pass the living wisdom from one generation to another, brings past experience to illumine the present. Maybe Updike has in mind that old-fashioned reliable fastener, the *hook and eye;* for Hook's eyesight is much remarked on. The old man has eyes that pierce the distance yet see what is near at hand only with difficulty. He has the vision that sees far, but his age makes it hard for him to integrate his wisdom with the needs of the present when there are so many who, like Conner, have full use of their eyes yet see nothing except what they want to see. He wishes to teach Conner to look beyond himself. For that very reason, Conner is obsessed with the notion that Hook is his enemy.

* * *

Hook's physical appearance, Christian faith, Democratic convictions, cigar smoking, and habit of deliberate speech (dividing the syllables of words) were all characteristics of Updike's maternal grandfather, who was a teacher for part of his life and who lived to be ninety.[2] From this personal starting point Updike shapes his

---

[2] In her short story "Translation" (*The New Yorker,* March 11, 1961, pp. 43-46) Linda Grace Hoyer, Updike's mother, describes her father as one who highly prized "the possibilities of memory" (p. 44). The title of this story refers to the "translation" to heaven of Elijah, with whom Updike's grandfather partly identified himself. In *The Poorhouse Fair* Hook's confrontation with Conner over faith in God echoes Elijah's confrontation with the priests of Baal (I Kings 18:20-40). Before the argument between the two men begins, Hook is talking to a group of the pensioners. He happens to mention the words "Baal and Mammon" when Conner breaks into the conversation. Conner has been unsuccessfully trying to light a fire, as the Baal priest tried to do on Mount Carmel. One of the pensioners now asks, "Is Mr. Conner with us?" (p. 95).

Incidentally, the Hoyer story shows that Updike's habit of emphasizing an important point by deliberately stopping short of stating it is a device that was familiar in the family. The story speaks of the ritual that took place whenever the ninety-year-old man had his feet washed: "Nearing the ritual's end, my father often quoted a part of the fifteenth verse of the tenth chapter

fictional character in order to drive home the point he wishes to make: that the *soul (anima)* of America is in danger of dying but still survives within the poorhouse wall. Hook's special interests are Roman history and nineteenth-century American politics. His long life is likened to a walk "down a long smooth gallery hung with portraits of presidents of the United States" (p. 143). Updike's own account of the present state of America is given in his description of the people who turn out to visit the fair:

> Heart had gone out of these people; health was the principal thing about the faces of the Americans that came crowding through the broken wall to the poorhouse fair. They were just people, members of the race of white animals that had cast its herds over the land of six continents. . . . History had passed on beyond them. They remembered its moment and came to the fair to be freshened in the memory of an older America. . . .
>
> The nation became one of pleasure-seekers; the people continued to live as cells of a body do in the coffin, for the conception "America" had died in their skulls. (pp. 158-59)

The last sentence is immediately followed by Hook's comment that Nero's age was likewise one of pleasure, peace, and perversion. Hook, here and elsewhere (p. 91), links Nero with Abraham Lincoln. He refuses to accept the popular image of Lincoln as a national hero and symbol of moral integrity, insisting that in private life Lincoln was an atheist, and in public life a front for the corrupt interests that showed themselves in the administration of "Lincoln's man Grant" (p. 95).

Hook's animus against Lincoln might be put down wholly to an ingrained prejudice against all Republicans were it not that Updike sets his novel deliberately a century after the time of the scandals arising during Grant's presidency.[3] When Conner objects that Lincoln

---

of Paul's Letter to the Romans: 'How beautiful are the feet of them that preach the gospel.' Here, the more important half of the exclamation still to be said ('and bring glad tidings of good things'), he stopped short, with one flawless white foot in the air" (p. 44). If confirmation were needed, this report also confirms how Updike learned in the home both familiarity with the Bible and also the importance of ceremony.

[3] A newspaper Hook is reading mentions that the St. Lawrence Seaway (opened in 1959) is "Less than a year away from its crystal anniversary" (p. 84). This would date the action of the book in 1973-74. The fifth printing of *The Poorhouse Fair*, though, reads "silver anniversary," and this might indicate that the year is 1984 — the year of Orwell's *dystopia*. But the latter reading would vitiate the point made by the reference to the new American era of peace and pleasure-seeking as being inaugurated by "The London Pacts" (p. 159), which must certainly refer back to the Treaty of London 1871, made in Grant's time. The 1966 printing, incidentally, contains some obvious printing errors.

was a Deist and and not an atheist, Hook replies that atheism "wears as many faces as Satan" (p. 104). The lesson which Hook sees in history is that humanism, or any creed which does not set earth in the perspective of heaven, allows self-interest to flourish under the cloak of altruism. He illustrates this by a story of a Quaker hypocrite who gained a reputation for sheltering runaway slaves, but had them labor for him in the summer without payment and then cruelly turned them out in the cold of winter. He concludes: "And no doubt he was a fair specimen of those so desirous to aid the negro" (p. 93).

Conner fails to understand why anyone should discuss such dead issues; yet, far from being dead, the issue is one of life and death within the poorhouse. He himself is the one who hypocritically claims to free slaves, and then shows himself to be without mercy. His argument with Hook over the existence of God is motivated by a deep desire to crucify the old man who has dared to assert independent views: "... he devoutly wished to pin his antagonist against the rock that underlay his own philosophy" (p. 109). He thereby proves the truth of Hook's accusation: "Your bitterness ... is the wilful work of your own heart" (p. 111).

While saying this, Hook "looked directly at Conner, his eyes greatly magnified by cataract lenses." The *great eyes* that can read the state of Conner's heart recall the biblical saying: "Man looks on the outward appearance, but the Lord looks on the heart" (I Sam. 16:7). And Hook's prophetically inspired accusation is true. For Conner began his argument with Hook in a moment of bitterness in feeling himself excluded "from the run of human hearts" (p. 108).

The truth of the heart is, indeed, the central issue of *The Poorhouse Fair*. America, says Updike, has lost heart though it possesses health. Conner's philosophy asserts that if health can be bought, then man's destination has been reached. He dreams of blank skies, which are really empty skies without radiance. He tells Hook: "The chief characteristic of the universe is, I would say, emptiness" (p. 113). And the result is a bitterly cynical view of life: "*We* are mostly monster. People speak of loving life. Life is a maniac raving in a sealed room" (p. 114).[4] So Conner finds nature to be unnatural, and life a state of being condemned to death. Yet, illogically, Conner clings to that other article of his humanistic creed — the goodness of man. He tells the pensioners that heaven will come on earth "because the administration of power will be in the hands of those who have no hunger for power, but who are, rather, dedicated to

---

[4] In the story "The Dark" (*MS*), the sealed room is an image of despair over the horror of death.

the cause of all humanity" (p. 196). But his hearers *have no illusions as to whose mercy they are dependent on.*

The unreason of Conner's creed comes from his belief that man will some day supersede the animal life which he finds so monstrous. Thinking of the slow progress of evolution that leaves the mass of mankind still with hateful animal natures, he asks himself, "When would they all die and let the human day dawn?" The actual outcome of putting his philosophy into practice, though, is that the people who come to the poorhouse fair are "just members of the race of white animals." They come to the fair because, within the poorhouse walls, there is refreshment. Among those who keep alive "the memory of an older America" is to be found that which alone constitutes sanity and freedom — "the run of human hearts," the *anima* which shows the human to be more than animal.

*   *   *

Within the poorhouse, the place of the old, the tired, and the dying, is the promise of a new life and a refreshed heart. This paradox illustrates Updike's argument that we know earth only when we know heaven too, and that shelter is found to be a blessing only when we have experienced the extremes of the weathers. Conner wishes to abolish pain and ugliness and decay, yet this means that he concludes life to be monstrous and maniacal. He wants to wipe out history and start with a clean universe innocent of the injustices of the past. Yet Hook points out to him that the old folk around him, those who are themselves ugly, deprived, and poor, do not complain of injustice but find their limitations a cause for thankfulness. Conner's philosophy of emptiness, in fact, makes him incapable of understanding the pattern of *things* in the world that floats on radiance. He condemns himself to boredom; and boredom is the parent of cruelty, as the example of Nero reminds us (p. 108).

Conner's rejection of the complex patterns of existence insulates him effectively from reality. Throughout the book he imagines himself to be in command precisely when he is most helpless. He is certain that his words have demolished Hook's faith. And then, grotesquely as he sees it, Buddy charges in to "rescue" him (p. 115). Similarly, after he has failed to light a fire in the poorhouse sitting room, a simple old pensioner named Fuller shows him how to open the flue. Conner is amazed at this "rescue," and still more amazed that the man "should presume to protect him" by stating to the company around, "We've built a fire" (p. 94). After the stoning incident, he thinks he has restored order by forbidding Hook his cigar. Hook's version of the affair was that the young man had been grievously stricken: "The weakness on his face after his henchman had stolen the cigar was troubling to recall; an intimacy had been there Hook must reward with help" (p. 185). That he might ever need the help of the poorhouse inmates, who are in total physical dependence on him, is something beyond the prefect's capacity to comprehend. Nevertheless, locked in the poverty of his view of life as emptiness, he receives their help all unknowing. Even the fantasy of naked girls on the seashore which he weaves as he thinks of the brave new world of the human dawn is derived from a passing remark of one of the pensioners, herself an ugly old woman (pp. 107, 124).

Hook argues against Conner's philosophy, but it is the pattern of *things* that silently refutes it. The weather mocks him. In the morning, looking at the sky, Conner is certain the day will be fine for the fair, thereby reflecting credit on him. "A few clouds dropping their shadows shouldn't matter. Certainly the immense bowl above could not be filled" (p. 40). Hook, experienced in weather, is skeptical of Conner's optimistic comments and the news that WNAM has predicted a fair day. He contents himself with observing that forecasters "can't quite pull a science out of the air" (p. 49). And the rain, less restricted, comes down in support of Hook.

The poorhouse building itself protests Conner's ideals. Built by Walter Andrews at the turn of the century, its well-carpentered structure proclaims a personal purpose at odds with the impersonal efficiency worshiped by its present prefect. In the "Archangel" shelter is offered in "bowers" of immaculate workmanship (*PF*, pp. 169-170). The details of carpentry enumerated by the Archangel are of the kind Hook remembers being lovingly fashioned by the craftsmen of his youth (*TPHF*, pp. 10-11). In his debate with Conner, Hook parries the argument that only an insane mind would think of the stars being made by "a young carpenter in Syria" by saying "there is no pro-fession so native to holy and constructive emotions, or so appropriate for God made flesh to assume" (p. 113). He also says that virtue "is a solid thing, as firm and workable as wood" (p. 111). Conner takes little notice of Hook's imagery. But Andrews' carpentered house, trimmed with "lace wheedled from pine planking" (p. 39), irritates him every day. (It is noteworthy that lace made from snow adorns the paradisal landscape in "The Crow in the Woods.")

Crowning the house is a cupola, once the music room and now the prefect's office. This room was originally built around the large piano which, since it cannot be moved, remains hemmed in by steel cabinets. Conner hates the symbolic height of the cupola and its high ceilings, for he comes "from a world of low ceilings" (p. 22). (Low ceilings gave comfort to William Young of "A Sense of Shelter" when he immersed himself in the Underworld.) Conner does not like to be reminded of the *above*. Furthermore, the music room had been chosen as the prefect's office by his predecessor Mendelssohn who — Conner reflects with distaste — thought of himself as God (p. 14). Conner *descends* to eat with his charges. But this condescending gesture of democratic goodwill only embarrasses the old folk. Mendelssohn ate raised on a dais; and he used to lead them in community singing, ending with hymns, prayers, and homilies on the omnipresence of death. They understood the nineteenth-century romantic music of this latter-day Mendelssohn, who looked so pious and dignified in life, and in his coffin as though he were finishing a prayer, although he spent his days drinking and neglected the care of the place. Conner, though "like many humanists . . . deeply responsive to music" (p. 124), is out of tune with the pensioners' tastes. He cannot perform to please them.

The ballroom wing of the house — the *west* wing — has been turned into the hospital. Conner takes special pride in his improvements here. But what human comfort there is in the space now turned over to the dance of death is provided by Dr. Angelo and the beautiful nurse Grace. Angelo is "godlike" (p. 36), but Grace wins their hearts. Against the rules, Grace brings some young friends during the fair in order to show "her poor sicklies" they are not forgotten. Their efforts to give physical comfort are clumsy, but their youthful presence restores the spirits of the bedridden, whose conversation afterwards leaps in pleasure. This act of *grace* brings them into the heart of the fair. It will not find a place in Buddy's statistics; yet its grace note registers.

Even the poorhouse wall has a voice to accuse Conner. Built by Andrews to say "Mine" rather than "Keep Away" (p. 39), it crumbles easily when hit by the soft drinks truck. Unlike the house itself it is not well built, being a shell filled with rubble. Conner feels that the fallen rubble is a public confession that he cannot keep the poorhouse in good order, and his attempt to clear it up leads to the debacle of the stoning. But, symbolically more important, at the moment when the wall is struck, Conner is looking at the blue firmament and does not see what has happened. The sound comes to his ears as thunder out of a clear sky. This was "the phenomenon which two millennia before had convinced the poet Horace that the gods do exist" (p. 66). Today, the very man who undertakes to prove the non-existence of deity is thus informed beforehand of the Wrath of Heaven against impiety.

* * *

The new prefect, unable to comprehend that the past is in living continuity with the present, misses the lesson taught by the Andrews building. He is unaware that his hurt surprise over the collapse of the wall that never said "Keep Away" betrays the hollowness of his illusion that old age and death can be kept away from society. Equally, he pays little attention to the views of the inmates of the poorhouse who cannot articulate their deepest convictions about the realm of the heart.

After Hook, with whom she is not afraid to argue, the most vocal of the old folk is Amy Mortis. "Women are the heroes of dead lands," thinks Hook (p. 160). Amy Mortis, whose name means a Friend of Death, sees no value in prolonging life, "when if we had any sense we'd let the Lord take us and start off fresh" (p. 30). She tells Conner that it won't do to try to make the poorhouse a little copy of the new world outside: "We're too told and too mean; we're too tired" (p. 43). Following the stoning of the prefect, in which she has taken part, she thinks that "if he killed her tomorrow it would be a blessing" (p. 142). In Hook's age group, she yearly makes patchwork quilts to sell at the fair. There will be no more, she insists, after this fair. Not only is she too old, but also she finds it increasingly difficult to obtain patterned material. These days, the blank skies favored by Conner are reflected in the cloth that women demand. Her sturdy realism challenges Conner's conclusions about the abolition of poverty by pointing out how rising incomes result in overcrowded poorhouses, since the aged are unwanted in homes where the little money they can offer is no longer a consideration. When Conner reluctantly admits that his dream of a heaven-upon-earth will not come in their day, she responds with a sprightly, "Well, then to hell with it" (p. 108).

Amy Mortis is homely and blunt. Another female pensioner, Elizabeth Heinemann, displays a gentleness of spirit that appeals even to Conner. Beautiful and blind, Elizabeth loves the rain, which clarifies her inner world. "You never feel alone when it rains," she says (p. 72). She startles the others by stating her belief that in heaven everybody will be blind. Death for her means going out of a house with few windows into the open air — losing mere appearance and gaining the shape of reality. Her understanding of the inward vision that is nourished by outward deprivation is the lesson that Conner most needs to learn; and, as though realizing this, she constantly appeals to him as she speaks. She tells him she is not convinced that he is an unbeliever, because everyone really believes in his heart. She asks him (who is so deeply jealous of Hook), "Don't you believe jealousy is the one *real* sin?" (p. 99). Her own blindness, she explains, has taken the burden of jealousy from her and made her presence turn others "toward gaiety and reverence." She has learned that everything has a voice and says "yes" to her.

As she walks down a corridor the walls on either side speak to her "like Mr. Conner speaking a moment ago" and tell her not to be afraid (p. 98).

Conner fails to listen to the direct words of Amy Mortis when she assures him that she has no delusions about whose mercy they're all dependent on, or when she argues that longer lives and increased prosperity mean more crowded poorhouses. And he is also quite incapable of understanding Elizabeth Heinemann's subtle language of the heart. His final point in the argument he has with Hook concerns a Peruvian Indian girl who was induced, under drugs, to have a vision of Christ. Hook replies that the experiment was a cruel one, but Conner pooh-poohs the idea and adds, "I think the report said the appearance told her not to be afraid" (p. 115). It is then that Buddy tries to rescue him by changing the subject. Had Conner heard Elizabeth Heinemann's description of the "yes" of the voice speaking to the spiritual ear, he would not have questioned the need for Buddy's intervention.

Hook is called "the man of thought." Two of the younger pensioners, Lucas and Gregg, are identified respectively as "the man of flesh" and "the man of passion" (p. 184). If Amy and Elizabeth are contrasting studies — common sense wisdom opposed to uncommon, spiritual insight — so the three men are complementary studies of three different aspects of the *anima*.

Lucas, a family man, shares his room with his weak-legged wife and a green parakeet wished on them by their daughter Joan. He irritates his sore ear with a match, and irritates Conner also by intruding upon him with complaints. He is the symbol of the nagging weakness and persistent demands of the body. When the parakeet escapes from their room, Lucas follows its random flight and finally catches it on the bed of a dying man in the west wing. Flesh, a green bird on the wing, is doomed to capture in the end. Its freedom is short-lived. Moreover, those who live only in the flesh do not find any permanent home for the heart. Joan had given her parents the bird simply because it had become a nuisance to her; and she, herself a bird in flight, has no settled home and a husband who is "not steady" (p. 166). Lucas' wife is named Martha, the biblical prototype of the this-worldly, busy woman, spiritually insensitive (Luke 10:40). But now this busy woman can no longer run about, for her principal strength has turned to weakness. Her husband gains his chief pleasure from his job of feeding pigs,[5] nourishing beasts reared to be killed. Flesh feeds on flesh.

---

[5] In "The Bulgarian Poetess" the writer Henry Bech explains that his second

Lucas appoints himself spokesman for the poorhouse inmates. He, the man of flesh, is the most obvious symbol of the decay of the body over which Conner and Buddy preside with distaste. Because he thrusts himself importunately before their eyes, they both dislike him. The first mention in the book of their wishing to kill the old people comes in connection with him. Buddy says to Conner: "Don't you think we could dispense with Lucas? He learns more than he tells, and physically, you must admit, he's a monstrous error" (p. 22). Buddy's words are a confession that the philosophy of the overseers of the poorhouse is that of the police state; and his phrasing anticipates Conner's view of human life as "mostly monster."

Gregg, the man of passion, is an electrician animated by a powerful psychic current, a current lethal as lightning in its erratic force. He is unmarried, dirty, foul-mouthed, ill-tempered, physically timid, devious, astute, imaginative — an illiterate romantic poet. But for all his surface unpleasantness, Hook sees in him the charm of the irresponsible boy. He has a child's amoral yet acute perception that shortcuts the processes of reasoning and finds a direct route to the truth. When Conner has the chairs of the pensioners tagged with their names, ostensibly to foster a pride in individual ownership within the corporate community, Gregg sees that they are being docketed, as pigs are by their owners. (He despises Lucas the pig-feeder, the animal-man who will not stand on his human "rights.") It is Gregg who carries the wounded cat inside the poorhouse wall and is livid with anger when it is shot on Conner's order: "I'll kill the c. sucker. I have rights" (p. 127). What enrages him is that the cat's body is left unceremoniously to lie in the rain. He knows the cat symbolizes their own helplessness and the fact that they are being treated like "stinking animals" and not like "humans." Reacting against such injustice, he protests the *right* of all life to kill in self-defense.

Gregg boasts, with accuracy, that he knows "what goes on in Conner's brain" better than does Buddy, who is "half a moron" (p. 12). He certainly understands "Birdbrain Conner" (as he calls him), where Conner fails to understand himself. He rages against Conner behind his back and, unerringly locating his weaknesses, ingratiates himself with him. Twice, he succeeds in humiliating the prefect without the other having the least notion of who is responsible. It is Gregg who initiates the stone-throwing at the broken wall

---

novel is called *Brother Pig,* "which is St. Bernard's expression for the body" (*MS,* p. 218). The identification between Lucas and the pigs he tends is made plain. "Lucas minded the stench of the pen no more than the smells of his own body" (*TPHF,* p. 166).

where, seconds before, Conner has been working beside him, feeling happy to be near so good a man. But, earlier in the day, Gregg has inflicted on Conner's pride a deeper hurt than the shame of having to flee before a hail of stones. All day Conner cannot put out of his mind the phrases of an anonymous letter he has received, signed "A 'Town's person.' " From his trust in psychology textbooks he cherishes the conviction that a warped spinster has written it. His naiveté (which seems to be shared by at least one critic) springs from his ignorance of the power of feeling, of the feminine in the masculine, which Gregg embodies. The letter is addressed to Stephen Conner — prophetic of the stoning which this disciple of progressivism is to undergo when accidental circumstances will turn him into a comic version of the first Christian martyr. The word "rights" stands out before his eyes. Yet the words in Gregg's letter that Conner cannot put out of his mind are these: "Yr duty is to help not hinder these old people on the way to there final Reward" (pp. 78, 178). The letter frightens him, because criticism from outside the poorhouse endangers his career. This particular sentence, though, touches him at a deeper level. It probes the inconsistency of his attitude which, consciously, is one of pride in having provided an efficiently run institution (the only reward worn-out bodies can expect), and which, unconsciously, is one of a desire to clear away decaying things (the reward meted out to the dying cat). With the letter in his mind, Conner thinks, "How much longer before people ceased to be fools?" (p. 78). Yet this letter, with its insistence upon the reward of an afterlife, echoes the biblical statement that the fool is the one who thinks in his heart that there is no God. And the psalm that opens with this assertion accuses the unbeliever thus: "You would confound the plans of the poor, / but the Lord is his refuge" (Ps. 14:1, 6).

*   *   *

Gregg, of course, has no thought of lecturing Conner on a biblical theme, any more than he recognizes the prefect as a secular Stephen, a pseudo martyr. Gregg represents only one fragment of the human spirit, the *anima*. The former Andrews estate is shown as a type of the *estate of man*. Outside its walls is a land controlled by soulless planners devoted to a cult of health beneath blank skies. Inside, the heart is still remembered, and the people of America enter to be refreshed, under skies that have shown the variety of weather, in order to walk once more in the paths of human history. The end of the novel records pieces of their conversation, brought together rather like the pieces of cloth in Amy Mortis' patchwork quilts. Many of them see in the fair only a quaint reminder of old-time life, but they are unconsciously drawn to experience *fair weather,* the climate in which the *anima* is nourished. When the day is over, the old people go off to bed, "for they had to rise early, to guard the gates of the deserted kingdom" (p. 184).

Updike's *anima* has nothing to do with the Jungian *anima,* but derives directly from Aristotle's *De Anima* in which the soul has three levels: the nutritive or vegetable (flesh-Lucas), the sensitive (feeling-Gregg), and the intellectual (thought-Hook). Confirmation of this derivation comes in *Couples,* where the central character Piet Hanema *(anima)* is said to be an Aristotelian (p. 93). While the existence of *anima* on any level — like the existence of all things — is a natural good,[6] in man the incompleteness of the soul, or its imbalance, is counted an evil. For Aristotelian man is a political animal, possessing a kingdom within him and needing to belong to a kingdom in which his selfhood may be developed. Therefore the inmates of the poorhouse know they must guard their kingdom's gates.

Conner's philosophy denies qualitative levels. The new prefect imagines that his predecessor had located his office on the top level of the Andrews House because he "had in part thought of himself as God" (p. 14). Conner thinks of no one as God; yet he now "reigns in the cupola" (p. 41) and, all unawares, sees himself as a young Prince who is to raise up a new kingdom. After the stoning, he calls to the pensioners' backs, "I know you all" (p. 134).[7] These are the words Shakespeare's Prince Hal addresses to Falstaff and his companions as they retire from his presence. The speech that follows (*King Henry IV,* Part I, sc. ii, 218-239) outlines the Prince's plan to "awhile uphold / The unyoked humour of your idleness" in order to have his royal glory break forth later in full splendor.[8] Evidently, this is how Conner thinks of his association with the poorhouse folk. He stoops to mingle with the unworthy, so that afterwards the world will applaud him.

---

[6] The following words on the bookjacket of *The Poorhouse Fair* express this notion: "The author seems to separate sense and existence; the chatter of the mob that comes to the fair in its sense illustrates the national decay that obsesses the pensioners, yet its existence, isolated by bits in the air, shares with grass and stones a positive, even cheering *anima.*"

[7] Updike underlines the importance of these words by using them twice again (pp. 141, 167).

[8] Echoes of this speech appear elsewhere in the book. For example, Prince Hal says: "If all the year were playing holidays,/To sport would be as tedious as to work" (ll. 227-28). Buddy protests to Conner: "What do these people want a holiday for, every day is a holiday for them?" (*TPHF,* p. 55). Yet, in fact, it is Conner who "ever since he could remember" had "hated holidays" (p. 178). No Prince, he is unable to alternate work with pleasant sport. He is bored with his work, and so finds holidays tedious.

In his princely role Conner sees himself occupying the place once held by another Prince, the Son of God. He is a secular Messiah, and not merely Stephen the disciple.[9] Looking down at the people gathering for the fair, a crowd seeming to him to be "a beast more monstrous than any he had told Hook of," he suppresses the memory of having been mocked and stoned with "the conviction that he was the hope of the world" (p. 158). Like Christ, though mocked and wounded, he has forgiven his enemies. Like Christ, he will lead those who have conquered the Beast (Rev. 15:2-4).

The pensioners, however, do not see Conner as their hope, but continue in the "hope laid up . . . in heaven" (Col. 1:15). Also, they regard their new prefect as a usurper and not as Mendelssohn's rightful heir. Mendelssohn retains their allegiance still, and not merely because of his kindness and his good spirit (fortified by secret drinking). Principally, they recall how he seemed alive after being laid out in his casket. He symbolizes the hope of immortality. The name Mendelssohn is linked musically with Elijah, the prophet translated to heaven. And Mendelssohn means also "the son of Mendel," Mendel being the man who found out how plant life (the vegetative soul) passes from one form to another. This last connection might seem rather remote, were it not that Lucas is mentioned as having had his farm requisitioned by a soybean combine that makes plastics; and Hook and he discuss how the coming of plastics has killed the craftsmanship associated with living wood. Lucas is specifically stated to have come to the poorhouse recently, within the time of the new prefect. So, under the new rule, life is destroyed — that same life Mendel showed to be capable of transformation with continuity. In the eyes of the poorhouse inmates, therefore, a reign of life has been followed by a reign of death. In the kingdom of the poorhouse, the only true king is the one who can guide his people "home" by knowing heaven as well as earth.

---

[9] In the interview recorded in the *Paris Review,* Updike explains that it is not only in *The Centaur* that he has worked in a "mythic mode." For example, "there is the St. Stephen story underlying *The Poorhouse Fair*" (*Art,* p. 104). He also mentions that his portrait of Conner was not meant to be a caricature, and furthermore "that Conner was a preliminary study for Caldwell in *The Centaur*" (p. 108). *The Centaur* is an exposition of the Chiron myth, chosen, he says, because this myth is "one of the few classic instances of self-sacrifice, and the name [is] oddly close to Christ" (p. 103). In the novel, Caldwell-Chiron takes the way of imitating Christ in self-forgetful humility, claiming nothing for himself and yet accusing himself of selfishness. Thus Conner is like Caldwell in the way that the Anti-christ is like Christ — the same traits are there, but turned to self-glorification instead of to self-denial. Conner dreams of being a Savior and actually becomes, all unknowingly, a tyrant and destroyer.

Updike's theme that true knowledge is the knowledge of the dividing line between *above* and *below, heaven* and *earth,* is very evident in *The Poorhouse Fair*. Almost at the very beginning of the book, Hook introduces the theme:

> "We fellas so close to the Line" — he raised his voice on this last word, inclined his head and lifted his right hand in a dainty gesture, the index and little fingers pointing upward and the two between curled down — "have our accounts watched very close." (p. 5)

Even Gregg's boiling anger is cooled by this admonition. The nearness of *the Line* makes the pensioners conscious that life is not cancelled by death but given meaning by it. Men are accountable for what they have done or left undone. Hook, concluding his argument with Conner, insists: "And if you have not believed, at the end of your life you shall know you have buried your talents in the ground of this world and have nothing saved, to take into the next" (p. 116).

Another *line* is disclosed in the poorhouse wall. Conner is surprised that this wall should crumble so readily when hit by the truck. But the wall, like the human body, is a mere shell and very vulnerable. Nothing physical which the individual calls "Mine" can last indefinitely. This truth Hook exhibits with his bent fingers. Part of us must go downward, though part may ascend. Those near to death, as the old folk are, cannot forget that the line between preservation and dissolution is a thin one. The pensioners who, as Amy Mortis comments, are old, mean, and tired, are those who can yet put heart into the healthy because they know both the fragility of flesh and the strength of spirit. The townsfolk, says Amy Mortis, take the poorhouse inmates to be fools; and Conner, by his overeager denial, betrays his agreement. At that moment, he knows she has weighed him over against Mendelssohn and found him wanting (p. 44). Only those who have contemplated the line between life and death have the wisdom required to rule in this kingdom, where the values of this world are reversed and what this world counts as foolish is declared wise in the sight of heaven (I Cor. 1:20). As she joins in stoning Conner, Amy Mortis sees in her mind Mendelssohn approving her action (p. 133).

The Poorhouse Fair closes with Hook wondering how he can instruct Conner in the wisdom the prefect has despised. The old teacher's eyesight, clear for distant views, cannot focus on the near at hand. He forgets what it is that he "must impart to Conner, as a bond between them and a testament to endure his dying in the world" (p. 185).

Hook has opened his bedroom door and seen "the blank green corridor wall across the way." Immediately he thinks of Conner and the weakness he has seen in the man. Now, Elizabeth Heinemann, perceptive in her blindness, knows that corridors are not blank. They say, "Yes." They say, "Do not be afraid." Conner, knowing only blankness and regarding only flesh (greenness), has been full of fear. Gregg saw that fear at the stoning and exulted in it — "Pieface Conner," he called him. Hook feels nothing but compassion for Conner. He recognizes in him a fellow intellectual, and sees him as a bright boy, easily hurt. When earlier that day Hook had looked over the patchwork quilts made by Amy Mortis, he had been amazed to see in one the pattern of his own childhood bedspread. He recalled how he used to go to bed, afraid of the dark yet knowing "that he must sleep, when the time came each day" (pp. 27-28). In those distant times, while he lay in the dark room under the bedspread, he could hear his father's voice as it drifted softly up the stairs. So the message he knows he must give Conner, and which eludes his memory now that he is so tired, is that we need not fear the dark. Conner too will come to the age when he is near to the Line, his unsettled accounts closely watched and his talents buried. But, in the darkness that must come to each life's day, there is more than emptiness. We are not in a sealed room. The voice of the Father can be heard, softly telling us not to be afraid. Even the man who has said "no" to life, can be persuaded to listen for the voice that says "yes," turning bitterness to gaiety and reverence.

10

RABBIT,
RUN

UPDIKE'S SECOND NOVEL IS PROBABLY THE ONE MOST widely appreciated, although *Couples,* by achieving something of a *succès de scandale,* has been the one to rise and stay over some months near the top of the best-seller list. *Rabbit, Run* possesses more of a plot than Updike's fiction generally has, and it also gives the feeling of pace and action. Updike himself says of it:

> I originally wrote *Rabbit, Run* in the present tense, in a sort of cinematic way. I thought of it as *Rabbit, Run: A Movie.* Novels are descended from chronicles of what has long ago happened, but movies happen to you in the present, as you sit there. (Jane Howard, p. 81)

We have already seen how the poem "Ex-Basketball Player" in *The Carpentered Hen* and the story "Ace in the Hole" in *The Same Door* are earlier approaches to the basic subject of this novel, namely, the high school athlete who finds adult life an anti-climax after his achievements in adolescence. The main ingredients of the plot in *Rabbit, Run* are already present in "Ace in the Hole." The short story tells how Fred ("Ace") Anderson, who a few years before had been a champion basketball player at Olinger High School, is dismissed from his job at a secondhand car lot. It is not the first job he has lost, and Ace is afraid to break the news to his wife Evey. On his way home he stops to pick up his daughter Bonnie from his parents' house, where she has been left for the day. His mother assures him that, if Evey walks out on them, Bonnie and he can come to live with her. Evey turns out to be angry as Ace had feared, and so, in order to break the mood, he turns up the

137

radio and makes her dance with him. She rejects coldly his suggestion that their next child must be a boy who can become another
champion. Yet, as she begins to pick up his rhythm in the dance,
"he seemed to be great again, and all the other kids were around
them, in a ring, clapping time" (*SD,* p. 26).

In *Rabbit, Run* the ex-champion is renamed Harry ("Rabbit")
Angstrom, and the town of Olinger is called Mt. Judge. The fundamental situation remains the same. There is also the same attitude
toward the athlete whose worries vanish when he feels "sure inside"
(*SD,* p. 14), and who believes that physical movement is the answer
to all problems.

Many of the details found in the short story are also skillfully
developed in the novel so as to give them a heightened significance.
The in-law tensions, the despair over the wife who does not cook,
the fears of a broken marriage, the debilitation of spirit in the secondhand car lot, the succession of dreary jobs, and the dreams of being
great again — all these elements emerge in a slightly different form.
Rabbit has not lost his present job, but he finds it difficult to endure, as he does his wife, who has taken to drinking and watching
TV instead of minding the home. Janice Angstrom, née Springer,
comes from a wealthier family than Rabbit's own. Her father owns
four used-car lots in Brewer (Reading), and her mother considers
her daughter to have married beneath her. Rabbit's son Nelson is not
such a champion-heir as Ace dreamed of. As Rabbit's own mother
does not allow her son to forget, the child will never make a player
since he has the small hands of the Springers. So the ignominy of
Rabbit's position presses in on every side. Here it is the husband
and not the wife who leaves the home. Going to collect Nelson
from his parents' house, Rabbit suddenly decides to clear out. When
the Springers call in the Episcopal minister Eccles, whose church
they attend, Rabbit tells him that he is not going back to Janice,
even though she is pregnant again. He has lost heart, in effect,
hoping that he can bring his wife to take from him the rhythm of
the dance. She is, he thinks, too "dumb" to learn.

From this point, the plot of *Rabbit, Run* passes beyond "Ace in
the Hole." Updike presses on to show, not an ex-basketball player's
temporary dreams, but the permanent consequences of the kind of
vision he cultivates. Rabbit finds consolation in Ruth Leonard, a
prostitute he meets through his old coach Tothero. Ruth has an affec-
tionate nature and delights him with her ample solidity of mind and
body, so different from Janice's "sallow density" and "stubborn smallness" (p. 54). When Janice gives birth to their baby girl June, Rabbit
returns full of good intentions. Then, after this reconciliation proves
unstable, Janice gets drunk and drowns June accidentally while

bathing her. At the funeral Rabbit appalls Janice and both their families by blurting out that she, not he, has killed their baby. Running away once more, he seeks Ruth. He finds her pregnant and hostile, demanding that he divorce Janice and marry her or she will get rid of the baby. So "with an effortless gathering out of a kind of sweet panic growing lighter and quicker and quieter, he runs. Ah, runs. Runs" (p. 307). And the book ends.

* * *

The epigraph Updike chooses for *Rabbit, Run* is Pascal's *Pensée* 507: "The motions of Grace, the hardness of the heart; external circumstances." The external circumstances of Rabbit's life, binding him (so he feels) like a net, are clear from the plot. The motions of grace over against the hardness of the hearts of the characters are less evident. Nevertheless, divine grace is constantly moving behind the scenes. The operation of this grace, and the way in which human hardness of heart turns away from its reconciling power, is the theme that knits the various episodes of the novel into a unity.

In "Toward Evening" the sacramental nature of the universe declares itself through the universal appetite for food. Here, the natural sexual appetite is the universal concern that opens human life to an understanding of that which is beyond the animal sphere. This biological urge carries with it a transcendent summons. Man who can lust after flesh cannot find an end to his desires except in the love of God.

Sexuality is certainly much in evidence in this book. Yet Updike's detailed descriptions of sexual intercourse, unlike so many similar passages in current writing, are not included merely for their own sake. At the same time, Updike is not a transcendentalist holding that physical actualities are no more than insubstantial shadows of a timeless and disembodied spiritual reality. Rather, everything that exists is good, although our misunderstanding of its true nature may so pervert natural good that it becomes hurtful to us. Thus sexuality in the novel is neither downgraded nor idealized. The sexual act is described both as a welling up of innocent joy and as an occasion when the weight of guilt makes itself known.

The key sexual symbol in *Rabbit, Run* is found already in "Ace in the Hole." In that story the word "hole" occurs when Ace is describing to Evey how he lost his job by damaging one of the cars when told to park another car in a space too small to hold it. He tells Evey: "Nobody could have gotten into that hole. Even if it had hair on it" (*SD*, p. 23). This explicit sexual reference explains the pun carried in the story title. Ace, in a hole of unfortunate external circumstances, escapes finally into a creative sexual relationship with his wife. With her he avoids the frustration of failure, through clumsiness, that cost him his job. That such is the meaning of his success in getting Evey to dance with him is clear, for Updike elsewhere writes: "What is a dance? A dance, we suggest, is a socially performed parable of sexual relations" (*AP*, p. 106). Earlier in the evening Ace had a foretaste of this moment of triumph, as the music of his car radio came on "warm" and "strong," making him sing with it, "On Blueberry Hill, my heart stood still" (p. 15). Now his heart is still with contentment. "Blueberry Hill" had been played on the radio by the Five Kings. Now he is king of his five senses. He feels himself "great." A good king, we remember, is called "the Great," and the perfect order of Ace's little kingdom suggests that he is King Ace the Great who shall have an heir to carry on the royal line.

Ace connects procreation with the children clapping at a basketball game. The same connection appears in *Rabbit, Run*. There Rabbit recalls how sexual experience came in the context of excitement among his high school classmates over school games. His first love, Mary Ann, used to wait for him after the game, and he would come to her, "a winner," in his father's car (p. 198). The game itself took on sexual significance in consequence. The ball had to be thrown into "the perfect hole" with "its pretty skirt of net" (p. 37). Now that Rabbit is too old for basketball triumphs, successful sexual games provide his sole link with those times when he felt much bigger. So the name Rabbit, with its double suggestion of speed and sex, is an apt one.

While Rabbit's prime asset had been his speed, he had also learned deftness in handling the ball, thanks to Tothero's coaching; and he had been a clean player, disliking dirty or revengeful play. The games he remembers now with most pleasure were not his spectacular wins, but those where everything seemed to come "just right," when he knew he could "do anything." One game in particular he remembers, though the name of the school where they played eludes his memory at first. Then the name comes to him, making him "perfect in joy." The school was Oriole High (p. 65).

Oriole — *gold:* Rabbit looks back to a golden age; yet that height of bliss lies behind him, almost forgotten. Tothero (Tot-hero?) is no longer a hero to the grown Harry; for the coach has lost his job, through drink and women, and is now a pathetic figure, dirty and unctuously moralizing — "in sad shape" (p. 67). Rabbit himself is only "demonstrating a penny's worth of tin called a frigging Magipeeler in five-and-dime stores" (p. 106). Although Tothero still greets him as "the great Harry Angstrom" (p. 41), the gold in Harry's life has turned to tin. So, on an impulse, he runs away from his home, where he feels nothing is right, where Janice — like Tothero — is taking to drink and is in sad shape. Then Ruth comes into his life. He asks her what she does, and she replies: "Nothing. Nothing" (p. 62). He is convinced that with her everything will be "just right," and that she will restore his certainty of being able to "do anything."

Ruth attracts Rabbit when he first meets her because, though her ginger hair is dirty and she has blemishes on her skin under the heavy make-up, "she is so good-natured" (p. 55). He tries to reassure her that she is not fat — she is "right" in proportion. When he goes to her apartment and they make love, he first washes the paint from her face, removes her ring, and refuses to allow her to use a diaphragm. Having stripped from her these reminders of the tawdriness and artificiality of modern living, he feels the wonder of "unadorned woman, beauty's home image" (p. 81). Earlier, he had jokingly recited to her his Magipeeler-Kitchen-Peeler sales-talk routine. Now, with her surface cheapness peeled away by him, she exhibits her natural goodness.

Through natural sexuality, then, Rabbit thinks he will be able to return to the age of golden innocence. As he embraces Ruth, he cries "in a silent exclamation" that "it is not her crotch he wants, not the machine; but her, her" (p. 78). His dream is of a human world of mutual love, and of the heart come home through womanly beauty. It is not surface prettiness that attracts him, either, for Ruth is plain. And it is not solely a matter of the body. He finds out that as a girl cooking had been her talent. Recently she has always eaten out, but he gets her to go back to this kitchen work, where she shows the talent for homemaking that Janice completely lacks.

Rabbit runs from his own home because he feels that he, the great Harry Angstrom, is wedded to the second-rate. Whenever he comes back from work to Janice he "senses he is in a trap" (p. 15) — he has married a Springer, and the trap has sprung. The clutter of their apartment room clings to him "like a tightening net" (p. 14). Among the litter there is always "the Old-fashioned glass" with its "corrupt dregs" that Janice leaves lying about. In spite of his wife's drinking he "keeps hoping that tomorrow she'll be his girl again" (p. 7); but her prettiness has gone and her mouth has become greedy. When he tells her he has given up smoking (he does not drink), she jeers, "What are you doing, becoming a saint?" (p. 9). That is why Rabbit suddenly bolts for freedom, and why he believes he can find in Ruth's ample goodness a space for the enlargement of his heart. Tothero has said: "A boy who has had his heart enlarged by an inspiring coach can never become, in the deepest sense, a failure in the great game of life" (p. 61).

Because of his fierce preoccupation with his feeling that life should be great and not squalid, free and not bound to the staleness of mediocrity, Rabbit has been judged by some interpreters of Updike to be a saint indeed, a hero of the spirit challenging all adjustments to bourgeois society that bind the self to external standards at variance with the integrity of its inward vision. But Updike would never exalt the *inside* at the expense of the *outside*. The name Harry *Angst*rom, of course, suggests existential *angst;* but the context in which this must be read is not that of Sartre's "nausea" over the meaninglessness of the world or of Camus' vision of the "absurd." Rabbit's sense of dread is the one described by Kierkegaard, namely, the fear of nothingness that is a consequence of man's having fallen away from grace. Where existential philosophy since Heidegger has taught that man finds meaning only within himself, Kierkegaard's existentialism insists that the subjective understanding is valid only when it coincides with "objective truth."

Rabbit's problem is that he trusts too blindly in the intuitions of a heart that has not been sufficiently, in Kierkegaard's phrase, "educated by reality." In this respect, he resembles Conner; and the result is a similar ignorance of the patterns of actual existence and a rejection of the healing that these could bring. Too often he says "no" to things, turning away from the "yes" which they are silently saying to him. His search for a home in sexuality, for example, is frustrated because he wants the hole without the accompanying net. He courts blankness, not realizing that this dream of perfection can lead nowhere except to embracing death. For instance, as he drives away after his first night in Ruth's apartment he thinks of how yesterday's sky was ribbed with clouds, and of how he had exhausted himself trying to head

> . . . into the center of the net, where alone there seemed a chance of rest. Now the noon of another day has burned away the clouds, and he feels nothing ahead of him, Ruth's delicious nothing, the nothing she told him she did. Her eyes were that blue. Unflecked. Your heart lifts forever through that blank sky. (p. 96)

Blankness and health had been Conner's touchstones of perfection. Although Rabbit has no trace of Conner's secularist philosophy, his imagination follows the same track, even to the point of envisioning his earthly paradise as a sand beach under a shining sky. His first flight from home occurs when he decides that instead of picking up Nelson from his mother's, he will simply drive down to the Gulf of Mexico. "He wants to go south, down, down the map into orange groves and smoking rivers and barefoot women. . . . Wake up with the stars above perfectly spaced in perfect health"

(p. 25). But, he does not reach "the huge white sun of the south," or even come nearer to it than West Virginia. Instead, he finds himself at the dead end of a lover's lane. Turning back, he heads for Brewer and sleeps under Tothero's roof. Then Tothero takes him to a Chinese restaurant and introduces him to Ruth.

As he drives on his romantic quest for the South, the car radio spouting romantic songs interspersed with commercials, Rabbit's mind turns to sexual fantasies involving the white skin of rich girls bathing in France. He avoids the coastal route. The stern waters of the Atlantic are too challenging. Moreover, "his image is of himself going right down the middle, right into the broad belly of the land, surprising the dawn cotton-fields with his northern plates" (p. 31). (This sexual image of America as a woman to be possessed continues unconsciously with him when, trying to amuse Ruth with his Magipeeler patter, he addresses her as "Mrs. America.") Besides the literal image of cotton-white skin, however, there is the more evocative symbolism of orange groves: green leaves for flesh, orange-ripe fruit for passion. Orange is an omnipresent color in this book — just as green was so prominent in *The Poorhouse Fair* — and Rabbit's evocation of the orange groves explains it, reminding us that oranges were love-gifts from Elizabethan times. In a wayside cafe where Rabbit stops for coffee, there are girls "with orange hair hanging like seaweed or loosely bound with gold barrettes like pirate treasure" (p. 32). Rabbit sees these girls as *mermaids;* and after seeing them, he is angry, because he senses his dreams are not going to be realized. Another Prufrock, he is one for whom the mermaids will not sing. As his romantic and foolish hopes fade, he finds the branches of trees closing round his car like a net. His vision of blankness, like all inward visions that wish to defy outward actuality, achieves the very reverse of his expectations.

From the road that leads to lover's lane there is only one way — back to the starting point. Rabbit might have learned his lesson on that day, but he was to try again the same road — both with Ruth and with Janice — and find himself again at dead end. He has ignored the motions of grace that might have cleared away the mirages called up by his romanticism.

One agent of grace appeared to him soon after he set out to seek the South. Stopping at a hardware store with two gasoline pumps outside (similar to the one Hook remembered in *The Poorhouse Fair*), he asks the old farmer who fills his tank for a road map. The farmer — "wearing glasses, a scholar" — does not give him the map, but gives him advice instead. "The only way to get somewhere, you know, is to figure out where you're going before you go there" (p. 28). Rabbit answers, "I don't think so," and the old man shows no surprise at his rudeness. But later, after getting a map, he tears it up. To him it becomes simply one more form of the net that everywhere closes around him.

The farmer had smelled of whiskey, and Rabbit dislikes this. "Everybody who tells you how to act has whiskey on their breath" (p. 28). Another adviser with whiskey on his breath is his old coach Tothero. At the Chinese restaurant, trying to impress, Tothero expands upon the responsibilities of his own calling. He says that the coach "is concerned with developing the three tools we are given in life: the head, the body, and the heart" (p. 60). Of these three, he continues, the heart is the most important. Because there can be achievement even in defeat, the will to achieve is what he has always tried to bring out in his boys. "Make them feel the, yes, I think the word is good, the *sacredness* of achievement, in the form of giving our best" (p. 61).

The advice is sound enough, in spite of the pretentiousness of the "bloated old bastard" (his hearers' judgment) who gives it; grace does not operate through perfect instruments alone. Yet the inadequacy of the instrument makes it hard for Rabbit to recognize that these words are a motion of grace. There is too much evident hypocrisy about Tothero, who talks about the sacredness of achievement but is really interested in winning by any means. Rabbit remembers how, "when Marty Tothero began to coach him he didn't want to shoot fouls underhand but that it turned out in the end to be the way" (p. 34). Similarly, when he goes to Tothero at the end of his failure to drive to the orange groves, the old coach does not listen to Rabbit's half-hearted suggestion that he ought perhaps to be getting back to Janice. Instead, telling him proudly that he has a girl for him, he takes him out to meet Ruth. Later on he is to insist that he had advised Rabbit to go back home where his duty lay. Yet, at the time, Tothero does say at least one thing better than he knows. After Rabbit explains that he has left Janice because she has become an alcoholic, Tothero answers: "Perhaps if you had shared this pleasure with her, she could have controlled it" (p. 42). Rabbit cannot follow this reasoning, but readers of Updike will recognize the theme of sharing as the principle of right rule (control) in the kingdom of marriage. Even old drunks can convey the messages of the spirit.

A teacher whom Rabbit does respect, up to a point, is the "big Mouseketeer" on the Mickey Mouse Club TV program. Rabbit and Janice both listen attentively while the "big Mouseketeer" says, "Know Thyself, a wise old Greek once said" (p. 9). They are impressed when this teacher links the wise old Greek with the God who gives us talents to use, saying: "So: Know Thyself. Learn to understand your talents, and then work to develop them. That's the way to be happy" (pp. 9-10). Some critics suppose that what is wrong with Rabbit is that he does not heed the big Mouseketeer and learn to know himself, learn to know his talents. Yet this teaching, for all its exploitation of God's name, is precisely Conner's philosophy in *The Poorhouse Fair*. Conner looks to the hope of man's being " 'integrated,' as the accepted phrase had it, 'with his fulfilled possibilities' " (*TPHF*, p. 65). It is perhaps worth noting also, in view of the epigraph to *Rabbit, Run*, that Pascal strenuously opposed the notion of self-knowledge as a path to truth. For him, nothing except a realization of our need of grace and forgiveness could put us in touch with reality. Rabbit, incidentally, is not entirely won over by the big Mouseketeer's plausibility. As he sees the performer pinching his mouth and winking after the speech, he understands that this is a frank admission: "We're all in it together. Fraud makes the world go round" (p. 10).

* * *

Talking about directions to the old farmer with whiskey on his breath, Rabbit has asked, "Suppose I go straight." He receives the answer: "That'll take you to Churchtown" (p. 26).

The straight road, the road of the heart, leads to *Churchtown*. But Rabbit, who has not figured out where he really wants to go, does not consider making for this destination. Nevertheless, we are told early in the novel that when the big Mouseketeer is speaking about God, "Janice and Rabbit become unnaturally still; both are Christians. God's name makes them feel guilty" (p. 9). In the Christian tradition, consciousness of guilt is the first step in the direction of grace. Among pagans who have no consciousness of guilt, says Kierkegaard, dread *(angst)* is not fully experienced. Mr. and Mrs. *Angst*rom, immature though they are, are capable of Christian experience both in its negative and its positive aspects. The negative aspect, *angst* (that is, fear without a known cause), is very evident at the beginning of the book. The first time we see husband and wife together — the time when they watch the Mouseketeer program — both are frightened; and Janice, "with unexpected earnestness," says: "Don't run from me, Harry. I love you" (p. 11). Her heart focuses her sense of dread on the precise danger that neither of them as yet realizes, for Rabbit has no conscious thought of running away when, shortly after, he leaves her to fetch Nelson.

Rabbit replies "I love *you*." How flimsy his profession is becomes obvious when he makes his decision to seek the orange groves with their barefoot women, and when his car radio announces commercials for "Lord's Grace Table Napkins and the gorgeous Last Supper

Tablecloth" (pp. 30-31). Janice has been betrayed at supper time, gracelessly deserted. The radio also carries news from Tibet that the whereabouts of the Dalai Lama, "spiritual ruler of this remote and backward land, are unknown" (p. 30). Rabbit's whereabouts also are unknown, and his domestic kingdom is left without its ruler, who has so little knowledge of his spiritual duties. The news is repeated: "Where is the Dalai Lama?" (p. 31).

When on his journey south he feels he is losing his way on the back roads, he prays that there may be a way through. "The prayer's answer is blinding" (p. 35). A car speeding towards him with its high beams on forces him into the ditch. He has been warned of the danger of the road he is taking. Finding himself unable to continue along the lover's lane, he wants to sleep for a while and then work out a route south, but another car behind him seems determined to prevent him from doing this, and "he turns instinctively right, north" (p. 37).[1] The journey back is quick and easy, signs and an all-night gas station appearing "magically" when he needs them. The music on his car radio is now "soothing," "lyrical," and "unadvertised." He wonders why his road home is so well posted with signs. "Of course, he didn't know what he was going toward, going down" (p. 38).

Thus, even when he runs away, grace is around him to warn him and guide him home. But, on returning, he does not go home. Instead he turns to his childhood guide Tothero, and gets diverted into another lover's lane with Ruth. But, though he has refused to go to Churchtown, Churchtown comes to him. The Christian community, in the person of the Reverend Jack Eccles, "traps" him by following him like a traffic cop in a patrol car, after he has made a surreptitious visit home to fetch some clean clothes. The green groves he had wanted to reach have taken the form of Eccles' green car into which he climbs. The car is, suitably, *olive* green. It promises peace, a peace that the world cannot give, if Rabbit will change into the penitent's white garments.

Young Jack Eccles (Ecclesiastes, or The Preacher) proves to be another imperfect instrument of grace. He is the third in an ecclesiastical series. His grandfather, the Bishop of Providence, was a near-Unitarian and his father rigidly High Church; both were equally successful and popular. His predecessor in this present parish was another much admired cleric. So he lives under a churchly shadow, haunted by the thought that he follows his calling to please an earthly father rather than a heavenly one, and conscious that he is being judged constantly to be inadequate for his position. His

---

[1] To turn *right* must, of course, be to turn *north*. See above, pp. 99-100.

insecurity is increased by his wife Lucy, a Freudian who loses no opportunity to remind him that she thinks Christianity a neurotic religion involving him in a daily retreat from reality. And he draws criticism also from beyond his own home and congregation. When he visits the elderly Lutheran minister of the Angstrom family, Fritz Kruppenbach, the latter comes in from mowing the lawn. Supper is being cooked in the house, and the smell of meat fills it. Standing in his sweaty undershirt Kruppenbach proceeds to tell Eccles that his job is not to run around trying to make everything smooth but to be an exemplar of faith, so that he can offer Christ to the people. Incensed, yet at the same time feeling guilty, Eccles escapes from the old man who has urged him to be hot for Christ. He cools himself with a vanilla soda in the local drugstore (p. 127).

Kruppenbach's opinion is that Rabbit's domestic troubles matter very little in a world filled with death and destruction and standing on the brink of the judgment of eternity. By bringing together grass cutting and meat, his house proclaims the Old Testament message that all flesh is grass (Isa. 40:6). His urging Eccles to be hot echoes the New Testament declaration that Christ rejects the lukewarm (Rev. 3:15). Dressed in his undershirt as though in vestments, he gives Eccles the stripped-down essentials of the faith he should be proclaiming. Rabbit himself is convinced that his professional instructor has no internal certainty about his faith but goes about wanting to be reassured "that he's not lying to all those people every Sunday" (p. 133). "Soggy" is Rabbit's private summing up of how Eccles strikes him (p. 299).

Eccles takes him to where it is soggy, too. He asks Rabbit to golf with him, and they go to a club where they walk on "soggy turf, raw and wet from recently thawing," down "in the pagan groves and green alleys of the course" (p. 129). In these surroundings, Eccles is transformed. No longer strained by having to present a front of piety, he is "animated" by "brainless gaiety." Here Updike presents us with a contrast between two approaches to existence, two views of the *anima:* the Christian and the pagan.

The Christian approach is indicated by the season of the year and its weather. It is the morning of Palm Sunday when Rabbit is encountered by Eccles. Earlier, Rabbit has looked from Ruth's room at the large gray church standing across the road from his apartment. The congregation is beginning to gather, and Rabbit, somehow heartened by the knowledge that people have left their homes to pray, says a surreptitious prayer for Ruth, Janice, and all the people he knows. On Tuesday he goes to play golf with Eccles. So this is Shrove Tuesday, the day when sin should be judged, penitence

declared, and absolution given after the imposition of penance.[2]
Signs of the day are all around, beginning with the ever-present
bulk of the mountain from which the town of Mt. Judge gets its
name. The thawing ground witnesses to the thawing of hearts hardened by sin. When Eccles gets out at the golf club, "his head across
the top of the car looks like a head on a platter" (p. 128). Jack
Eccles becomes John the Baptist, calling men to repentance. On
the course "Eccles flits in his grubby shirt like a white flag of forgiveness, crying encouragement, fluttering from the green to guide
him home" (p. 131). Rabbit is angered by Eccles making him try
over again when he fails. What he objects to is the assumption
"that his strokes are past counting" (p. 132). He wants to win on
his merits, and is irritated by the thought that he needs grace.

This golf game recalls the golf game in the short story "Interces-
sion," from *The Same Door*. There, a guilt-ridden man named Paul
plays golf with an imaginative boy. Paul is infuriated because the
boy will not play by the rules and refuses to count wasted shots;
and still more infuriated because the boy keeps insisting that *his*
way is better than Paul's way, that his father has told him not to
bother, but to concentrate upon getting tuned up. Paul is certain
that he is "destined" to beat the boy. But when a shot that he feels
is certain to land on the green hardly rises above the ground and
suddenly vanishes "as if a glass arm from Heaven had reached
down and grabbed it" (p. 208), he gives up. Everything seems to
him to be under a curse. The story, evidently, is about the issue with
which St. Paul wrestled: the curse of the law and the way of grace
which the Father has offered beyond the reach of legalism.

If the mute actions of Eccles suggest the Christian themes of
law and grace, forgiveness and repentance, his whole conduct does
not. After asking Rabbit whether he wishes to return to Janice,
Eccles accepts easily Rabbit's refusal. Rabbit is annoyed "at the way
this minister isn't bawling him out or something; he doesn't seem

---

[2] Shrovetide begins on Saturday, which is the day Rabbit comes back from
his attempted escape to the south and seeks sanctuary at Tothero's house. No
direct mention of the day's being Shrove Tuesday occurs while Rabbit and
Eccles are playing golf among the pagan groves. Rabbit's imagination is pre-
dominantly sexual as he tries to guide "the hard irreducible pellet that is not
really himself yet in a way it is" (p. 131) to the hole on the green. He finds
himself comparing the irons, "thin" and "treacherous," to Janice, and the
woods, "fat" and more sympathetic, to Ruth. But he also sees his grandfather
in the sky, staying there so that Rabbit will not be "the Fosnacht." The reference is to a German custom connected with *Fastnacht* (Shrove Tuesday),
in which the last person downstairs is called the Fosnacht or fool. So the hole
is more than pagan sexuality; it is also "home," and a remembrance of the
loving care of the grandfather who, Christlike, bears the shame belonging to
others.

to know his job" (p. 102). When he goes to Eccles' house he sees "a little porch imitating a Greek temple" (p. 115) and a cold silver room containing "one of those clocks with a pendulum of four gold balls that are supposed to run practically forever" (p. 116). Here is a pagan world, with its love of lucidity and its aspiration toward eternity. It is not surprising that its owner should take him out among pagan groves. Eccles' wife Lucy answers the door dressed in orange pants — "a fine-grained Ruth" (p. 117), Rabbit thinks. The orange groves are right within reach; and Rabbit slaps the pants, "a cupping hit, rebuke and fond pat both, well-placed on the pocket," afterwards making a face, "a burlesque of penitence" (p. 118).

Because Lucy does not tell her husband about the slap, Rabbit guesses he has judged her rightly. "A sharp vanilla cookie," he thinks to himself (p. 123). Now "vanilla" is etymologically the same as vagina. Eccles himself likes vanilla sodas into which — completing the sexual image — a scoop of maple-walnut ice cream has been put. For him, indeed, drugstore counters are places where he becomes "titillated silly" (his wife's verdict) with teenagers' talk about "how far" you can "go" on dates and still love Jesus (p. 189). Thus Eccles' house not only looks pagan. It is also a place where there is a pagan preoccupation with sexuality. When Rabbit first enters it, Eccles calls out that Joyce, his three-year-old daughter, is getting into bed with him. "Lucy opens her eyes and says to Rabbit proudly, 'See?' " (p. 117). She has just been explaining her Freudian view that sex determines all family relationships.

Updike uses a literary source to comment on the Eccles household: Hilaire Belloc's *Cautionary Verses.* Lucy dislikes her husband's reading "those hateful Belloc poems" to Joyce, because they introduce the topic of death. She mentions in particular, "that damn pony Tom" (pp. 120-21). Belloc's "Jack and his Pony, Tom" describes how a boy kills his pet pony by feeding it unsuitable food. While Belloc is being discussed, a cake Lucy is baking begins to burn; and soon Eccles is telling Joyce she should not be asking for another cookie. Is it Jack's choice of diet (poems about death) or Lucy's (herself a "cookie") that will harm the child? Joyce also comes downstairs complaining that she is afraid of the "li-un." The reference is to the poem "Jim: Who ran away from his nurse, and was eaten by a Lion." "Joyce, are you a good girl?" Rabbit asks. She shakes her head but answers, "Yes." "And is your mummy good?" The child says *yes* to this too, and then runs away. Answering for her mother as well as for herself, Joyce says out loud that she is good, but by running away silently denies it. This interchange is explained by another Belloc poem, called "The Lion." "The Lion, the Lion, he dwells in the waste, . . . And a good little child will not play with him." Rabbit is sure that Lucy is no good little child, and would willingly play with the lions of passion.

The Belloc poems are comic parables, written, "For people such as me and you/Who pretty nearly all day long/Are doing something rather wrong." In Updike's handling of the theme there is a biblical reference in the background, namely, that death is the consequence of sin, and that sin is the consequence of lust (James 1:15). Later in the novel, Rabbit refuses Lucy's invitation to come into the house with her, making it clear that he thinks she is propositioning him, "and reaches his apartment clever and cold with lust" (p. 242).

Rabbit sees that, as both Joyce and her mother tease Eccles over the Belloc poems, at the same time they are testing him, impudently yet fearfully. He wonders "why Eccles doesn't go for it; drive a wedge in this chink of fear and make discipline. Not that he could do it either" (p. 122).[3] Rabbit's immature Christian vision has some notion of the need for a disciplined life, but it remains mostly at the level of feeling. In Kierkegaardian terms, it hardly progresses from the aesthetic sphere of existence to the moral-religious spheres. Rabbit tells Eccles, "I *do* feel, I guess, that somewhere beyond all this" — he gestures toward the "un-grandest" landscape of Brewer — "there's something that wants me to find it" (p. 127). Also, standing on Mt. Judge with Ruth, he thinks "that if there is this floor there is a ceiling, that the true space in which we live is upward space" (p. 113). On the strength of this instinctive conviction that earth can be truly known only in relation to heaven, Rabbit is called by Eccles a mystic who can give other people faith (p. 144).

The result is that Rabbit begins to pride himself on being a spiritual person, superior to others — to Eccles, for instance, who for all his theological training must come to him to have his doubts removed. "I'm just lovable," he says to Lucy, with hardly any irony (p. 208). But it is to Ruth that he confides his most prized piece of acquired wisdom: "If you have the guts to be yourself, other people'll pay your price" (p. 149).

---

3 Rabbit himself is, of course, the type of undisciplined child so often described in children's books. Belloc's poem "Jim," for example, begins: "Now this was Jim's especial foible./He ran away when he was able." But Rabbit's name suggests another and better-known undisciplined youngster — Peter Rabbit. Perhaps in unconscious recollection of Beatrix Potter's story, Eccles and his wife refer to Rabbit in front of their children as "the naughty man." Updike refers to this parallel between Harry Angstrom and Peter Rabbit in the *Paris Review* interview, adding: ". . . only lately do I see that Brewer, the city of brick painted the color of flowerpots, is the flowerpot that Mr. McGregor slips over Peter Rabbit" (*Art,* p. 104).

Before he says this to her, Ruth has realized how things stand
with him. She thinks:

> That was the thing about him, he just lived in his skin and didn't
> give a thought to the consequences of anything. . . . For the
> damndest thing about that minister was that, before, Rabbit at
> least had the idea he was acting wrong but with him he's got the
> idea he's Jesus Christ out to save the world by doing whatever
> comes into his head. (p. 149)

Eccles, through his well-meaning attempts to win Rabbit over
through the appeal of love without discipline, has encouraged Rabbit to live on the aesthetic level, the level of feeling, and to avoid
the rigor of moral realism. On the golf course, he offers Rabbit a
gardening job with one of his parishioners, a Mrs. Horace Smith:
"Flexible time. That's what you want, isn't it? Flexibility? So you
can be free to preach to the multitudes" (p. 128). But Rabbit is
no Jesus, and not even an innocent Adam; and firmness, not flexibility, is what he requires. Among the "brainless flowers" of Mrs.
Horace Smith's garden, Rabbit's mind runs along the pagan path
of Horace's *carpe diem*. He thinks of the scented blooms in terms
of Oriental prostitutes and cheap enticing girls in flashy clothes.

When Rabbit is called back at the time Janice is having her baby,
he is at first stabbed with guilt, feeling sure that "as a consequence
of his sin Janice or the baby will die" (p. 196). But after his
daughter is born and his wife seems ready to take him back as
though nothing has happened, this mood quickly passes. He is full
of elation as he goes to Eccles' church when Janice gets out of the
hospital. He thinks he will pray for forgiveness, but he is too happy
to do so. The sermon is about Christ in the Wilderness and his
confrontation with the Devil. Rabbit scarcely listens for he has no
taste for the dark aspect of Christianity, "the *going through* quality
of it, the passage *into* death and suffering that redeems and inverts
these things. . . . He lacks the mindful will to walk the straight line
of a paradox. His eyes turn toward the light however it glances into
his retina" (p. 237).

Instead, Rabbit is captivated by "the beauty of belief" (p. 235).
His is an aesthetic, pagan vision that seeks the illumination of selfhood without consciousness of guilt. Looking at the women and
girls around him in their Sunday best, he thinks that he has come
into a field of flowers ("brainless flowers!"). Soon he has recognized
Lucy Eccles — so luminous a vision that he is surprised to find,
when she turns, that her face has features on it. In his euphoria, he
believes that she wants him, wants to take him from Janice. Invited
by Lucy after church to come in for coffee, he feels big as he

refuses, saying: "No, look. You're a doll, but I got this wife now" (p. 242).

With complacency comes cruelty. Lucy Eccles, whether justly rebuffed or unjustly insulted — or both at once — is hard enough to react with unforgiving hatred. But Rabbit hurts the vulnerable too. Ruth is aware that the gentleness he displays in love-making (so long as he is pleased with himself) is not kindness. On one occasion, angered by the thought that she has been a whore, he insists on using her like one; and Eccles, phoning him soon after, cannot believe that the rough voice that answers is really Rabbit's. Similarly, he attempts to force Janice to give him sexual satisfaction after the birth of her baby, at a time when she is worried about not having milk enough to feed it. Repulsed, he leaves her in anger. She is bitter about his calling her dumb and about his being too stupid to see that anyone besides himself has feelings. Her despondency leads to her drinking, and so to her acccidentally drowning the baby.

At the funeral, common grief softens hard hearts: Rabbit's, Janice's, and even the hearts of the antagonistic in-laws on both sides. Then, at the close of the service, the words about "Casting every care on thee" ring in Rabbit's head. He feels sudden illumination, unusual strength. He has seen the truth and wishes others to see it too. "Don't look at *me,*" he says. "I didn't kill her. . . . *She's* the one" (p. 293). As "heads talking softly snap around at a voice so sudden and cruel," he is amazed. Up to this moment he has felt only forgiveness, but now he hates; he hates especially Janice's "dumb" face. Overwhelmed by the enormity of the injustice being done to him, he turns and runs. Finally, finding Ruth, he meets a judgment that confounds him. For Ruth also has her moment of illumination. She says: "I see you very clear all of a sudden. You're Mr. Death himself. You're not just nothing, you're worse than nothing" (p. 301).

*   *   *

Ruth's words are exact. After the baby's death Rabbit has a dream in which he stands on a large playing field or vacant lot and sees the moon blotting out the sun, "lovely life eclipsed by lovely death." In his sleep he is greatly excited, thinking "he must go forth from this field and found a new religion." Then he wakens to find Janice bending over him, and realizes "that he has nothing to tell the world" (p. 282).

Rabbit's romantic soul has followed the quest of *nothing:* the blank skies of the South, with its huge white sun; Ruth's delicious nothing that she says she does; and the luminous view that concentrates itself into the figure of Lucy Eccles. In his dream this nothingness resolves itself into the less than nothingness of death. The white sun has been eclipsed by the dead disc of the pale moon, so beloved by romantics. The religion he imagined he had to announce to the world has turned out to be nothing. Eccles had said he was a mystic able to give people faith, but Rabbit "never would have thought of it himself. He doesn't think much about what he gives other people" (p. 144).

This unwillingness to give is, finally, the root of Rabbit's inadequacy and the cause of his declension into the kingdom of death. While he works in Mrs. Horace Smith's garden among the brainless flowers he at least catches a glimpse of the natural world where a right order rules. "Sun and moon, sun and moon, time goes" (p. 135). In the garden the opposites of lightness and darkness succeed each other and guarantee a cosmic rhythm in which death does not eclipse life but leads to ever-renewed resurrection. Rabbit loves to lay the seeds in the ground: "The simplicity. Getting rid of something by giving it to God. God himself folded into the tiny adamant structure" waiting to burst into new life (p. 136). But though Rabbit gives trustingly to the God immanent in nature, he refuses to give anyone — God or human being — who makes moral demands on him.

Rabbit's reconciliation with Janice after the birth of their baby is short-lived because of his indifference to the sacrifices parenthood demands. With his mind set on making love to Janice, he is irritated at the baby's refusal to sleep, making instead "an infuriating noise of strain, *hnnnnnah ah ah nnh*" (p. 242). Like Tom's horse in the Belloc poem, this little living creature whinnies to explain that it is being fed on a diet that will kill it, that the nourishment of self-giving love is being denied it. Nelson too becomes fretful and whiny. He is sensitive to "the threat the infant is trying to warn them of" (p. 243). It is then that Janice discovers she has no milk. And the crib begins to look like a coffin.

The desire for enjoyment without cost to himself first sent Rabbit journeying south in search of orange groves. A similar expectation of being able to enjoy an "orange" world at home, when frustrated, drives him away again from his wife and children and sets in motion the events leading to his daughter's death.

In the hospital, Janice speaks of wishing Rabbit could come into bed with her. "It seems to me you're pretty sexy for somebody in your shape," says Rabbit (p. 204), and Janice replies that she's just got this terrible thirst for orangeade. Soon, however, she thinks only of caring for her baby; Rabbit finds her tastes have changed. Rebuffed in his love-making, he thinks of the streets "stretching bare" under the street lamps, puts on his "suntans" and leaves her. His decision echoes the journey south to the orange groves, when he thought of himself driving down the belly of America towards the sun. In the morning Janice starts drinking in order to numb her consciousness of being abandoned once more. She smashes an orange juice glass in the sink. Then she turns in horror to discover June's crib "smeared with orange mess" (p. 262). She swears at "this awful baby," and fills the bath, wishing she could get into it herself. Her wish in her spirit to be cleansed from orange mess is answered by the spirit she has turned to for help.

Before Rabbit left the apartment, Janice asked him if he could not think of how she felt. He answered: "I can but I don't want to, it's not the thing, the thing is how *I* feel" (p. 248). It is true that his aesthetic scale of values does give way momentarily to moral ones on occasions when reality breaks in forcibly. When he was called to the hospital at the time of June's birth he saw himself as "the runner, the fornicator, the monster" (p. 201). And after June's death this feeling becomes greatly magnified. "He wants jail: to be locked in place" (p. 286). Yet, once he has assured himself that Janice and not he bears the guilt, he runs away with an easy conscience. "Janice and Eccles and his mother and his sins seem a thousand miles away," and he wants to tell Eccles: "I'm on the way. I mean, I think there are several ways: don't worry" (p. 297). But this is before he has the final confrontation with Ruth.

* * *

In order to postpone deciding how to reply to Ruth's ultimatum to either marry her or else lose both her and her baby, he goes out to get himself a sandwich at the delicatessen. The "opposites" become clear to him:

> Janice and Ruth, Eccles and his mother, the right way and the good way, the way to the delicatessen — gaudy with stacked fruit lit by a naked bulb — and the other way, down Summer Street to where the city ends. He tries to picture how it will end, with an empty baseball field, a dark factory, and then over a brook into a dirt road he doesn't know. He pictures a huge vacant field of cinders and his heart goes hollow. (p. 305)

In his mind the several ways he has earlier imagined now narrow down to two: the way of life and the way of death. The way of life presents itself in three modes: the right, the good, and the delicatessen (the natural appetite). But he has come to the point where, as Ruth has told him, it is "too late" to make a choice that can be either right or good. For so long he has played with thoughts of the right and the good, but always he has taken the way of satisfying

his appetite. (The delicatessen is described in sexual images —
"gaudy," "stacked," "naked.") So, though his appetite has taken
him outside, he does not go to the delicatessen.

There is only one other way to take. He thinks that he will go
around the block, but then neglects to turn *right,* and instead steps
down off the curb and begins to run. So he goes on toward that
huge vacant field which had featured in his dream of death eclipsing
life. The field of cinders over a brook and reached by a dirt road
he doesn't know is, indeed, a precise picture of hell. He, who has
tried to have life on his own terms, is finally forced to take the way
of death without hope.

The choice of death has become inevitable since he clings blindly
to his old belief that external reality must retreat before internal
feeling. "He feels his inside as very real suddenly, a pure blank space
in the middle of a dense net" (p. 306). Not knowing what to do
or where to go, he seems to have become "infinitely small," and is
reminded of being blocked at basketball and having to pass the ball
to others, leaving, in effect, "nobody there."

The street he crosses, looking down to its "unseen end," is
Summer Street. The narrative of *Rabbit, Run* begins at Shrove Tide
and ends in high summer. Yet Rabbit will not enjoy the autumn
fruits that have been ripening in the summertime. He visualizes them
in the delicatessen window, and he leaves them behind as he runs.
Nor will his path bring him to Churchtown, which once he could
have reached had he gone straight. The church opposite the window
of Ruth's apartment is there, and it too he passes by:

> Afraid, really afraid, he remembers what once consoled him by
> seeming to make a hole where he looked through into underlying
> brightness, and lifts his eyes to the church window. It is, because of
> church poverty, or the late summer nights or just carelessness,
> unlit, a dark circle in a stone facade. (p. 306)

Mrs. Springer, with her unfeeling realism, at one time remarked
to Eccles: "Well if the world is going to be full of Harry Angstroms how much longer do you think they'll need your church?"
(p. 154). Yet the Harry Angstroms of this world — the men of
angst who are really afraid — are the ones who most need the
light that proclaims on earth the light of heaven. When for them
that light has gone out there is no other way to take except "the
other way, down Summer Street to where the city ends" (p. 305),
and where the heart goes hollow.

11

THE
CENTAUR

IN THE CENTAUR *UPDIKE BREAKS WITH HIS USUAL*
custom of preserving a wholly naturalistic story line. Except for
"Archangel," in *Pigeon Feathers,* this has not happened before; and
only "Four Sides of One Story," in *The Music School,* exhibits anything similar since. Whereas, as we have seen all along, the symbolic
dimension of Updike's fiction is normally suggested indirectly,
through hints carried in the narrative which the reader is expected
to pick up for himself, here symbol is laid side by side with realistic
description. Olinger in one sentence becomes Olympus in the next.
George Caldwell, high school teacher in General Science, merges
into Chiron the wise centaur, instructor of the young heroes of
Greek mythology.

Because the mythological elements in the novel are so obvious,
so striking, it is easy to overlook the fact that *The Centaur* is
basically another Olinger story. Updike tells us (*Olinger Stories,*
Preface, vi) that writing it was a not wholly successful attempt to
say farewell to Olinger and move on elsewhere. Perhaps the thought
that he was reflecting on his childhood world for the last time
made him particularly anxious to re-create the past with precision.
At any rate, *The Centaur,* presented as Peter Caldwell's account of
how things were when "I was fifteen and it was 1947" (*TC,* p. 47),
is crammed with detail plainly carved on the author's memory. From
the sequence of the gradients on the roads between his home and
school to the feel-in-the-hand of a certain "painted china figurine
of a smiling elf with chunky polka-dot wings" (p. 277), there are
a thousand items brought out of his past. The result, though never

156

mere reminiscence, is a vividly re-created scene, "a patch of Pennsylvania in 1947" (p. 293).

So this is the most personal and the least "invented" of the novels. The mythological sequences, intriguing and illuminating though they are, serve chiefly to give us insight into Updike's belief that the truth about any landscape does not lie on the surface but is found when observation deepens into vision.

* * *

The recorded patch of Pennsylvania, 1947, is a three-day sequence: Monday morning to Thursday morning in the second week of January. Two short stories, published in the month before *The Centaur* appeared, give the opening and the closing scenes of the plot. In the novel they form two chapters and are realistic narratives along the line of other Olinger stories. The story "After the Storm"[1] appears almost unchanged as Chapter VIII, apart from the addition of an extended introductory section (*TC,* pp. 265-270). "On the Way to School"[2] has, however, undergone many small but important changes when it appears as Chapter II. These changes provide a valuable pointer to Updike's intentions in shaping *The Centaur* within the framework of an explicit mythology.

The narrative of Chapter II describes how George Caldwell starts off on a cold Monday morning in January from the farm near Firetown and drives with his son Peter to Olinger High School. George's usual reluctance to return to work after the weekend is increased because he suspects he is ill. The unspoken fear of cancer surrounds them as his family urges him to see Doc Appleton if his condition is more than imaginary. He is worried about being late, yet he stops on the way to pick up a decrepit hobo and makes a detour into Alton (Reading) in order to accommodate him. All morning, Peter has been angry with his father for his obstinate ways, particularly because he will not put on the expensive pair of leather gloves Peter has bought him as a Christmas present, instead letting them lie on the back seat of the car. Now, sure that they will be late, he scolds, "What do you *see* in these bums?" (p. 91). They reach the school in time, but Peter discovers that the hobo has stolen the gloves he had saved so hard to buy. With the comment, "Well, he needs 'em more than I did," George Caldwell walks into the school, wearing a hideous blue knitted cap (that shames Peter because it was snatched out of a trash barrel), "consuming the cement walk with generous strides" (p. 92). Peter muses:

---

[1] *Esquire,* January, 1963.
[2] *The New Yorker,* January 5, 1963.

My father provided; he gathered things to himself and let them fall upon the world; my clothes, my luxurious hopes had fallen to me from him, and for the first time his death seemed, even at its immense stellar remove of impossibility, a grave and dreadful threat. (pp. 92-93)

So ends Chapter II. The short story, on the other hand, continues with three additional sentences: "Without him, I would cease to exist. Stunned by this lesson, I entered the school. In the crowded corridors, he had already disappeared" (*The New Yorker*, p. 67). In these three sentences the theme of *The Centaur* is condensed, and the reason for the introduction of the myth of Chiron is explained.

On the bookjacket of *The Centaur,* we are told that the novel was originally planned to be a "contrasting companion" to *Rabbit, Run.* George Caldwell, the devoted husband and father, certainly makes a very evident contrast with Harry Angstrom, the rabbit that breeds and runs. The most far-reaching difference between them — apart from differences in age, occupation, and temperament — is that Rabbit lives in his skin and does not care what he gives other people, while George Caldwell is a man who walks with "generous strides." The schoolteacher's intense concern for others and his disregard for self-interest is, indeed, a constant source of dismay to those who know him — and to his own family in particular — since it leads him into conduct seemingly quixotic and even irresponsible. All the same, whatever the embarrassments his selflessness provokes, he proves to be the antithesis of the man in *Rabbit, Run* who is seen as Mr. Death himself. At the beginning of Chapter II in *The Centaur* Peter records what his home continually gave to him: "I always awoke to the sound of my parents talking, voices which even in agreement were contentious and full of life" (p. 47).

In effect, then, *The Centaur* tells the story of Mr. Life. As his father leaves him to walk into the school, Peter describes him in terms that could be applied to God, who is the source of all goodness and whose gifts, falling ceaselessly upon the world, are given in love to his children. Yet, at this very moment Peter realizes that his earthly father, though standing in relation to him as a type of the Heavenly Father, is human and for that reason mortal. Chapter II ends with Peter's realization of the "grave and dreadful threat" that the possibility of George Caldwell's death presents to him. The short story "On the Way to School" goes on to explain the "lesson" Peter learns by going to school on this memorable Monday morning. "Without him I would cease to exist." Yet, immediately, his father *disappears.* So Peter understands that physical absence does not mean having to be "without" the supporting presence of his father's love. Neither the threat of death, nor the brute fact of death which must inevitably follow some day, will leave him fatherless.

This explicit statement of the "lesson" is omitted from the novel, because the lesson is spelled out much more fully there. The narrative of the three days shows us Peter and his father together under stresses that gather in blackness and then dissolve into un-hoped-for relief. The narrative ends on Thursday morning, with George Caldwell going back to school and Peter recovering in bed from a feverish cold he has caught. The threat of death from cancer has been removed, for the doctor has phoned to say that the X-ray plates he has taken are clear. Peter's father is not going to "disappear" for the present. At the same time, Updike introduces via the mythological story of Chiron an interpretation of the rela-tionship between Peter and his father on another level — a tran-scendent one. On this level the fact of death is seen not merely as a personal problem for the individual, but as a cosmic question de-manding an answer as to how biological existence meshes with the life and death of the spirit. And man's consciousness of death as an evil is probed in connection with human responsibility before God, where the willing sacrifice of one's life for others may prove to be the way of bringing life out of death.

The contrast between *The Centaur* and *Rabbit, Run* is not simply a contrast between two men, one self-sacrificing and the other not. The pair of books can also be taken as parables of the different spheres of life defined by Kierkegaard. *Rabbit, Run* describes the consequences of choosing to live in the aesthetic sphere. *The Centaur* goes on to examine life lived in the moral-religious sphere, which for Kierkegaard is reached only by those willing to exercise freedom of choice and accept the discipline of suffering, sacrifice, and death.

* * *

As we have already noted, the epigraph prefixed to *The Centaur* is a quotation from Karl Barth describing man as that being who stands between the conceivable creation called earth and the inconceivable creation called heaven. By choosing to call upon Greek mythology to provide a vision of "heaven" above "earth," Updike has found a way of presenting man in his "middle" place without explicitly asking the reader to accept a specifically Chris-tian estimate of the universe. We shall see that this does not mean that he avoids any appeal to the Christian view of man and his destiny (which is, in any case, clearly assumed by the Barthian reference), but only that such a view is not directly presented.

However, it cannot be overlooked that the particular myth taken to illustrate the theme of the novel is one which echoes the central motif of the Christian story: a blameless life freely offered in order to expiate sin against the divine order. Such is the sacrifice made by Chiron, the noblest of the Centaurs. Chiron has been wounded accidentally by a poisoned arrow which leaves him in perpetual pain. He offers to exchange his immortality as an atonement for Prometheus, who has incurred the wrath of Zeus by stealing the sacred fire from heaven; and Zeus accepts the exchange. Updike makes full use of the Chiron myth's implications for the Christian imagination. By casting George Caldwell as Chiron and Peter as Prometheus, he sets their story in the context of sacrifice and atonement, and thus is able to raise the question of the purpose of existence and the nature of the universe. The cosmic theme, in fact, is introduced in the very first chapter of *The Centaur,* which describes the wounding of Chiron and also presents George Caldwell in his role as teacher of General Science.

The book opens on Chiron's wounding. George Caldwell has his ankle pierced by a metal arrow in the classroom, without seeing which of his pupils is responsible for the cruel joke. He has the arrow removed by the garageman Al Hummel (Hephaestus), and hurries back into school, where the principal Zimmerman (Zeus) is waiting, reproaching him for being late for class. Zimmerman then sits in the room while Caldwell gives a lesson on the evolution of the solar system and the coming of life to earth.

On the level of strict realism, the incident of the arrow strains the reader's credulity. It is, perhaps, the only place where Updike's use of the Chiron myth breaks the artistry of the story. But it makes an exciting beginning, and it establishes quite firmly the Caldwell-Chiron parallel, putting everything that follows into perspective. In this chapter, too, the reader is introduced to the technique that Updike employs, with its unannounced transitions from Olinger to Olympus — from the empirical world to the mythic. Sometimes the scene switches back and forth within a single sentence. For example: "An implacable bolt, springing from the center of the forehead above the two disparately magnifying lenses of the principal's spectacles, leaped space and transfixed the paralyzed victim" (p. 31). Here Zimmerman's disapproving reception of George Caldwell, as the teacher returns late to the classroom after having the arrow removed from his ankle, is pictured as Zeus hurling his thunderbolts.[3] The next sentence completes the comparison: "The

---

[3] Zimmerman is described as looking at Caldwell through the disparately magnifying lenses of his spectacles. We have already seen how *magnifying lenses* are used by Updike in *The Poorhouse Fair* to suggest the transition from human to divine gaze (see above, p. 125). Here the two spectacle lenses are

silence as the two men stared at each other was louder than thunder."
This imagery is reinforced when Zimmerman, noticing the arrow
which Caldwell now carries in his hand, asks sarcastically why he
should be carrying a lightning rod on a cloudless winter day.

George Caldwell's science lesson begins with a description of the
beginning of the universe, the genesis of earth, the coming of life, and
the introduction of certain death — as opposed to random extinction — by the introduction of co-operative life with the volvox *that
dies sacrificially for the good of the whole.* The cells that came together to make the volvox, says the teacher, "were the first altruists.
The first do-gooders. If I had a hat on, I'd take it off to 'em" (p. 42).
The lesson ends, as the buzzer sounds, with the announcement of
the appearance of "a tragic animal" called Man (p. 46).

Throughout the period the class is inattentive, and George Caldwell finds it hard to concentrate on what he is saying. He writes on
the board the weight of the sun in tons: 1,998,000,000,000,000,-
000,000,000,000. "The zeros stared back, every one a wound leak-
ing the word 'poison' " (p. 37). Zimmerman whispers to a plump
girl and looks down her blouse. "His lechery smelled; the kids were
catching fire" (p. 38). The room seems to dissolve into a disgusting
chaos. Live trilobites curl on the floor, a girl turns into a huge purple
parrot, an athletic but stupid student called Diefendorf turns into a
centaur, and the whole room smells like a stable. Caldwell has been
distracted by Diefendorf's efforts to tickle the girl sitting in front of
him, "a smutty little tramp from outside Olinger" named Becky
Davis (p. 38). At last, just before the buzzer goes, he strikes
the boy with the arrow. He sees Zimmerman making furious notes,
and is dismayed. He finds he loathes the story he has been telling.

This chapter is set on the Thursday before the Monday morning
recorded in Chapter II. It reinforces the details of that morning, as
we can see from the additions made to the short story in the novel.
In "On the Way to School" George Caldwell says he feels something inside him like a clot of poison. The novel adds the remark
"I can't pass it," and comments that "this detail seemed to balk"
his wife (p. 47). When Hummel removed the arrow in the garage,
Caldwell had smelled the arrow to see whether it was poisoned; but
he could not tell. In the short story the reluctance of Peter's father
to go to work is connected in the child's mind with the dreariness of
"the long haul" between Christmas and Easter. In the novel an

---

disparate, representing the two levels of the human (Zimmerman) and the
divine (Zeus).

Clearly, the technique employed in *The Centaur* is no real innovation. The
use of levels of meaning beyond the literal one is simply made more explicit
in this novel than in others.

additional reason is given: "Zimmerman's after my hide" (p. 68).
And Peter remembers that his father had told them that he had
struck a boy with Zimmerman in the room (p. 48).

Peter's role as Prometheus is also accented by details added in
the novel. The short story describes his psoriasis (his "humiliation"),
which covers his body with scabs but mercifully leaves his face and
hands free. The skin condition fluctuates with the seasons — it is
especially bad in January — and Peter regards it as a curse laid on
him by God. In the novel his scabbed belly is said to look "as if
pecked by a great bird" (p. 52). The reference is to the punishment Zeus inflicted on Prometheus, that of being chained to a rock
and having his liver pecked by a great eagle. Also, on this Monday
morning of Chapter II, Peter puts on a red shirt: "I would carry to
my classmates on this bitter day a gift of scarlet, a giant spark, a
two-pocketed emblem of heat" (p. 55). This description is in the
short story also, but the novel expands the reference and includes the
information that Peter rarely wore it, because it showed up the white
specks that fell from his afflicted scalp. However, "a generous impulse brushed the risk aside," and he puts it on. Taking the risk upon
himself, Prometheus brings the gift of fire to mankind. While Chapter I does introduce us to the double vision of Olinger-Olympus, it
focuses upon the "conceivable" creation called earth. It ends by
announcing the coming of that "tragic animal" man, who (judging
from the sample population found in the classroom) is evidently a
bestial creature with the morals and the smell of Swift's Yahoos.
Chapter II, on the other hands, actually takes us to where we have
a glimpse of the "inconceivable" creation called heaven. It shows
us human beings who are subject to the divine curse and who know
the fear of death, but who nevertheless exhibit the pulse of life
and are moved by a more than earthly impulse towards generosity.
Says Peter, looking back to his boyhood days: "It was good. We
moved somehow on a firm stage, resonant with metaphor. . . . Yes.
We lived in God's sight" (*TC,* p. 70). Even the hobo they picked
up on the road was in George's magnanimous eyes a gentleman and
an artist. Peter's father could see the divine image in the least lovable
of his fellow creatures. The hobo was, on the stage resonant with
metaphor, the god Hermes. "Annh — I cook," he says when George
asks him what his profession is (p. 82). Hermes had cooked at least
once, for as a baby he roasted two of the cattle he stole from Apollo.
He retains his artistry in theft, as he proves by taking the gloves un-
noticed. And his role as messenger of the gods is revealed as he
stands by the Alton road "looking like a messenger" (p. 90).

* * *

By providing a Mythological Index at the end of the book, Updike allows us to see how thoroughly he has saturated his story with mythic elements. Furthermore, he prefixes to the novel the story of Chiron as given in Josephine Preston Peabody's *Old Greek Folk Stories Told Anew*. This familiar book has been through many editions since 1897, and it may have been Updike's starting point in finding myths suitable for his purpose. However, less than half of the fifty-six headings in the Index are to be found in it, and it seems that Updike has turned also to H. J. Rose's *A Handbook of Greek Mythology including its extension to Rome*, where all the rest occur. The account in the novel of Chiron's begetting and childhood (pp. 21-23) follows very closely the account given in Rose's work. In addition to secondary sources, though, Updike has also made use of primary ones. Hesiod's *The Works and Days* and *Theogony* and Pliny's *Natural History* are the most evident of these.

Some of the mythological parallels in the novel are comic. There is a lady teacher at Olinger High, a stern disciplinarian whose charges are "unnaturally still" and who has "yellow pencils thrusting from her tangled hair" (p. 19): she is Medusa. Some parallels are ingenious. Hades in his underworld is the janitor Heller working in the school basement, where on one occasion he picks up some seeds and asks Peter and his father how they got there: the incident recalls Persephone and the pomegranate seeds. Some are over-ingenious. Peter wonders why Doc Appleton (Apollo) has in his vestibule a small dark print portraying some kind of torture: it is evidently the flaying of the satyr Marsyas who had dared to challenge Apollo to a contest in musical skill. Other mythological parallels make one point of contact only. Peter's mother Cassie is Ceres only because of her love of the land, and his grandfather Pop Kramer is Kronos only because his age connects him with an earlier time — symbolized by a clock that he has inherited from his father.

But myth is mostly put to work in a way that advances the reader's understanding of the story. Diefendorf is in turn centaur, merman, and Hercules. As merman he is the leading member of the school swimming team which George Caldwell coaches. His loutish nature is characteristic of the majority of centaurs, and, though he professes to be fond of Peter's father, he is continually hurting him. It is Diefendorf who damages the only possession George Caldwell is really proud of — the shining chrome grill of his '36 black Buick. The boy's car stalled and was being pushed by the Buick when Diefendorf stupidly braked; and the resulting damage (so we can guess from the design of the Buick grill) must have been the equivalent of having kicked his teacher in the teeth. We are never told who shot the arrow in the classroom, but since it was

Hercules who shot Chiron by misadventure, Diefendorf must have been the one. Diefendorf ends up as a teacher, however, and so his admiration for George Caldwell must have been genuine enough — one centaur instructed and improved by another. Peter, who as well as being Prometheus is Chiron's daughter Ocyrhoe "tormented with prescience" (p. 96), knew that such would be Diefendorf's destiny.

As Chiron, George Caldwell was deserted as a child and left to fend for himself. His mother had transformed herself into a linden tree to avoid suckling him, though he imagined her branches bent over him in affection. Now, being forced to go parentless into the world is a cause for bitterness. Venus (Vera Hummel, wife of the garageman) excuses her cynicism on this ground after she has savagely lampooned the characters of her fellow gods in Chiron's hearing (pp. 25-28); and Peter, when he feels that his mother has allowed him to go away from her even a distance of ten miles, reflects that this "rejection" on her part makes him "vengeful, proud, and indifferent: an inner Arab" (p. 139). But in Chiron's case rejection leads not to bitterness but to compassion, and his undeserved poisoning by the arrow increases his sympathy for the suffering of others. He tells Venus that her husband's fall upon Lemnos has purged his heart of bitterness (p. 27), and of all his students he sees that the one most in need of his affection is Achilles, who will himself die from an arrow wound (p. 95).

Chiron-Caldwell honors Zeus, yet fears him and does not trust him. He tells Venus that we worship the gods not for what they do but simply because they are (p. 25). In this he follows the early, amoral valuation of the gods exhibited in Hesiod's *Theogony*. It is Hesiod's account of the origin of all things from Chaos that forms the basis of his instruction as he teaches the children of Olympus, where each day's lessons begin with hymns to Zeus, the present ruler of heaven. Also, Hesiod's description in *The Works and Days* of the successive ages of the world, descending from the Age of Gold to the Age of Iron, is much on his mind. Hummel the garageman remarks to George Caldwell, as he removes the arrow, that these are bad days. "It's no Golden Age, that's for sure," replies George (p. 17). In the garage is a sign warning people: "Protect Your [Eyes] You Won't Be Given another pair" (p. 10). In the sign, instead of the word "Eyes," is a drawing of two eyes. The drawing of the eyes recurs through the book, and is linked in Chiron-Caldwell's mind with the suffering of life lived under the eyes of the gods. This reflection echoes a passage in *The Works and Days* (ll. 267-273) in which Hesiod says that the eyes of Zeus see everything, and that, while unrighteousness seems to triumph all around us, perhaps Zeus will not allow this state of affairs to continue indefinitely.

Chiron-Caldwell's problem is that he cannot believe that Zeus, from what he knows of him, really cares about justice. All the evidence indicates that the affairs of men are run by an overlord who is unscrupulous and devious. In his hope to discover the truth about the universe, he therefore turns to the search for truth about the nature of the world, of this earth, apart from the gods. He turns, in fact, to Pliny.

Pliny thought Greek beliefs concerning the gods' rule over human affairs to be the cause of continuing ignorance and superstition. His *Natural History* was an attempt to describe the facts that could be known about the realm of nature and of men apart from superstition, using observation as our only guide. In *The Centaur* are inserted chunks of the *Natural History* (pp. 93-95). These deal specifically with those herbs that are poisonous and those that bring healing — Chiron's chief concern — and show Chiron's agreement with Pliny's conviction that traditional views of how to use them retain much that is superstitious. Yet, how can mortals winnow truth from falsity? Chiron observes the flight of an eagle, said by Pliny to be thought to signify death to an herb-gatherer within the year (*Natural History* XXV, xxi), and wonders whether the omen is a true one for him (p. 98).

George Caldwell the science teacher continues the search for truth along the line Pliny had initiated. The facts that science can provide, however, do not give an answer to the question of whether the universe we inhabit takes any account of values of good or evil, and so they leave a moral vacuum empty of hope for mankind. In the short story "Lifeguard" the narrator notes "how severely humanism has corrupted the apples of our creed," since "the little scabs of land upon which we draw our lives to their unsatisfactory conclusions are suffused by science with vacuous horror" (*PF,* p. 213). The lifeguard says that because of this he can hardly bear the thought of the stars. George Caldwell has a similar reaction after giving in the classroom at Olinger the scientific account of the genesis of our planet. The truth about the human meaning of the world must be found elsewhere than within the sphere of earth itself. And for Caldwell the personal meaning of existence is a dark mystery, the nature of which is somehow bound up with his relation to Zimmerman.

* * *

The story of Harry Angstrom in *Rabbit, Run* begins with a consciousness of *angst;* so, too, does the account in *The Centaur* of the

three days spent by Peter and his father. Peter, still in bed on the
Monday morning, hears his parents talking:

> "Cassie," he said, "don't be frightened. I don't want you to be
> frightened. I'm not frightened." His voice blanched in repetition.
>
> "You *are* frightened," she said. "I wondered why you kept getting
> out of bed." Her voice was white too. (p. 47)

Angst, says Kierkegaard, is the lot of all men since Adam; and its
only cure is faith. Otherwise it issues in despair, the course of which
Kierkegaard outlines in *The Sickness Unto Death.* The question
which is raised by the fear of cancer is precisely whether George
Caldwell has the sickness unto death. Everyone, says Kierkegaard,
is set upon the road of despair; and even Christians who have faith
are "somewhat" in despair, though they can find deliverance from it.
One sign of hope in the Caldwell household — very different from
the Angstrom household — is that its members do not live within
their own skins, thinking that "the point is how *I* feel." Their first
concern is for the other person. Thus Chiron, seeing the eagle flying,
thinks first whether the omen portends evil for his charges, and only
when he is reassured on this point, sees that it is flying on his left and
therefore threatens him. George and Cassie try to reassure each
other, and Cassie is concerned that their talk shall not frighten the
child.

In "Pigeon Feathers" young David Kern has his first awakening
to the sickness unto death, and among the spiders' webs in the outhouse his fear of spiders for once seems trivial (*PF,* p. 123). Spiders
seem to symbolize death for Updike.[4] George Caldwell speaks of his
consciousness of death-bringing sickness as "a clot of poison" (*TC,*
p. 47), "a poison snake" (p. 48), and finally as "a spider in my
big intestine" (p. 48). He feels the spider to be more than physically
caused, and to have emanated out of the hatred of his students
towards him. On this last point his wife refuses to agree, insisting:
"It's love. They want to love each other and you're in the way.
Nobody hates you. You're the ideal man" (p. 49).

Cassie Caldwell's argument here reflects a story in *The Same
Door,* "The Alligators." In this story the hostile acts which are
directed against a little girl who comes from Maryland to the fifth
grade in the elementary school at Olinger turn out to be a disguised
form of love, covered over by the embarrassment children feel over
displaying their true emotions. Like Elsie, the mother in "Pigeon
Feathers," Cassie is a "real femme." Intuitively she reaches through
appearances to grasp the truth of human feelings. Unhappily, though,

---

4 See also the story "The Dark," in *The Music School.*

her trust in the goodness of the natural — both in the land and in humanity — fails to make contact with the outlook of either her husband or her son, who alike read the face of nature as death-bringing rather than as life-sustaining. Although both approaches have their validity, they cannot come to terms on a rational level. In "Pigeon Feathers" Elsie and George quarrel over the use of artificial fertilizers. In *The Centaur* husband and wife quarrel over clocks. George insists that an electric clock he has bought gives the right time, rather than Pop Kramer's hand-made timepiece. Cassie shows her conflicting emotions by tearing the electric clock off the wall — and then holding it to her breast as though it were a baby (p. 70). Her action makes Peter fear for her and also makes him afraid of her.

On the mythological level, George Caldwell's preferring the electric clock to his father-in-law's traditional one is Chiron's distrust of the old gods, a pious impiety. "Time and tide for no man wait" is one of Pop Kramer's favorite sayings, one which George Caldwell frequently repeats, but always with irritation. He explains: "I was a minister's son. I was brought up to believe, and I still believe it, that God made Man as the last best thing in His Creation. If that's the case, who are this time and tide that are so almighty superior to us?" (p. 63). Mythologically, the situation is this: Kronos has fallen and Zeus now reigns in heaven. But then the question arises as to whether Zeus will not fall in his turn, not now to make way for another ruler in heaven but to declare the heavens to be empty. In that event, man will be free from the watchful eyes of the gods. Yet his freedom may be only to stand helpless before death, with life a "vacuous horror." Both Peter and his father face this fearful possibility. They cannot rest in Cassie's delight in the beauty and peace of nature, or in her father's placid assurance of traditional wisdom, packeted in ancient proverbs.

In "Pigeon Feathers" David comments that he has so often heard his father say, "This reminds me of death" that he has never stopped to consider what it meant (*PF*, p. 127). In both this story and *The Centaur* his father constantly refers to his own death as "getting the garbage out of the way." George Caldwell, so we read in *The Centaur,* was "rarely a formally humorous man" (p. 17). Speaking about life as garbage is seriously meant, if casually uttered. There is in him a deep piety that never forgets the Christian God (as Chiron never forgets Zeus); yet his searching honesty, directed by his scientific training, will not allow him to rest in an untroubled faith such as Pop Kramer possesses — and far less in the quasi-Greek

belief in the "soul" of nature that his wife entertains.[5] Peter comes
to share his father's view of nature as basically rot and filth. The
man-made city calls him, and the countryside repels him. Besides,
in his skin condition nature speaks to him of ever-present disease.
His psoriasis seems to him to be something allergic to life itself.
Getting up from his bed, he thinks resentfully about his mother
having engineered their move to "this primitive place," the farm.
"She loved nature. I stood naked, as if exposing her folly to the
world" (p. 52).

Peter's "humiliation" has been inherited from his mother. It does
not mark her, except on her hands, where "some of my mother's
fingernails were eaten down to the quick by what looked like yellow
rot" (p. 53). The experiences of the first two days described in the
novel impress on him how all life is decaying and how death presses
in from the extremities of existence to the center. Failure, fear, death,
and sex seem to make one putrefying mass.

*   *   *

After school on Monday Peter and his father see Zimmerman's
report on the class of the previous Thursday. At the end of the principal's caustic account of Caldwell's lesson, it points out that striking a student is a cause for dismissal. It seems a death sentence,
and one that will be repeated in the doctor's examination. Doc
Appleton, saying that belief in the soul leads to misuse of the body,
proclaims (like the big Mouseketeer in *Rabbit, Run*): ". . . know
thyself, George" (p. 130; ellipses in the text). After the X-rays have
been taken at the hospital, George and Peter are ready to go home;
but the Buick "dies" on them, and they are forced to spend the
night in Alton. A drunk accosts them, hugging Peter and accusing
his father of being "an old lech" lifting boys off the street. The
drunk then jeers, "Are you ready to die?" (p. 157). Escaping to a
hotel, Caldwell explains to the clerk that they need shelter but have
no money. Having taken the strangers in, the Samaritan clerk dies
during the night.

On Tuesday evil seems omnipresent. Three scenes show it. First,
Peter is in Minor Kretz's Luncheonette when his father comes in
with more bad news. He has seen Mim Herzog, a school trustee,
coming out of Zimmerman's room with her lipstick mussed; and he
fears she will have him dismissed to protect her reputation. Peter's
companion in this scene is Johnny Dedman, a flunked senior, who
has been showing him a deck of pornographic cards. Dedman claims
that Hitler is alive and living in Argentina — waiting as he (Dedman)

---

[5] In "Pigeon Feathers" George Kern's having taken chemistry at college is
directly placed over against Elsie's having taken Greek (*PF,* p. 122).

is for the next war. So the word from Minor's place (the abode of King Minos of Crete) is that the living are dead men governed by lust and dreams of violence, and that evil alone proves to be indestructible.

In the second scene, Caldwell goes to an incompetent dentist, one of his old students who has failed to qualify as a doctor and who now pulls his tooth before the Novocain takes. The third scene is in the school auditorium in the evening. The crowd that is gathered there to watch basketball is "menacing, odorous, blind." George Caldwell meets some ex-star players, now failures, and sees them as living corpses. He feels himself surrounded by "waste, rot, hollowness, noise, stench, filth" (p. 251). Just before, Zimmerman has met him and told him suavely that he can be spared from the school if he is finding the work too much for him. The "subtle prick" of the principal's words has opened a hole releasing "dust, lint, spittle, poverty, stuck-together stuff in gutters — all the trash and chaos behind the made world" (p. 249). But, since Zimmerman has turned away without letting the axe of dismissal fall, the teacher is left bewildered. Another blow falls on him, though. He notices that Peter is sitting — not accidentally — beside Penny Fogleman, and "the Foglemans were the kind who would eat your heart and then wash the rest down the sink" (p. 254).

So during these two days George Caldwell finds within himself all the symptoms of a sickness unto death while there arise around him multiform emblems of death, "the many visages which this central thing wears" (p. 251). The mythological dimension of the story spells out the situation with precision.

In the events of both days the gods appear to conform to the cynical picture of them painted by Venus for Chiron's benefit (p. 26): Hermes as a "thieving tramp"; and Dionysus as a "drunken queer." Chiron, however, refuses to let cynicism dominate his vision, and he finds good where others find only evil. For example, the deformed and sinister Charon is supposed to refuse to row the dead to the underworld if they come without the required obol, leaving them to wander forever as homeless ghosts. But Caldwell finds Charlie (Charon), the hunchbacked hotel clerk and uncle of Iris Osgood (Io), kind to him and Peter when they ask for his services without being able to produce the fee. Yet, though the mean aspects of the lesser gods do not trouble Chiron-Caldwell, he cannot bring himself to trust Zeus-Zimmerman, the All-Ruler, although he gives him the respect required by his position. This fundamental doubt about the universe being justly ordered is what makes him sick of life and yet unwilling to die.

Caldwell's concern over this question of the right ordering of the universe is indicated by the fact that he has been raised a Presbyterian but has become a Lutheran like his wife. He associates the Calvinistic God with Zimmerman and "with everything murky and oppressive and arbitrary in the universal kingdom" (p. 232). At the basketball game in the school auditorium he comes across Vera Hummel (Venus) talking to the Reformed minister, an ex-soldier called March (Ares or Mars). Chiron judges Ares to be "the most vicious of all" the gods (p. 27). He tries to engage this man whose faith is like "metal dead" (p. 237) in a discussion on predestination. He is rebuffed, and, as March turns back to the lover's "bower" he has woven with Vera, Caldwell thinks that the minister's sculptured face is one to make even Nero look tame. And he feels "heavy and giddy with his own death" (p. 253).

Until he can be sure that the universal kingdom is not ruled by a God possessing Zimmerman's duplicity and requiring the service of March's dead-metal faith, George Caldwell carries death around with him. At best, he can joke about his fears and say, "The Lord loves a cheerful corpse" (p. 231). But he cannot banish his fear for others. He sees Peter falling prey to one of the Fogleman clan, as Prometheus is fated to endure the eagle Zeus sends to feed on the Titan's liver. Through his mind there runs Pop Kramer's phrase: *time and tide for no man wait.* Time (Kronos) is destructive of humanity. And another phrase keeps recurring to him: *ignorance is bliss.* He is a teacher, yet his knowledge as a man of science, dedicated to removing superstition, has simply left him with a universe from which human meaning has vanished. He tells Zimmerman: "I never studied. I never thought. I've always been scared to. My father studied and thought and on his deathbed he lost his religion" (p. 249).

Caldwell's sickness unto death is, in the last resort, a despair of possessing faith. His father, though he was fifth in a line of Presbyterian ministers, died shorn of hope in eternity because of his lifetime quest for knowledge. So the question that torments Caldwell is whether the pursuit of truth leads inevitably to the destruction of belief in a God of goodness and to the triumph of a desolation of heart beside which brute ignorance must seem a blessed state.

The fears which trouble George Caldwell trouble his son as well. When his father disappears into the school on that Tuesday morning, he is seized by terror (p. 170). There follows an imaginary obituary for George Caldwell, one that might have been read by Peter in the local paper if his father had died then. Following the obituary, we encounter the vision of Peter as Prometheus, chained to his rock, rent between fantasy and realism: his father's colleague Phillips

(Pholos the centaur) tells him how Thanatos the death-demon carries off the dead; the town, foolish and vague, cannot remember his father ever having lived; the students file past to view his scabs, and attribute them to his having syphilis; Diefendorf instructs him on the sex act, assuring him that this is all women want; Johnny Dedman brings out his dirty cards; Penny, his girl, promises to pray for his father and afterwards tells him she has forgotten to do so. So death and forgetfulness, it seems, have the final word. In life, love seems only a disguise for lust. Finally, his father seems to give him a lesson in organic chemistry whose conclusion is that the life-death cycle is without meaning or purpose. Peter tries to tell his father that he has hope for more, but his father seems only (like the Sibyl in the jar) to want to find rest in death. And Peter, passionately voicing his trust in life in order to convince his father, is aware that the words he utters are a lie.

However, not all the hours of the two days are filled with fear. An oasis in the desert of despair is found in the person of Doc Appleton's twin sister Hester (Artemis), who teaches Latin and and French, and has long cherished an unspoken love for George Caldwell. Stumbling over lines of Virgil, Peter is guided to translate a passage in which Venus, standing for an instant naked — *vera dea, a true goddess* — reveals herself to her son Aeneas. When Peter is defeated by the word *incessu* ("in gait"), Hester explains that there is a "style" to divinity (p. 185). After school, she speaks to Peter's father, for she senses that a cloud of pain hangs over both father and son. Caldwell asks her to say something to him in French, because the sound always cheers him when he is depressed, and he is at present down "in Old Man Winter's Belly." She responds with: *"Dieu - est - très - fin.* It's the sentence I've lived by" (p. 194). He agrees banteringly, but almost immediately begins to recite to her part of a poem he learned in childhood and had forgotten till this moment, a poem beginning: "The great Jehovah wisely planned / All things of Earth divinely grand." He says he feels this poem to be a "very happy" one.

Thus Hester Appleton, as the chaste goddess Diana, teaches Peter that Venus is not simply the "born whore" she is commonly judged to be (p. 27). And, as the spinster who has accepted without bitterness her restricted life, she calls back faith into Caldwell by confessing her own. Both father and son need to recognize the reality of true divinity present in a universe that seems to be trash and chaos. Hester provides Peter with a hope in the life of love that is beyond lust, and Peter's father with the recovery of strength from a forgotten past at a time when he is conscious only of loss.

On Tuesday evening Peter is given a revelation of love. On the stairs outside the overheated auditorium, he shows his girl Penny the shameful secret of his psoriasis, but she simply says that she already understood he "had a skin thing." He presses her to confess whether she minds, and she replies, "If you knew what love was you wouldn't even ask" (p. 246). He recalls that on Monday morning he had awakened from a dream about Penny in which she had turned into a tree. He had understood this to be a transformation brought about by her wish to shelter him, thinking at the time: "she would sacrifice for me" (p. 51). Now he tells her of this dream and how he had wanted "to cry and pray" (p. 244).

Peter's dream follows the same mythic pattern as that of Chiron's mother willing to be changed into a linden tree. While Chiron had never known with certainty whether his mother's action arose out of rejection of him or of care for him, Peter's unconscious mind has no doubt that the motive of transformation was one of womanly self-sacrifice; and he consciously recognizes this same tenderness in Penny's free acceptance of his blemished skin. So, pressing against her thighs, he finds that the mystery of sexuality — "the secret the world holds at its center" (p. 246) — is not at enmity with unselfish love. At that moment he looks through the window, and, "wonder following wonder," finds that it is snowing (p. 247).

Later, when Peter and his father leave the school and set out for home, the snow becomes a great wing of infinitesimal feathers (recalling the wing of the heavenly being in "Archangel" who offers shelter and beauty to all). Peter sees in the complex pattern of the falling flakes a whole universe of beauty and order. The snow falls over the town "with a sort of ultimate health" (p. 256). The snow, it seems, brings a remedy for the sickness unto death that has tormented father and son during the past two days.

Once again, then, Updike makes falling snow the vehicle of a message from heaven. Once again, too, Updike stresses that the message from heaven is effective whether or not people comprehend it. He describes how, as the snow falls, Olinger becomes another Bethlehem: "Behind a glowing window the infant God squalls. Out of zero all has come to birth." But the cry of the baby is not heard outside. "The world goes on unhearing" (p. 239). And yet, within the auditorium, although no one knows about the snow, the atmosphere changes. "Things are not merely seen but burst into vision" (p. 239). Now, this is the time when Peter's father walks through the crowd filled with thoughts of death. Nevertheless, he finds grace working where he least expects to find it. Just as he is sure Zimmerman is moving in to destroy him, the principal says, "You're a good teacher," and walks away (p. 250). Immediately before, Zimmerman has referred to St. Paul's words about speaking the truth in love (Eph. 4:15). Caldwell cannot believe that "this amazing statement" is other than a part of Zimmerman's cat-and-mouse game with him, but his fears are mistaken. This time, the unjust judge has pronounced a just verdict and stands by it.

Messages from heaven, as we have seen, invariably say, *Run on home*. But, also, God decides to give his gifts *in My way, in My time*.[6] Although by Tuesday evening Hummel has repaired the Buick and father and son start out in the snow for home, they are not to reach their destination for another twenty-four hours. Before that happens, they will have been granted a vision of the workings of grace.

They drive out of Olinger and pass the Jewish Cemetery where Abe Cohen, a bootlegger of Prohibition days, lies in a splendid tomb. On the next hill the car becomes stuck fast in the snow, and they are forced to get out and walk back to Olinger. Numbed by the cold, Peter feels his body vanish by stages, until only a tiny speck of consciousness remains. Then his father, who is walking in front of him to shield him from the wind, places on his son's head the old blue wool cap that Peter has hated so much because it symbolizes his father's poverty and total lack of self-regard.

Reaching Olinger, they spend the night at the Hummels. Peter wakes in the morning to see blue skies and a day so perfect he thinks *"This morning has never occurred before"* (p. 271). Going downstairs, he feels full grown, and is served an ambrosial breakfast by Vera, a trim housewife with apron and a bandana covering her hair, who, he says, "served me like a wife" (p. 272). His father spends the morning at the school (closed because of the storm) bringing his books up to date, while Al Hummel is out clearing the roads which have become blocked during the night. The car is freed, they buy provisions, and by early evening they are near home. For the third time, though, the car fails to take them all the way. They leave it stuck in the snow and walk to the house, arriving to find everyone well and busy, and adequately supplied with food. The X-ray report has been given by phone. George does not have cancer. Fevered but content, Peter is put to bed and dreams of his early childhood, waking the next morning to hear the familiar contentious exchanges between his parents as his father gets ready to return to school. Caldwell thinks he can hang on for another ten years until he gets his pension. Before leaving, he comes upstairs to see Peter, saying: "Yeah, I've always been lucky. God takes care of you if you let him." And he tells his son not to worry

---

[6] See *Pigeon Feathers*, p. 120.

about his old man, for: "I've never made a decision in my life that wasn't one hundred per cent selfish" (p. 292).

Snow from heaven, bringing to a halt earthly busyness, allows man to know that he is in the care of a Providence ordering all things in a fashion beyond his comprehension. Man cannot find this through his own efforts. Even Peter's vision of a universe of order and beauty, a vision stimulated by the falling snow, breaks down because it demands too much from the human imagination. Peter tires of following the pattern of the snow and begins to feel cold and damp. "Revelations have skinned Peter's nerves and left him highly irritable" (p. 257). Human intelligence overreaches itself (as both Kierkegaard and Barth insist) when it tries to read the mysteries of heaven from an earthly standpoint. In the Hummel home on Wednesday, Peter picks up a copy of the *Reader's Digest* containing the two articles "Miracle Cure for Cancer?" and "Ten Proofs That There Is a God" (p. 276). He puts the magazine down, depressed by the thought that there *is* no cure and no proof. The answers to the final questions of existence are not to be picked up cheaply. They must be won by following the exacting path of faith.

The road back to Olinger taken by Peter and his father on Tuesday night is a parable of this path of faith. Most of all, the road introduces the theme raised in "Dentistry and Doubt," namely, that salvation comes by grace and not by works. This is the teaching of St. Paul — whose name Zimmerman had invoked earlier that evening — and it is indicated by the introduction of the Jewish cemetery. There, Abe Cohen, "priest" of the Prohibition era, lies entombed, a reminder of the Law of Moses and its prohibitions. No one, say St. Paul, obeys the Mosaic Law; and, in breaking the Law, we die. We cannot save ourselves by good works; but God has provided another way, the way of grace, to let us live. This teaching, adds St. Paul, is judged to be absurd and foolish by the wise of this world, both Jews and Gentiles, but it is God's way of salvation (Rom. 2—5; 1 Cor. 1:18-25).

Failing to climb the hill by their own efforts, father and son have been forced to turn round (to be converted), and find strength in weakness. Peter has raged at his father several times since they set out together on Monday morning, asking him why he is so "silly." Now he walks, sheltered by his father's graciousness, and crowned with the blue cap which he has thought so shameful and absurd when it was on his father's head. Along the way, the pine trees stand like "dark angels."

The following day brings the fulfilment of the promise which faith offers: a morning of light, when all things are made new (Rev. 21:5). Joy comes in the morning.

The final chapter of *The Centaur* describes Chiron accepting death — which is also George Caldwell accepting life out of death.[7] Still obsessed by the brutishness of the human landscape, and still thinking that in a dirty world "ignorance" may be the ultimate bliss, Chiron-Caldwell remembers an incident from his childhood. Walking beside his minister father, he had passed by a saloon from which "there welled a poisonous laughter that seemed to distill all the cruelty and blasphemy in the world." But his father had smilingly said to him: "All joy belongs to the Lord." As he recalls this incident, all that is not joy falls away from him, and "he discovered that in giving his life to others he entered a total freedom" (p. 296). Suddenly, the universe is welded for him into a radiant unity. As Chiron, he discovers this in mythic form. Sky and Gaia (mother earth) seem to mate again in his "upright" body; that is, the Golden Age is restored. As Caldwell, he reads the message in moral-religious terms: "Only goodness lives. But it does live" (p. 297).

In Zimmerman's report on Caldwell's science lesson there had been the dry remark: "The humanistic values implicit in the physical sciences were not elicited" (p. 110). This sentence had puzzled Peter, but his father had seemed to pass it off lightly. Yet the doubt about there being any human meaning in the universe is the cause of the poison in George Caldwell's bowel, being directly connected with his inability to trust Zimmerman in his role of Zeus at Olinger. As they drive away from the school on Tuesday night, Peter's father remarks to his son (with the insight given by the snow around them): "I've never gotten to the bottom of Zimmerman, is I guess my trouble" (p. 257). Peter replies that there is no bottom to get to, and asks why his father is so "superstitious."

Doc Appleton had commented that George's trouble lay in the fact that he was a learner rather than a teacher. But to be sure that faith in a universe ruled by a divine Providence is not superstitious is a lesson George finds hard to learn. Yet, so long as he cannot affirm this (the humanistic values implicit in the physical sciences), he thinks that all learning is futile and that ignorance is bliss. Finally, he knows that he has learned his lesson and can escape from his poisoned existence.

Chiron, in the last pages of the book, finds that "he must order his mind and prepare his lessons" (p. 298). The lessons are four in number: first, Zeus alone is to be worshiped; second and third, the rivers of the dead and the daughters of Nereus are to be named; fourth, a hero is to be defined as a king sacrificed to Hera. The

---

[7] "By the way, I must repeat that I didn't mean Caldwell to die in *The Centaur;* he dies in the sense of living, of going back to work, of being a shelter for his son" — Updike in *Art,* p. 92.

interesting fact is that the first three lessons are contained in the poem George Caldwell recited to Hester Appleton: "The great Jehovah wisely planned / All things of Earth divinely grand." The poem speaks of God's rule over earth in the first stanza, and in the second stanza (which is all Caldwell remembers) it goes on to speak of the rivers that flow out of the past into the unknown future. Chiron's lessons simply reverse the order of the verses, beginning with the rivers and going on to name the Nereids, each of whom represents a region of the world.

A teacher, as *The Poorhouse Fair* makes plain, is essentially a transmitter of wisdom from one generation to the next. He can pass on only that which he has himself proved to be true. Thus Chiron, having carried in his own body the infection of poison, could instruct those who were themselves to be poisoned. And, having accepted death to self-will, he could convey to others the lesson that they must learn in order to find life.

* * *

The Centaur is so much the story of Chiron-Caldwell and his fight against the sickness unto death that the reader is likely to judge the part played in it by Prometheus-Peter simply as a witness to the heroic stature of the title character. Yet, though the novel is presented as a memory of three days in Pennsylvania in 1947, there is also a good deal of stress laid upon Peter's view of his own life as it is being lived at the moment of his telling his father's story.

In the two short stories published prior to the publication of *The Centaur* and appearing in the book as Chapters II and VIII, the adult Peter simply looks back to his fifteenth year. In the novel he addresses his story to his "love," a Negro mistress, and thus sets the narrative of 1947 within a present-day frame. The frame shows what has become of Peter after his father disappeared, that is, now that Peter has left his father's house and has taken responsibility for his own actions. And it would seem that what Peter confesses to his mistress about his relationship with her is related to Chiron's fourth lesson: the definition of a hero as a king sacrificed to Hera, the patroness of marriage. In mythic terms, Peter's concern is over the conflict between the service of Hera and the service of Venus.

Venus is presented in a less than flattering light in the first chapter of *The Centaur*. The goddess speaks of herself as a whore and begs Chiron to mount her. Chiron meets her, as Vera Hummel, in the basement of the school; and, later in the book (p. 276), Peter refers to Vera's love life as giving rise to legends that circulate like dirty coins in the student underworld. When he gives his science

lesson in the presence of Zimmerman, George Caldwell asks if anyone knows the name of the only star in the solar system. A dull
girl replies, "Venus," and the boys snigger: for Venus means to
them "Venereal, V.D." (p. 36). Caldwell's reaction is summed up
in his estimate of the sexually precocious Becky Davis: "Dull. Dull
and dirty" (p. 38). So Venus seems to be simply a name for lust.
And in the chapters following, lust becomes for both Peter and his
father one of the dreary faces of death. There is a girlie calendar
on the wall of the garage where they go on Monday night to see
whether the Buick can be repaired. Soon Caldwell is saying, "This
reminds me of death" (pp. 153-54).

On the last lap of their journey home on Wednesday evening
Peter, walking behind his father, sees the planet Venus in the sky
and asks whether one can steer by it. His father says he has never
tried, but agrees that the North Star is hard to find. Shortly after,
he turns around to be sure his son is still following him. Peter, who
has been finding that his father's stride is too great for him to keep
in the footsteps, is startled. "I felt so alone," he comments (pp.
284-85).

Peter's reflections about his life with his mistress carry the implication that, by making Venus the star of his solar system, he
has ceased to follow in his father's footsteps and so is *alone*. He is
troubled now with dreams that carry the death-quality of those first
two days away from home. "Last night I dreamt that Hitler, a white-
haired crazy man with a protruding tongue, was found alive in
Argentina" (pp. 46-47).[8] In the lengthy introductory section of
Chapter VII (which is not found in "After the Storm"), he elab-
orates his sense of having lost his heritage. He is proud and glad
of his love. Yet, he says,

> I miss . . . the sudden white laughter that like heat lightning bursts
> in an atmosphere where souls are trying to serve the impossible.
> My father for all his mourning moved in the atmosphere of such
> laughter.
>
> . . . I grow frightened. I consider the life we have made together
> . . . and its rather wistful half-Freudian half-Oriental sex-mysticism,
> and I wonder, *Was it for this that my father gave up his life?* (pp.
> 269-270).

However, there is another love which Peter serves: his art. In the
hotel at Alton where his father takes him on Monday night, Peter

---

[8] See above, pp. 168-69. Dedman's fantasy has entered Peter's unconscious
mind with the further detail that evil not only lives on but also mocks humanity's efforts to bury it.

imagines that he is a lover yearning to possess the City.[9] (In mythic terms, Alton is Athena — patroness of Athens and of the civilized arts — and Peter is Priapus, the ugly fertility god and son of Dionysus by Venus.) The City rejects him, and he begins to dwindle away. Before shrinking to nothing, he gets into bed, offering a prayer asking blessing for himself and his family; and in bed he begins to grow as large as the universe, until his father's coming into the room brings him back to normality. His father says: "Don't worry about your old man, Peter. In God we trust" (p. 168). This vision of the City introduces the ambition which Peter has of being an artist, and suggests his subsequent frustrations in following his career.

Peter's misgivings about his present style of life are directly related to the incompleteness of a vision that cannot see the self in its real size within the world, and that cannot go to sleep saying, "Don't worry. In God we trust." Thinking about his father and his father's father (whom he never knew), Peter exclaims, "Priest, teacher, artist: the classic degeneration" (p. 269). This scale of values is precisely the (reversed) order of Kierkegaard's three spheres of existence: the aesthetic, the moral, and the religious. Kierkegaard's teaching was concerned to proclaim: "Away from the aesthetic!" But Peter has chosen to follow the aesthetic.

In making Peter's mistress a Negress, Updike indicates Peter's wish to explore the dimension of life that keeps wholly to the human level without awareness of the divine — to explore, in Kierkegaard's terminology, *the pagan*. Here the symbolism of black instead of white (which has, of course, no relation to empirical judgments about racial characteristics) indicates the choice of the unconscious in preference to the conscious, the instinctive in preference to the ethical and the rational. Peter says that he would like to become a Negro for his love's sake, forgetting "everything but the crooning behind my ribs." But, he adds, "I cannot quite make that scene. A final membrane restrains me. I am my father's son" (p. 269). By what he was, by how he lived, his father has made him unable quite to be a pagan, one unaware of "the infinite qualitative distinction between time and eternity." He knows that there is an unbridgeable gulf between hearing the crooning behind the ribs and the laughter that breaks out where souls are trying to serve the impossible.[10]

From his confession to his love that he is still his father's son,

---

[9] For Updike's early belief that Reading (Alton) was the archetypal City see above, p. 33.

[10] The imagery here echoes Kierkegaard, who spoke of humor being the way into the religious sphere of existence and called Christian faith in the incarnation a faith in the absurd.

Peter moves back to the Wednesday morning when he saw Vera Hummel, for all her scandalous reputation, dressed as a neat housewife and serving him food like a wife. He has now left behind his early love, Penny Fogleman, who might have taught him the further stages of the lesson he began to learn from her about the possible union between sexual love and sacrificial living, between the service of Venus and the service of Hera. Even his present love is not altogether without a link with the remembered past. He describes Penny's eyelids as being "vaguely Negroid" (p. 117).

Penny represents the path that might have taken Peter through to being a king sacrificed to Hera, since it is through her that he became in adolescence certain of the reality of sacrificial love. The connection is not only on the naturalistic level, either, for Penny, in her role as Pandora, belongs to the Promethean myth; and Updike has given us a typically indirect indication of the fact.

The third lesson of Chiron is to name the fifty daughters of Nereus. This list of names is set down in full for no very obvious reason. The reason may well be to draw our attention to Hesiod's *Theogony* from which the list has been taken (ll. 240-64); for in the *Theogony* there is a long account (ll. 40-105) of the creation of Pandora by the command of Zeus. Zeus sends her to earth in order to bring about the ruin of mankind after Prometheus has brought to earth the gift of fire. Hesiod writes of Zeus laughing at the thought of his plan:

> *As the price of fire I will give them an evil,*
> *and all men shall fondle*
> *this, their evil, close to their hearts,*
> *and take delight in it.* (ll. 57-60)

Pandora, of course, brings to earth a jar (or box) that, once opened, spreads abroad all the ills that plague men; one good thing alone, hope, remains within the jar.

In *The Centaur*, Pandora's box turns out to be the "nothing" where Penny's legs meet, which Peter, in his adolescent eagerness, tries to touch, causing Penny to say, "No, please" and to draw away. Here is the delight that can also be a potent occasion for evil in the world, as *Rabbit, Run* illustrates. The *nothing* of femininity, pursued for its own sake, can lead as it did in the life of Rabbit Angstrom to a death-seeking romanticism. Peter himself feels frightened by the half-Freudian, half-Oriental sex-mysticism that is beginning to dominate his existence. And his "vast canvases — so oddly expensive as raw materials, so oddly worthless transmuted into art —" (p. 268) give him no comfort, since he is uncertain that what he wishes to say in paint can ever be said.

Peter recalls how, on that Thursday morning when his father went off to school leaving him in bed with a fever (a sickness not unto death), he saw the scene from his window, a patch of Pennsylvania in 1947, and how he wished to paint it. He wanted to spread himself over the face of nature, "in the hope," he thinks, "that, my submission being perfect, the imprint of a beautiful and useful truth would be taken" (p. 293). Yet, can the aesthetic vision ever capture a truth either beautiful or useful if it does not know the service of the impossible, if it does not embrace the possibility of self-sacrifice and of a love that reaches beyond earth to heaven?

Updike has presented in his narrative the essential difference between *nothing-life* (which is shaped and ruled by a personal God, Creator of heaven and earth out of nothing) and *nothing-death* (the void which is "vacuous horror"). The zeros of the sun's weight depressed Caldwell's spirit when he gave his lesson about the genesis of the earth, because his scientist's mind could not contemplate the "nothing" out of which all life emerged. In the same way, Peter was oppressed by the "nothing" of woman. Yet it was from the "hope" that lay in the "nothing" that he was to discover human love and the meaning of divine grace, through the knowledge of self-sacrifice that will surrender all for "nothing," die to live.

The Centaur leaves Peter's dilemma unsolved. It allows the life of Chiron-Caldwell to stand clear in its own light. By so doing, the book is in itself a partial answer to the question of whether the aesthetic vision must inevitably remain closed to the moral and religious dimensions of life. But it leaves open the human question — which is the specific question perplexing the man Peter as he looks back to his adolescence — as to how the pursuit of the artist's vocation and the demands of mature responsibility in the individual existence are to be reconciled.

12

OF
THE
FARM

IF THE CENTAUR *IS INDEED UPDIKE'S FAREWELL TO* Olinger, the fact that his next novel returns immediately to the same setting is one requiring some explanation. *Of the Farm*[1] is the record of three recent August days spent at the farmhouse from which Peter Caldwell and his father had set out for the three days away from home in January 1947. The son of the house, here called Joey Robinson, tells how he drives from New York to visit his widowed mother. His father has been dead for a year; and, though failing in health, his mother lives on alone at the farm. Joey is thirty-five. Newly divorced from his first wife Joan, he has re-married in June. Peggy, his present wife, is also divorced. She and her eleven-year-old son Richard accompany Joey to see the farm for the first time and to become acquainted with Mrs. Robinson.

In spite of the setting, *Of the Farm* is not an Olinger story, because it is not a story of the past, of how it was. It is not even a continuation of the past into the present. Certainly, Mrs. Robinson seems to be an older Lillian Dow ("Flight"), an Elsie Kern ("Pigeon Feathers"), and a Cassie Caldwell (*The Centaur*). Joey Robinson's early memories parallel those of Allen Dow, David Kern, and Peter Caldwell. Peter Caldwell, however, was fifteen in 1947. He would have been only thirty-three in 1965 when *Of the Farm* was published. Joey's life is discontinuous with Peter's, then, and represents what would have happened had the boy raised in the farmhouse turned from art to moneymaking.

---

[1] New York, 1965.

In *The Centaur,* as Peter lies in the bedroom of the hotel at which he and his father are staying in Alton, his father comes upstairs and explains that he has met a man willing to offer a creative young person like Peter a job in advertising that leads to a salary of twenty thousand dollars a year. Peter shows no interest, and George Caldwell chuckles: "The hell with him, huh? I guess that's the attitude to take" (p. 167). The career so quickly turned down by Peter has been accepted by Joey. Joey's own account of his work is as follows:

> I work for a firm which arranges educational programs for corporations on such matters as tax minimization, overseas expansion, federal contract acquisition, and automation. My specialty is advertising dollar distribution, which is to say, broadly, corporate image presentation. (*Of the Farm,* p. 109)

Joey's mother wanted her son to become a poet "like Wordsworth." Updike parodies the jargon used in the world to which Joey now belongs, showing nicely how its ugliness is a universe away from the simplicity of Wordsworthian poetry. So he indicates the folly of Joey's choice, which has involved him in what Mrs. Robinson forthrightly refers to as "that prostitute's job" (p. 156).

By turning to the service of Mammon, Joey has put himself on the road leading away from the life of self-sacrifice, and so from the service of Hera. Peter Caldwell was drawn aside from following in his father's footsteps by the attraction of romantic love, yet he knew himself to be still his father's son. But Joey's father (also called George) has not just disappeared; he is dead. And Joey is not just "nesting" with a mistress.[2] He has turned out wife and children to make his mistress his wife. Joan, his son Charlie, and his two daughters are as though they were dead, for they have gone to Canada, to "another country." His mother, too, knows herself to be marked down by death.

Joey's divorce has parted him from the good life lived in God's sight. There is now no possibility of return to the "white laughter" that Peter knew in his parents' home (*TC,* p. 269). When Peggy married Joey, she carried flowers "not white," and Joey had a sense of "falling" when the marriage vows were sworn (*OTF,* pp. 10-11).

The "fall" is into a disordered married state. Recalling the mar-

---

2 This is the word Peter's mother used to describe lovers seen in the Museum grounds at Alton when Peter, as a little boy, asked her what they were doing (*TC,* p. 266). Peter refers to the "nest" he and his Negro mistress have made for themselves. The same image occurs also in *Rabbit, Run.* This image from the animal world reduces love to the purely aesthetic (or pagan) level where the notion of guilt has not come into consciousness.

riage ceremony, Joey thinks, "We were all displaced" (p. 9). And, in fact, their names are displaced echoes of the partners in the Maple stories. *Joan* has become the discarded wife, and *Richard* the boy whom Joey identifies with his former self. (Richard is embarrassed because he cannot call Joey anything else except "he.") The restoration of right order is impossible in this family situation. Joey cannot become a child again and grow into a husband for his ex-wife Joan. There is only the possibility that, by coming back to the place where he can see the difference between the boy he used to be and the man he has now become, he can reach self-knowledge and find how best to live with his mistakes.

The epigraph prefixed to *Of the Farm* is a well-known comment by Sartre:

> Consequently, when, in all honesty, I've recognized that man is a being in whom existence precedes essence, that he is a free being who, in various circumstances, can want only his freedom, I have at the same time recognized that I can want only the freedom of others.

The subject of freedom, however, is not discussed in the novel from the standpoint of Sartre's ontological analysis of essence and existence but is presented in terms of Karl Barth's exposition of the freedom that should issue from the right relationship between man and woman. Joey's divorce and remarriage provide the background against which he, his mother, and his second wife, through the tensions of living under one roof for three days, search for the meaning of freedom. Directly or indirectly, the subject of freedom dominates all their light conversations and their often furious arguments. And the farm itself — an omnipresent witness to the past that has shaped Joey's conscious and unconscious attitudes to life — adds its mute testimony to their debate as they strive to solve the riddle that perplexes them.

* * *

As usual, Updike provides the reader with a pointer to his use of a hidden source, but drops it in an inconspicuous place. Joey, Peggy, and Richard arrive late Friday afternoon at the farm and leave on Sunday afternoon. On Sunday morning Joey and his mother go to the local Lutheran church, where a young minister preaches on the creation of Eve. The text is Genesis 2:18: *And the Lord God said, It is not good that the man should be alone; I will make an help meet for him* (pp. 149-150). And the sermon itself occupies nearly six pages. Obviously, these pages are important for our understanding of the whole book.

What is not so obvious is the importance of two quotations from Karl Barth that are in the sermon. Yet these two sentences provide the key to the way in which the theme of freedom is developed in *Of the Farm*. They also show how this novel follows naturally from the previous one, beginning where *The Centaur* leaves off.

The Barthian epigraph to *The Centaur* speaks of man on the boundary between heaven and earth. It is taken from *Dogmatics in Outline*,[3] which is an exposition of the Apostles' Creed. The context of the quotation chosen by Updike is a discussion of the meaning of belief in God as Creator of Heaven and Earth. This theme is central to *The Centaur,* where the whole story is about living "in God's sight" — that is, on earth under heaven. The sentences quoted in the sermon recorded in *Of the Farm* are taken from Barth's multi-volume *Church Dogmatics,* from a section entitled "Freedom in Fellowship."[4] In this section Barth expounds the Genesis account of the creation of Eve. He says that God calls his human creation not only to himself but also to one another. Man is called in freedom horizontally as well as vertically, and Adam first understands his freedom on the horizontal, human level in relation to his helpmeet Eve. The theme of freedom for others, though introduced in the words of Sartre, is, then, actually developed by Updike along the lines of Barth's "Freedom in Fellowship." Where *The Centaur* dealt with man's vertical freedom, *Of the Farm* deals with his horizontal freedom. Man's first duty is to his Father in Heaven, and his second to his neighbor on earth. And man learns love for his neighbor through his basic experience of one who is like himself and yet unlike, namely, through woman.

Creation, says Barth, implies an order commanded by God. And it follows that man cannot be man (or woman be woman) outside this divine order. The relationship between man and woman, he continues, may be compared though not equated with the relation of heaven to earth.[5] Man and woman are not the same, and so they cannot be equal. In the created order woman follows man, and man has the primary responsibility for maintaining this order. There is no claim here that man is superior to woman; what is claimed is simply a partnership in which neither can usurp the role of the other. Maintenance of the right order requires strength in the man, who learns from the woman how to be kind in his strength. The man who does not want the woman to stand at his side as a partner (helpmeet) but likes to play the cruel tyrant and force her submis-

---

3 (London, 1958), p. 59.

4 Vol. III, Part 4 (Edinburgh, 1969), p. 54.

5 *Ibid.,* p. 176. Barth is considering here, in particular, the New Testament text, ". . . the head of the woman is her husband . . ." (I Cor. 11:3).

sion is weak and disregards the right order. Through the mask of his cruelty the woman quickly enough sees the weakness written on the tyrant's face, and, knowing that he really wishes to be dominated, rules him through apparent submission.

The sentences from Barth quoted by the Lutheran minister in *Of the Farm* are these: "Successfully or otherwise, she the woman is in her whole existence an appeal to the kindness of Man. . . . For kindness belongs originally to his particular responsibility as man" (*OTF*, p. 153).[6] The preacher does not go on to quote Barth's words about the other side of the picture, when man through weakness surrenders his responsibility. But Joey does provide a concrete illustration of Barth's thesis in this direction. "I think of myself as a weak man," he says (p. 61).

Discussing Joey with Peggy, Mrs. Robinson speaks about his having "this unexpected cruel streak." As a child, she explains, he would torment his toys, "trying to make them confess. His father thought it was the effect of war propaganda." Then there was the way he treated his pet, a puppy called Mitzi. He used to tease her until she would run and hide in a drainpipe near the chicken shed. One day, having grown larger, she was unable to turn around in the pipe and became stuck. Joey was scared, but finally the dog had the sense to back out. All the same, although he was so relieved that Mitzi saved herself, "whenever he felt a bit mean he would take her down there and show her the hole and pretend to put her in the pipe again. I thought that that was ungentlemanly," says Mrs. Robinson (p. 137). The adult Joey still exhibits his capacity for cruelty, especially in the verbal bullying by which he tries to wring a confession from his victim (usually Peggy). This form of cruelty is frequently described by Updike. It is found already in "Sunday Teasing" (*The Same Door*), and it is increasingly emphasized in the Maple stories.

But there is another side to the cruelty which Karl Barth spells out. The tyrant is he who, instead of serving the order, makes the order serve himself. But the tyrant "need not be cruel or bad-tempered. There are quiet, gentle, easy-going tyrants who suit women only too well, and it is an open question in which form the male tyrant is worse and more dangerous."[7] Joey's example shows that the two forms of the tyrant may well co-exist in the same person. The greater part of the narrative in *Of the Farm* is taken up with the friction arising as Peggy and Joey's mother argue their respective views of freedom in marriage. Their difference in temperament and

---

[6] *Ibid.*, pp. 180-81.
[7] *Ibid.*, p. 177.

beliefs leads from polite needling to open quarreling. But, at the very end of the book, both women agree that Joey is "a good boy" (p. 173). It would seem that this agreement is more deadly than the previous bickering, and that their consensus is accurate simply insofar as Joey is willing to remain an *easygoing* tyrant who will please himself by pleasing his women, without thought of the responsibilities demanded by adult freedom.

The relationship between Joey and his mother finds its point of greatest tension in her desire for a country life which made her insist — against the wishes of husband, father, and son — on bringing the family to the farm. Her love of Nature, emphasized in "Pigeon Feathers" and in *The Centaur,* is not the instinctive love of working on the land which characterized her own mother, but is one with her love of Greek. It is a platonic love (Nature with a capital "N"), as *Of the Farm* makes clear; for the practically-minded Richard asks at the beginning of the book, "What's the point of having a farm nobody farms?" (p. 4). In this regard, it is one with her love of Art and her dislike of the bourgeois standards represented, in her eyes, by Olinger. Joey, like Peter and like George (in both books), cannot understand this love; but he does come to see something of its positive worth.

The story which stands in the closest relation to *Of the Farm* is "Flight," in *Pigeon Feathers.* This short story is about Allen Dow's love for the Olinger girl Molly Bingaman when he was seventeen, and about his mother's strenuous opposition to the association of her son with this "stupid" girl. (Mrs. Robinson insists that Peggy is a stupid woman; and Joey, like the boy Allen, cannot deny this.) Allen, dismayed by his mother's fury and by the general disapproval he finds around him of his chosen love, first torments Molly and makes her cry, and at last breaks with her when he finds she comes to him too easily. They never reach the point of sexual intercourse, but Allen discovers from her — and this is the reason for his joy in her — that a man can "bury a humiliation in the body of a woman" (*PF,* p. 63).

"Flight" is so called because Allen's mother fancies that her son, through his artistic talent, is going to fly like a bird beyond the mean limits of Olinger. In this story the platonic vision of Lillian Dow fuses with Allen's discovery of romantic love. Allen is his mother's son in refusing Molly Bingaman when the ideal image threatens to become a limited reality. *Of the Farm* repeats the same pattern. Joey cannot share his mother's love of the beauty and peace seen on the face of nature, but he does respond to her wish for him to be a poet. Like his father, he is a city boy at heart, and at this point he asserts his independence and goes to make a career for himself in New York. But he marries Joan because she is a poetic image belonging to the world his mother wishes for him. When he first met her, he says, "she suggested, remote and lithe and inward, the girl of 'The Solitary Reaper' and, close-up, seemed a cool Lucy whose death might give me cause to sing" (p. 109). However, marriage with the remote, inward, and cool woman of romantic poetry proved a disappointment. A platonic ideal is ill-suited to the intimacies of bed and board. And, having decided not to be a singer, Joey turns from his Wordsworthian fancy for the far-away-and-long-ago and discovers another woman in whose body he can forget his humiliation.

Joseph in the Old Testament is the favorite of his parents. He is taken off to Egypt, gains wealth and position by advising Pharaoh on "dollar distribution," and eventually is able to help his family. But Joey Robinson is only Joseph in a diminutive form, a weak Joseph who does not afterwards achieve reconciliation with his family and rescue them from poverty. Instead, he has filled his parents' home with costly and unsuitable gifts, sent "usually in haste and late," and seeming, as he says, to be "cheap·substitutes for my love and my presence." He sees these objects as "scintillating dregs of my corruption" (p. 15).

Joseph in the Bible was a dreamer. And Joey too dreams. In particular, he has a recurring dream which began when he first thought of divorcing Joan in order to marry Peggy. In his dream (p. 48) he is a small boy standing in front of the farmhouse and looking up over the grape arbor on its south wall. The grapes are green and he thinks he has come to call on a playmate. Peggy's face, blurred by the screen, appears at a window upstairs. She is wearing a loose orange nightie and smiling at him. Her smile seems to promise forgiveness, and he forgets all the dismal hours he has spent at the farm. Her gayness makes the farm gay as it has never been in his waking experience.

The romantic vision of Peggy in Joey's dream is another ideal, like that of Joan the Wordsworthian girl, except that it is erotic instead of platonic. The orange nightie is the orange of passion which Rabbit Angstrom sought. The green grapes, the boy waiting for his playmate,[8] and the smile seeming to promise forgiveness

---

[8] The word "playmate" has now entered modern mythology through its use by *Playboy* magazine. So Updike is able to draw on both the literal meaning of the word, belonging to pre-adolescence, and the special meaning reflecting the erotic-aesthetic *Playboy* "philosophy."

and reconciliation with his past — these symbols relate to a "blurred" aesthetic world where moral issues are resolved without pain, without effort, without the stern demands of maturity. (Kierkegaard, we may note, sees the essence of the aesthetic approach to existence in the *erotic,* just as marriage is the essential repudiation of the aesthetic ideal.) In waking life, Joey finds in Peggy a counterpart of his dream as long as he is making love. But whenever he is not either buried in her body or thinking of it, the familiar frustrations of existence return with new force. Far from reconciling him to the farm, Peggy stands in complete opposition to it. Although he feels it to be his fault that it is so, he blames her because he cannot "see both her and the farm at once" (p. 170). And his mother views Peggy as an implacable rival: "That woman. She's fierce. She'll have me dead within the year" (p. 139).

The name Peggy has personal associations for Updike, ones going back to childhood when he, a boy of five, was to take a present to a children's party. The intended present was the little figurine of a winged elf mentioned in *The Centaur.* But Updike, saying Peggy was an *animal,* refused to give this image of the imaginative soul, and decided to take her candy instead. Throughout Updike's fiction, candy connotes the shallow triviality of our civilization.

Peggy and Mrs. Robinson clash on the first evening of the visit. Joey's mother explains how she has not been supposed strong enough to have a baby, but has had Joey; and how, not wanting her only child to be an Olingerite but a *man,* she has persuaded husband George to let her have the farm. Peggy replies: "He gave you Joey and the farm; what did you give him?" (p. 30). Mrs. Robinson is taken aback, but at last says, "Why, his freedom!" When Peggy asks whether you can give another person freedom, Mrs. Robinson says that only God can, really, but that other people can by not denying it. This argument continues throughout the visit, at various peaks of vehemence. Peggy insists that she herself is the first woman Joey has met who has allowed him to be a man — and Joey, telling the story, comments: "This was her secret song, the justification with which she had led me to divorce" (p. 112). His mother says that no doubt they mean different things by the word "man," and Peggy retorts that they must, because of what Mrs. Robinson did to her husband when she ran to the farm as though to a giant lover. Joey's retrospective comment is that perhaps they were both right and both wrong. "Their conversation seemed a collision in darkness to me but my mother's darkness was nurturing whereas Peggy's was cold, dense, and metallic" (p. 135).

Peggy, with her red hair and "pelvic amplitude" and "quick health," is a Venus figure like Vera Hummel in *The Centaur*. Angered by the constant arguments and by Mrs. Robinson's breaking plates in the kitchen to relieve her frustration, she says she is leaving at once and goes upstairs to pack. Richard runs after her to persuade her to change her mind, and Joey's mother remarks: "Cupid interviewing Venus" (p. 119). But Peggy is also a woman who seeks power. In Barth's terminology she is the "rebellious" woman, that is, one who rebels against right order and is "submissive" only to gain her ends. Joey's view of Peggy as having "led him" into divorce is accurate enough; and his conclusion does not conflict with his memory of how Peggy, once she knew he was contemplating parting from Joan, begged him to leave her and return to his wife and children. She has trusted the weakness of the man to make him turn in gratitude to her because of her "submission." Mrs. Robinson tells Joey that Peggy is very interested in seeing round the farm, especially since she has seen that building developments are going on at its edges. Joey agrees that Peggy is thinking of how much it would fetch, for she has always been a good "window shopper" (p. 140). He remembers, too, the first time he met Peggy. Joan was dressed in (romantic) blue and Peggy in wheat yellow, and, "when Joan said, *This is my husband,* Peggy's hand stabbed mannishly towards mine and she grinned with startling width, as if incredulous" (p. 173). The occasion that triggers his memory is Peggy's agreeing with his mother that he is a good boy. From the very beginning, therefore, Peggy has taken the male's place in defiance of the created order. She was a window shopper shopping for a weak man who did not want to take a husband's responsibilities; and she found him.

* * *

Going into the bedroom on Saturday night, Joey commiserates with his wife who has gone to bed earlier because her period has started. "Poor girl. You need a baby." "I have one. Two, counting Richard" (pp. 144-45). Soon she is tender again, but he is not to be placated. He taunts her about her first husband: "So you laid for a Yalie. I'll be damned."

The immediate cause for Joey's nastiness is the fact that Peggy has momentarily dropped the pretense that she is the woman who is proud to make him a man. Behind the realization that his new wife's submissiveness is not real, however, lies the greater fear engendered by the thought that he has betrayed Joan and his children for nothing. He married Peggy because he saw her as infinitely desirable, the embodiment of a Venus whom all the world must desire; but he is tortured by the thought that he has not won her, that he is only one in a succession of anonymous males who have been granted the "freedom" of Peggy's body since she was nineteen. His jibe about Yale is prompted by Richard's innocent remark earlier that his father had stayed overnight on different occasions after his mother's divorce. Peggy's former husband, Dean McCabe of Yale, is a menacing figure to him, because Joey has never discovered the precise circumstances of the divorce, and he fancies that McCabe pities rather than envies him.

Joey's life at thirty-five seems a series of mistaken choices. His "prostitute's job" is described on the same page as his mother's wish that he be a poet like Wordsworth. ("Getting and spending we lay waste our powers.") He has turned away from an artist's vocation in favor of a money-earning position which Peter Caldwell rejected contemptuously at the age of fifteen. In *The Centaur* George Caldwell went into a lavatory in the school and saw a four-letter word on the wall that had been altered so as to read BOOK. The fact depressed him. "Could his son have done it?" (p. 247). Joey's progress seems to have been in the opposite direction. The judge's chambers in which he was married to Peggy suggested a lavatory, and his most successful conversation with his wife is in four-letter words. The only relic of Christianity left in Peggy's vocabulary seems to be the use of the word "know" in the sexual sense found in the Bible. But Joey sees no way in which his regress can be halted. He confesses to his mother that he knew, even before it was too late to change, that he was making a mistake in divorcing Joan. But — unlike the wise dog Mitzi who saved herself from the drainpipe — "I was damned if I'd back out" (*OTF*, p. 138).

Joey remains an imaginative man. The poetic impulse has not died in him. Yet the powers of the imagination that might have enlarged his life have not been disciplined or directed into true creativity. Since he met Peggy, his mind has turned mostly to romantic-erotic images similar to those occupying the thoughts of Rabbit Angstrom in *Rabbit, Run,* though having a greater sophistication. The chief difference is that, for Joey, Rabbit's orange-haired mermaids have materialized in the form of his red-headed mistress-wife. Like Rabbit, his fancy merges Woman into Landscape. He sees Peggy as the cottonfields of the South and as the distant land of France — and as other regions Rabbit's limited imagination prevented him from envisaging (p. 46). On the Saturday of his visit, Joey goes to mow the large field across the road from the farm. Sitting on the tractor under the sun's heat he feels his mowing to be a sexual act and thinks: "My wife is a field" (p. 59). In the thought of Peggy being a landscape over which he can glide he always experiences a sense of freedom that has become for him a necessity of life (p. 47).

The romantic imagination can provide a giddy sense of life. But its final discovery is always, as Rabbit found, the chill emptiness of "lovely life eclipsed by lovely death" (*RR*, p. 282). Joey's picturing of Peggy as "a variety of landscapes" begins with sunny lands and ends with Antarctica (the land of suspended life) and with a river scene suggesting the waters of the Styx (*OTF*, pp. 46-47). Similarly, his mowing ceases to be a triumphant sexual conquest, as the gathering clouds above him seem to present "the anatomy of a dead marriage" (p. 82). However, the romantic man can even enjoy the thought of lovely death eclipsing life and can luxuriate in the thought of being a lost soul. Mrs. Robinson tells Joey that she sees her son's ruin in Peggy's eyes. Joey thinks: *"Ruin.* It pleased me to feel myself sinking, smothered, lost, forgotten, obliterated in the depths of the mistake which my mother, as if enrolling my fall in her mythology, enunciated" (pp. 140-41). Here Joey exhibits the true romantic's indifference to reality so long as he can turn it into material for aesthetic self-gratification.

Nevertheless, Joey's imagination has not decayed so much that it is totally insulated from reality. Tired from mowing, he goes to bed on Saturday night and dreams he is still in the field and that the tractor stumbles over something. Thinking he has shattered a nest of pheasant eggs, he stops and dismounts. He is suddenly in a strange bleak landscape, smoldering like a dump. (The scene reflects a science-fiction story which Richard has been telling him about. It is also the biblical image of hell: Gehenna, the garbage dump outside Jerusalem in the Valley of Hinnom.) Joey picks out of the dirt "a hunched homunculus, its head sunk on his chest as if shying from a blow." The little being cries out: "Don't you know me, Daddy. I'm Charlie." Charlie is his son by Joan. Joey clasps him to his chest and vows "never to be parted from him" (p. 146). He wakes to find his mother calling him, asking whether he is coming to church.

An imaginative man, such as Joey still is, may learn both through dreams and through going to church the tragic consequences of the wrong choices he has made.[9] Nevertheless, those wrong choices can-

---

[9] It is by no means certain, of course, that the churches will give the teaching that they ought to provide. In spite of the fact that he both quotes Karl Barth and takes the outlines of his sermon from Barth's *Church Dogmatics,* the Lutheran preacher fails to measure up to the size of Barth's teaching. Sometimes he asserts precisely what Barth denies, particularly when he says that woman is *less* than a man — somewhere "in between" a man and a child — and when he attributes woman's beauty to her possessing a dreamlike quality.

not be reversed. Since weak men have renounced their responsibilities, they have laid upon their sons burdens too heavy for their small shoulders — making them homunculi. Joey wonders whether his Charlie will become "like Richard, a little husband" (p. 120).

Seeing Richard as a small replica of himself — and as one who is stronger in relation to Peggy than he is — Joey tries to tell him about himself and his mistakes. At least, such is his unconscious desire. Consciously, he knows only that he wants to gain Richard's trust and affection. So he tells him a bedtime story he has told before to seven-year-old Charles, warning him that to an eleven-year-old the story may seem childish. Richard replies: "That's O.K. I enjoy childish things" (p. 129), and Joey wonders whether the boy realizes he is echoing the Bible.

Joey tells of a frog who was "like a tiny king inside his castle inside his body" (pp. 129-131), and who went down inside himself searching for a treasure. He started when the leaves were falling, becoming smaller and smaller as he descended, until at last he reached "the dungeon of his guts" where he was sure the treasure was. Then he disappeared. In the spring he awoke in the darkness, ran upstairs, threw open the lids of his eyes, and looked out. "And the sky was blue. End of story."

The story is interrupted by comments from Richard and also by thoughts that come to Joey while he is telling it. Describing how the frog sends out his tongue to spear "a poor fly," Joey thinks of "Poor Joan." As he speaks of the dungeon of the guts, he hears Peggy talking to his mother. When Richard says the story is like Doctor Seuss, Joey says that he meant it to be like Dante. The story finished, Joey kisses Richard and says: "O.K., frog." As he goes downstairs, he is "touched, enclosed, by a faint familiar tint of vapor" that he assumes "would reveal some nostalgic treasure unlocked by the humidity within the stones, plaster, wood, and history of the house." But he finds that this thought has been given him by the smell of a damp towel lying on the landing. From the towel comes "the hoarse scent of Peggy's wet hair" (p. 132). (She had been caught in the rain at the end of the afternoon he was mowing the field, and had been soaked.)

As Joey talks to Richard in the bedroom he is troubled at the "unthinking non-Christianity" of the boy and his mother and he blames himself for not having dared to teach the boy a bedtime prayer. So, although he does not realize it, he gives Richard a sub-

---

These comments show the minister's unthinking acceptance of current romantic and pagan ideas, and they are no doubt the cause of Mrs. Robinson's remarking acidly that he has given an unusually "*young*" sermon" (p. 154).

stitute: a Christian story of heaven and hell (Dante) disguised as a fanciful animal story (Doctor Seuss) and having some affinity with Freudian symbolism. (Peggy goes in for amateur psychology.) The treasure in the guts is the sexual fulfilment he has sought in Peggy, and which has caused him to "disappear." He has ceased to be a king in the kingdom of marriage, and has lost himself as a man. Yet, as Richard is quick to understand, disappearance is not necessarily identical with death. There may be a springtime resurrection, and an upward ascent that once more puts man in touch with heaven. Before Joey descended into the dungeon of the loins he had seen the sky, but had used his vision merely to capture and destroy Joan. A second chance to rule as king in the light of heaven will not come for him, he thinks. He knew that already when he decided to divorce Joan. So he made up the story originally for the benefit of his child. Now he tells the same story to his substitute child. His kissing Richard is his blessing given to one who cannot call him "father" and yet who may find in him a spiritual father who instructs him as a father should. "O.K., frog" says Joey before he leaves Richard, pressing home the moral that Richard is to identify himself with the frog in the parable.

However, Joey's understanding of his own message is so dim that as he *descends* the stairs of the house he actually thinks he is to find the treasure that he has just explained in the story *cannot* be found by descending. He is dismayed to find that the treasure is only the mirage which has already deceived him — the scent of a whore.

* * *

In the symbolic language of his own imagination, Joey is declared to be the weak tyrant; to be the lover who deludes himself into thinking he can combine the orange of mature passion with the green of childhood; the father who crushes his child under the wheels of his desire, who promises never to leave him and yet consigns him to hell; the would-be poet who has exchanged his creative vision for the flesh-pots of Egypt; the seeker of a heavenly treasure who has become the plaything of a whore, a whore for whom he is willing to sell his mother's life and squander his inheritance.

The farm itself provides another set of symbols, symbols giving Joey an opportunity to come to self-knowledge. Although *Of the Farm,* unlike *The Centaur,* does not use an explicit mythic pattern to interpret the naturalistic story line, yet Joey realizes that his return to his childhood home has drawn him, whether he likes it or not, into the orbit of his mother's "mythology." During the three days of his stay, the values by which he has set his course in New

York are weighed in the balance over against a wholly different way of life, against values of a very different kind.

When in *The Centaur* Peter and his father return on the Saturday after the storm, Cassie Caldwell greets them with the words: "My heroes" (*TC*, p. 286). Mrs. Robinson welcomes the car from New York with the cry of "Pilgrims!" in which "a faint irony" is just audible (*OTF*, p. 7). This greeting may be read in the light of a remark made by the narrator of the title story in *The Music School*. This story is told by an unfaithful husband who remarks about himself and his friends, "We are all pilgrims, faltering toward divorce" (p. 190). For Joey and Peggy that particular pilgrimage has ended, but they are still pilgrims along the road continuing on the other side of divorce into an uncertain future.

On the way to the farm, Joey tells Richard that he will have to ask Mrs. Robinson for the answer to his question about the point of a farm which nobody farms. Out of his pertinacious intellectual curiosity, Richard does. Mrs. Robinson replies that the land, like people, becomes tired and needs a rest (p. 24). Later, she draws Richard into a fantasy of making a "people sanctuary" where those who have become misshapen by city living can grow into their human form again (p. 71). Richard, who is precocious in his grasp of scientific information (he prides himself on taking after his father), is fascinated by the world of nature so totally new to him. He wants Joey's mother to teach him how to name the wild flowers on the farm. Mrs. Robinson tells him that it is not enough to look them up in a book, because the art lies in matching the picture to the real specimens. When Joey goes to mow his mother's field, Richard is elated at Mrs. Robinson's suggestion that he is not too young to learn to drive the tractor. Peggy's categorical refusal, and her insistence that the idea is an *insane* one (pp. 71, 93), leads to the first burst of hostility between the two women.

Joey has always hated the farm, and he left it in order to find his freedom. He has felt justified in leaving the country for the city by the fact that his father shared his viewpoint. What he has not realized is that, unlike his father, he has failed to find a sphere in which to exercise a like responsibility. His father did not farm, but he stayed for his wife's sake in a place he disliked, and so kept his family together.

The sermon of the Lutheran preacher (following a line of thought initiated by Barth) points out that Adam's first work was to name the animals. The preacher adds, "Is not language an act of husbandry, a fencing in of fields?" (p. 151). Joey would have followed that Adamic work had he become a poet — a life as necessary and as rewarding as either farming or teaching. His "prostitute's job" does indeed provide him with the means of supporting a family (and, now, two families) but it prevents him from knowing man's proper place and responsibility, because it substitutes pride of possession for sacrificial sharing. That is why his expensive gifts to his parents seem, when he sees them in the farmhouse, to proclaim his corruption. They witness to the truth that he has never given himself. When he tells Peggy that he never liked the farm, she replies: "Oh, I think you do like it. You like it the same way you like me. It's something big you can show off" (p. 122). And Joey reflects that her disillusioned estimate is nearly true.

The farm, then, is not the place to which Joey can, or should, return permanently. Knowing himself from early years to be a city boy, he has had no alternative except to leave it. Yet, returning to it for these three days, he finds in it a reminder of the right order he has betrayed. His mother's "mythology" is one that he could never adopt for himself; yet, through her intense devotion to the order of nature, he and his little counterpart Richard are brought to a place where they are continually confronted with realities which the city allows them to forget.

In the Epilogue to *The Centaur,* Updike tells how Chiron is set by Zeus among the stars and therefore "assists in the regulation of our destinies, though in this latter time few living mortals cast their eyes respectfully toward Heaven, and fewer still sit as students to the stars" (p. 299). Joey's mother does follow a "mythology" which acknowledges an orderly pattern in the universe. And being brought into a life where the stars matter, the pilgrims from New York City are given a glimpse of earth seen in relation to Heaven. They are directed to the virtuous life.

* * *

Hook, in *The Poorhouse Fair,* thinks of virtue as residing in the manliness that gives firmness to society by pursuing "invisible goals," so that "it can be written that the woman takes her life from the man." Hook believes women to be "the heroes of dead lands" (p. 160). Mrs. Robinson, when she first appears at the farmhouse door, is wearing a man's sweater over her blouse. It is Joey's grandfather's sweater — as though she is making explicit Hook's judgment that today "there is little store of virtue left" (p. 160). In dead lands, the woman has to take over the man's place, unwillingly, so that some trace of virtue may be kept alive.

Joey senses the absence of virtue as he listens to Peggy accusing Mrs. Robinson of having taken the farm as her giant lover, and so of having deprived both Joey and his father of their masculinity. Peggy is sitting "in the wing chair where . . . [his] grandfather had pontificated" (p. 133). Joey reflects: "Her cigarette smoke insulted the room" (p. 135). The insult consists in her having symbolically declared herself head of the house. But Joey never thinks that the disorder is caused by his own refusal to assert his responsibility for keeping right order. Idly reading a P. G. Wodehouse novel (his childhood occupation), he sits between the two women as they argue about the meaning of freedom, silently rejecting the "mythology" he sees in each of the conflicting views, yet never using his freedom to reconcile wife and mother.

It is Richard who displays eagerness to learn from the farm how to be a strong man. When the boy asks Mrs. Robinson how to identify the flowers, he is taking up Adam's work of naming. He pleads with his mother to be allowed to learn to drive the tractor: "Just a lesson, Mother; just Lesson One, Léçon Première?" (p. 92). And it is he who has courage to tell Peggy that it would be "impolite" to leave the house in a temper (pp. 118, 120). Joey feels jealous of the "little husband's" strength.

Peggy herself, having said that there is nothing for her to do in this dreadful place, starts hoeing in the garden, trying to imitate Mrs. Robinson's work (p. 89). The sight of her standing in her fashionable New York clothes, flushed from her efforts, makes Joey and Richard burst out laughing; but Joey's mother is impressed. She has already seen a resemblance to her own mother (Mrs. Hofstetter) in Peggy, and later she tells Joey that Peggy is "more your style" than Joan. She adds, "The Hofstetters always had high-stepping women" (p. 156). Peggy comes from farming country in Nebraska, and she is in her own fashion as spirited as her new mother-in-law.

The heroic quality evident in Richard and the two women is not evident in Joey, who is most reluctant to take up the man's part. He objects to being asked to mow the fields, asking why they cannot pay someone else to do the job. "It's our place," his mother tells him. He retorts: "It's your place" (p. 33). Giving in, he mows the large field, but, anxious only to be gone before the Sunday evening traffic starts, goes back to New York with the rest untouched. As for mothering his mother, he comes upstairs on Friday night, seizing Peggy's wrists to make her listen to him, and saying in anger: "I'm thirty-five and I've been through hell and I don't see why that old lady has to have such a hold over me. It's ridiculous. It's degrading" (p. 45). He has just come from exercising his mother's dogs, and Peggy remarks that he smells like a puppy. The comparison is apt.

Joey, while spending his days in the service of advertising dollar distribution, had sold cheaply the most valuable assets in life: his poetic gifts, his capacity for work, his responsibility to wife and children. But, most damaging of all, he has come to accept the value of everything in terms of possessing something "big." Peggy realizes this, and his mother confirms Peggy's judgment when she says that in Peggy Joey has bought "an expensive bit of property" (p. 140). Talking to Richard, Mrs. Robinson compares Peggy to a flower, saying that flowers have to be bright when "the point is" to attract bees (p. 124). How Joey thinks of flowers we learn when he is looking at the field he has mowed and thinks: *"the first advertisements"* (p. 164). He wonders if he can use the notion in his work. Jesus asked his hearers to consider the wild flowers of the field (Matt. 6:28). Joey considers them, and hopes they will make money for him.

Understanding that Joey cannot see both Peggy and the farm at once, and certain that he will part with the land to keep the expensive property he has married, Mrs. Robinson pleads with him: "Joey, when you sell my farm, don't sell it cheap." He replies: *"Your* farm? I've always thought of it as our farm" (p. 174). His words end the book.

The answer may seem conciliatory, and yet it is, as he admits, "teasing" — that is to say, cruel. The circumstances that have brought his mother to challenge him thus directly are sombre ones. As Joey and she are on their way back from church she has a heart attack. Joey and Peggy are both frightened, though not frightened enough to put off their return to New York. Joey, far from taking the man's share of the responsibility for mothering his mother, shows little consideration for her "heart." He knows he cannot give a direct answer, and so gives one "that with conspiratorial tact declared nothing and left the past apparently unrevised." It is language understood in the family; but it closes the past, and closes it unkindly. After church Mrs. Robinson has expressed disapproval of the minister's sermon — a disapproval directed at the speaker rather than at his words — saying: "No, Joey, it seems to me whenever a man begins to talk that way, he's trying to excuse himself from some woman's pain" (p. 154). She explains that the minister is known to have "a roving eye." Joey responds by changing the subject, attempting to excuse himself from his mother's pain. While he speaks to her, his mind is on New York, "the living memento of my childish dream of escape," as he refers to it. He feels the City calling him, and, though he is "ashamed," he will not stay.

The full cruelty of Joey's attitude to his mother is suggested by an earlier exchange between Peggy and him. Peggy, angered at his holding her past against her, tells him that he has made his choice to marry her and must take responsibility for it. She tells him:

". . . don't tease me like you did that dog. Don't keep showing me the hole" (p. 170). Peggy has the health to fight him and expose his tyrannical weakness; but his mother now has not, for all her spirit. And in effect, he is also showing her the hole, that deep hole going into the earth that is death and into which she is soon to be pushed without the possibility of backing out.[10] His apparent kindness in granting her earlier plea to think of the farm as "ours" only brings back her own words, "It will be yours soon enough" (p. 33). He has made his decision, in spite of having "apparently" left the past unrevised. It is the decision of a weak man who, excusing himself from a woman's pain, creates a dead land.

*   *   *

Apart from the sermon in the church, little is said in *Of the Farm* that directly introduces the subject of faith. Rather, what is stressed is the unselfconscious paganism that Peggy has passed on to Richard (pp. 70, 129). The problem that Updike raises — though only in passing, because *Of the Farm* is about the right order *in* creation rather than about the right relation of earth to heaven — is one to which he gives serious attention in his next novel *Couples*. It is the problem of whether belief in heaven can persist at all once man has consciously acted in defiance of the right order in creation. Joey has never made the decision to cut himself off from his childhood Christianity. Although his mother is surprised when he consents to go with her to church, expecting him to refuse (p. 148), he has expected to accompany her as a matter of course. He explains that Peggy and Richard will not accompany them because Richard "didn't bring the right clothes" (p. 147). There seems to be no need to give any excuse for Peggy.

Once again, it is Joey's unconscious mind that shows his spiritual condition. His reflection about the flowers of the field, recently cut down by the mower and growing again, refers on the surface to his scale of values as an advertising man. But the words "flowers, the first advertisements" are set in italics — always an indication in Updike's writing that more is being said than the literal reading requires. As Joey looks at the flowers he also sees dead grass (p. 164). The flowers and the grass have publicity value. What do they say? Perhaps the words of Isaiah are relevant:

> *A voice says, "Cry!"*
> *And I said, "What shall I cry?"*

---

[10] Death as "that deep hole" is an important image in "Pigeon Feathers" (p. 139). And we have seen how the hole, at first a sexual image, becomes an image for death in *Rabbit, Run*.

> *All flesh is grass,*
> *and all its beauty is like the flower*
> *of the field.*
> *The grass withers, the flower fades,*
> *when the breath of the Lord*
> *blows upon it;*
> *surely the people is grass.*
> *The grass withers, the flower fades;*
> *but the word of our God will*
> *stand for ever.* (Isa. 40:6-8)

The word advertisement, after all, means in its basic sense either "warning" or "turning to." The flowers cry out their warning, calling to men to turn to the God whose word stands fast while men lose strength (Isa. 40:29-31). The refrain of the chapter in Isaiah which speaks of the flowers of the field is, "Have you not known? Have you not heard?" Joey has heard, though in his weakness he does not know what he hears.

The flowers grow and are cut down in the field where he has reaped the crop of summer weeds alone. He is the man who remembers a girl reminding him of Wordsworth's Solitary Reaper. Wordsworth himself was not certain what the girl he saw was singing. Perhaps it was of "old, unhappy, far-off things,"

> *Or is it some more humble lay,*
> *Familiar matter of today?*
> *Some natural sorrow, loss, or pain,*
> *That has been, and may be again?*

Familiar enough is Joey's "matter of today": a lost wife and lost children; the pain of a marriage felt to be a union with a whore — "You and me and Richard and Dean McCabe and four dozen other gentlemen not specifically identified" (p. 169); the sorrow of a dying mother. Once he had thought that death could bring him to song. But the poet in Joey is dead too, or at least has disappeared. And the flowers will soon be forgotten in the streets of New York where the demand is for something "big" to show off, and where the imagery of either Isaiah or of Wordsworth counts for nothing in comparison with "corporate image presentation."

13

EROS

INCREASINGLY, UPDIKE'S WORK HAS COME TO CONCEN-
trate upon pilgrims faltering toward divorce, and upon those other
pilgrims who have reached the place of their pilgrimage but are still
uncertainly questing. In *Pigeon Feathers* the theme of the complete
or threatened breakdown of marriage is explicit in only one story,
"Dear Alexandros." In *The Music School* ten of the twenty stories
take this for their subject. So far as the novels are concerned, only
The Centaur breaks the line running from *Rabbit, Run,* through *Of
the Farm,* to *Couples* — and it breaks the line only partially.

We have seen how relating the *outside* to the *inside* — internal
feelings to the objective world of things — was already a major
interest for Updike while he was writing chiefly about the remembered world of childhood and adolescence. Now, as he grapples
with the adult world of the present, he is investigating a complex
problem in the same area. The *inside / outside* contrast appears
again, only this time it is presented in terms of the internal passion
we know as love and the external social contract we know as
marriage. Here divorce is the end product of the belief that the
inside and the outside are essentially in conflict; and remarriage
after divorce witnesses less to a wish to reconsider this belief than
to a hope that to every universal rule there is at least one exception.

An important influence shaping Updike's approach to the whole
subject of love and marriage is that of Denis de Rougemont's classic
treatment of the subject in his book *Love in the Western World.*[1]

---

[1] Published in France in 1939; a revised and augmented edition appeared
in 1954. Quotations are taken from the second English edition, entitled *Passion
and Society* (London, 1956).

In a long review of a collection of de Rougemont's essays,[2] Updike examines this author's thesis. He spends most of the review outlining and criticizing *Love in the Western World,* presenting its central argument as follows:

> The love-myth, simply, is the daughter of a creed that holds Creation in contempt. She stands in the same relation to fruitful marriage as does Dualism to the Christian Monism precariously hinged on the dogma of the God-man. Her essence is *passion itself;* her concern is not with the possession, through love, of another person but with the prolongation of the lover's state of mind. Eros is allied with Thanatos rather than Agape; love becomes not a way of accepting and entering the world but a way of defying and escaping it. Iseult is the mythical prototype of the Unattainable Lady to whom the love-myth directs our adoration, diverting it from the attainable lady (in legal terms, our "wife"; in Christian terms, our "neighbor") who is at our side. (*AP,* p. 285)

The review insists, giving special consideration to the story of Tristan and Iseult, which holds a central place in de Rougemont's book, that this interpretation of the idea of passionate love as a *heresy* and a *myth* is over-ingenious. It grants, however, that "de Rougemont is dreadfully right in asserting that love in the Western World has by some means acquired a force far out of proportion to its presumed procreative aim" (p. 299).

In the Foreword to *Assorted Prose,* Updike takes back his reservations about de Rougemont, saying that the latter's "overriding thesis seems increasingly beautiful and pertinent" (*AP,* ix), and adding that "corroborating quotations leap to my eyes wherever I read." (He proceeds to quote samples from Freud, Vassilis Vassilikos, T. E. Hulme, and Paul Valéry.) De Rougemont's thesis is plainly visible in Updike's own retelling of the tale of Tristan and Iseult in one of the short stories collected in *The Music School.*

"Four Sides of One Story" presents the Tristan romance in modern dress with the original setting showing through. (For example, King Mark refers to the alchemists at his court and also orders his wife to have psychoanalysis.) Eros as the creation-renouncing courting of Thanatos is illustrated in Tristan's statement that marriage is the death of love, and in his proud confession that because their love is a guilty one, he and Iseult can seize "a purity that will pass without interruption through death itself" (*MS,* p. 93). What is particularly interesting, however, is that details confirming Updike's acceptance of de Rougemont's reading of the Tristan romance also link "Four Sides of One Story" with other Updike stories. Like

---

[2] *Love Declared* (New York, 1963).

Rabbit Angstrom, Tristan is heading south and thinking about mermaids; like Janice Angstrom, Tristan's wife Iseult of the White Hands has taken to drink; like Joey Robinson, Tristan is "charmingly boyish" (p. 94) and given to tormenting; and like Peggy Robinson (in Joey's description of her in the months before he had finally decided to leave Joan and marry her), Iseult the Fair is desperately anguished and begs her lover to return to his wife and children.

Thus the de Rougemont theory of passionate love or Eros is not something brought in and applied to Updike's fiction from the outside. Whether at any one time Updike either accepts fully or rejects partly this theory as a conclusive analysis of love in the Western world, he writes in full awareness of the *force* that makes the phenomenon we have come to call "falling in love" something quite different from a simple biological drive.[3] And the effects of this force, making Eros a romantic quest for death rather than a turning towards life and the solid world of created things, is something he continually documents. For him the connection between Eros and Thanatos is never very far out of sight,[4] and in his later fiction this connection becomes an increasingly important theme.

*   *   *

Notable among the recent short stories exploring aspects of Eros is "Museums and Women."[5] Its narrator turns out to be the William Young of "A Sense of Shelter." Though now a man, William still seems to cling to his adolescent desire for indoor weather.

Museums and women have been linked in William's mind since childhood, when his mother used to take him frequently to a "provincial museum." This museum was set in a garden whose "paradisical grounds" contained "exotic flora, and trees wearing tags, as if freshly christened by Adam" (p. 57). Inside the museum, though, the conglomerate exhibits seemed sad, inducing in William a mood of dread which he connected with the "ghostly hunt" on which his mother had started him. He believed "she was pointing me through

---

[3] The divinity student in "Lifeguard" says: "It is not true that our biological impulses are tricked out with ribands of chivalry; rather, our chivalric impulses go clanking in encumbering biological armor. Eunuchs love. Children love. I would love" (*PF*, p. 217). From the context of these remarks, however, the reader gathers that it is the *student* who speaks — that is, someone who has not yet fully learned his lesson. His confidence in being master of his subject is actually a sign of his comparative ignorance of it.

[4] The poem "Erotic Epigrams" (*TP*, p. 79) makes an almost complete identification between Eros and Thanatos. The second of the three "epigrams," incidentally, is about Tristan and Iseult.

[5] *The New Yorker*, Nov. 18, 1967.

these corridors toward a radiant place she had despaired of reaching" (p. 57).

This same museum appears in *The Centaur,* where Peter Caldwell tells his mistress of similar memories. Peter connects the sense of dread he felt inside the museum with the omnipresence there of death. "So much death; who would dream there could be such a quantity of death?" (p. 267). He remembers especially a life-size statue of a naked green lady standing in a pool and holding to her lips a scallop shell. Water dripped from the far side of the shell, and Peter used to imagine that during the night, the statue would slant the shell toward her and drink. Peter's romantic dream of there being a magic in darkness capable of satisfying desires denied in the prosaic light of day makes contact with the "ghostly hunt" for an ideal beyond the real that characterizes William's memories of his first museum and the first woman in his life.

The possibility of William's ideal "radiant place" becoming actual came with his falling in love with a classmate.

As in "A Sense of Shelter," William confesses that his love for the girl was originally his mother's idea. His mother had praised her "spirit" (recalling Mrs. Robinson's remark in *Of the Farm* that high-spirited women were the choice of the males in her family). But, though they came together on school trips to the museum, William never declared his feelings to the girl; and so he felt that external circumstances had come between him and this possible embodiment of his mother's ideal for him.

Becoming a university student, William met at the college museum the woman he was to marry. Standing at the top of the museum steps and suggesting something "mute and remote," this girl seemed to him "the very gatekeeper of the temple of learning that must be the radiant place" (*The New Yorker,* p. 59). Later, and now married, he discovered in a "faraway museum" a small marble nude asleep on a marble mattress. Like his wife she was "fair, and finely formed, and mute" (p. 59). And at that moment an "ideal other women" entered his life.

Two other living women feature in William's story of museums and women. The first, a friend of a friend, was momentarily brought close when she stumbled against him as they descended the ramp of the Guggenheim Museum of Modern Art in New York. The second was brought by him to another New York museum "which was once a mansion and still retains a homelike quality, if one can imagine people rich enough in self-esteem to inhabit walls so over-ripe with masterpieces" (p. 60). They had been making love, and had the sensation of being hosts in a house worthy of their pride in each other. William remembers the moment as one when he had "come to the limits of unsearchability." Here, he says, was "My woman, fully searched, and my museum, fully possessed" (p. 61). Later he saw her again, for the last time, in another museum where she was now working. They had parted, and the woman, though tearful at the thought of how William had allowed their love to come to nothing, refused to blame him. Leaving this museum, William reflected: "And it appeared to me that now I was condemned, in my search for the radiance that had faded behind me, to enter more and more museums, and be a little less exalted by each new entrance, and a little more quickly disappointed in the familiar contents beyond" (p. 61).

In Plato's *Symposium* Socrates explains love (Eros) to be the child of a divine father (Plenty) and of a human mother (Poverty). This Eros is always in search of a heavenly perfection that cannot be found on earth. Just so, William Young explains that what we seek in museums is the opposite of what we seek in churches. Churches give us the consolation of "previous visitation." But museums draw us to seek "the untouched, the never-before-discovered." He mentions his discovery of the marble nude on her mattress as being the "thin keystone" to the arch of his story. Here is the ideal disclosing itself in the radiance of its untouched perfection. Yet, at the moment of discovery, William is "disturbed by a dread and a premonition of loss"; and he asks "Why?" (p. 59). Without answering his own question directly, he compares this "ideal other woman" with his wife.

When he marries her, William's wife seems to him to be the radiance his mother had led him to look for in museums. Yet, evidently, this marriage is not the end of his quest. The marble woman leads him to believe that the ideal must be found in "another woman as yet untouched." He continues in his search and finds a mistress, who at the time of discovery seems to be his marble woman come to life. (When he looks at "my woman, fully searched" in "my museum fully possessed," he remembers how recently, after they have made love, he has seen her asleep on a mattress; but now she is wide awake.) The conclusion of the story is that the Eros-ideal is never realized in time and space. Women and museums entered and possessed do not bring the ideal nearer. Instead, they spread over our existence dread and a sense of loss. The marble woman on the marble mattress, William insists, looked asleep and not dead. Yet the continued pursuit of the Eros-ideal in the actual world where we have our existence means progressive disillusionment, turning the romantic dream into tears over a dead love, and bringing the seeker-after-radiance to the point where he knows that the radiance has faded behind him.[6]

Throughout William's story the image of *falling* emphasizes the instability of the Eros-ideal. At the college museum, William sees his future wife standing "on the edge" of a fall. "I heard the volume of emptiness calling to her, calling her away from me, so full of talk" (p. 59). In the Museum of Modern Art, he learns how modern ways of living encourage us to fall. There, on the *descending* ramp, "was a rather slender and low concrete guard wall that more invited than discouraged a plunge into the cathedralic depths below" (p. 60).

Both women and museums, says William, "suggest radiance, antiquity, mystery and duty" (p. 57). William is, as he confesses, "by nature dutiful and reverent" (p. 58). He is not a bold adventurer, deliberately courting a fall. Nevertheless, his quest for the Eros-ideal leads him to seek an "ideal other woman." The marble dream-woman calls him to awaken her, to search and possess her untouched shape. But when he takes a mistress, this awakened woman of flesh and blood cannot be returned to the world of dreams. She makes demands which force him to "retreat" from this "beautiful boundary" between the ideal and the actual (p. 61). When he returns to see her in the museum where she has gone to work after their parting, she tells him not to come teasing her, and he finds that he cannot give her a good reason for his having dismissed her from his life: "Cowardice. I've always been timid. A sense of duty. I don't know" (p. 61). He has chosen to keep the laws of marriage at the cost of offending against the natural laws of human kindness.

The worship of Eros, it would seem, must inevitably lead to cruelty. The pursuit of this ideal is destructive of the real. In particular, it ignores the real situation of marriage, where love between one man and one woman involves responsibility to the family. William records that in the museum-mansion where he walked with his mistress as though it were their home, she expressed displeasure over a chest painted with "pubescent cherubs" (p. 60). The thought of children spoiled that moment when love seemed complete because it carried a duty beyond the service of Eros.

---

[6] The story also nicely illustrates Kierkegaard's thesis of the difference between the aesthetic and the moral-religious spheres of life. The religious sphere, says Kierkegaard, is the sphere of *repetition* ("previous visitation"), the aesthetic is the sphere of the *possibility of everything* ("the never-before-discovered"). Kierkegaard sees the aesthetic manifested most fully in the *erotic*, as typified in the Don Juan story. The poet of aesthetic possibilities, Kierkegaard insists, is fated to be unhappy, a prey to *angst*.

"Museums and Women" presents, in a concentrated and most explicit form, the view of romantic love that Updike unfolds in so many other stories. But it is especially emphatic about the essentially self-centered nature of the Eros-ideal. Both de Rougemont and Karl Barth note that while Christianity sees human love fulfilled in the love of *the other* — the actual neighbor — the Eros-ideal presupposes that all love is self-love. The worship of Eros finds no place for mutual self-giving. Instead, man hopes, through devotion to a love that is pure only when it is unconsummated, to find his own "feminine soul." Only a love that scorns earthly limitations will allow him to restore the original wholeness of the self that is a primal unity, a unity split by the grossness of matter into bisexual components.

Speaking of how he first courted the woman who was to be his wife, William comments: "I felt in her an innocent and sad blankness where I must stamp my name" (p. 58). His wife-to-be introduced him in a Boston museum to a sculptured figure she loved, a headless Attic sphinx with an S-curve in the body and tail. The head, which would complete the curve, he afterwards found in the Louvre. He adds: "So, too, the women were broken arcs of one curve" (p. 60). This belief in finding a completed whole through the exploration of successive women is one disregarding the individual person in favor of a disembodied ideal of the primal self. When William says his final farewell to his ex-mistress, he notices the headless sphinx on his way out. In actual life in the here and now, it is a cruel dream to believe that we are in search of a perfect unity of the self. Following this dream, we must always hurt those we profess to love.

Museums and women, so William's story begins, are "mutually transparent" even in their letters. "E" 's and "M" 's blend and complement one another (p. 57). Once we attend to the letters of the words, we see something which William does not say but which Updike, presumably, wishes us to notice. *Use, muse, wom(b), won, me, men:* this is what the letters say.[7] But William, by stressing the "M" 's and the "E" 's, lays the emphasis upon the *me*. It is through *me* that museums find their *use,* and by *me* that women are won. The service of the Eros-ideal to which William gives himself is, above all, the quest for the self stamped on the blankness of women. Eros-led, the man seeks the "spirited" woman under ever-changing forms in order to discover the depth of his own *anima* or feminine spirit. The radiance, antiquity, and mystery of the feminine ("Thou

---

[7] In *Couples,* Piet Hanema analyzes his name in this fashion, seeking to define himself thus: *"me, a man, amen, ah"* (p. 13).

art noble and nude and antique," said Swinburne to his romantic ideal Dolores) awakens his hopes of bringing broken arcs into a perfect circle persisting beyond death and decay. At the same time, the Eros-ideal has no place for duty; and, in seeking the completed curve, it mercilessly sacrifices the arcs.

William comes to see "that nothing about museums is as splendid as their entrances" (p. 61). Within, the hoped-for discovery is inseparable from dread and loss. That is why Christianity teaches that love is to be sought through Agape rather than through Eros. In William's Eros-dominated vision, both museums and women appear to be *nameless* and *continuous*. Agape demands that the neighbor be loved as an individual, a partner in a partnership where duty is remembered with kindness.

* * *

Explaining the mutually transparent nature of the two words of its title, "Museums and Women," William Young notes that "Both words hum" (p. 57). No explanation of what it means for a word to hum is given; but this is to be found in the story "Eros Rampant." In this story, Richard Maple is dreaming when he is distressed to hear a humming. He awakens to locate it "as a noise from the transformer on the telephone pole near their windows." He then realizes: "All night, while its residents sleep, the town communes with itself electrically" (*Harper's Magazine,* June, 1968, p. 64).

The reference to the telephone pole supplies the needed link for the reader to understand the significance of humming. That the telephone pole is an important image for Updike can be seen from his naming the second collection of his verses *Telephone Poles.* The title poem in that collection contains the lines: "What other tree can you climb where the birds' twitter, / Unscrambled, is English?" (p. 43). This explanation recalls a similar one in *Rabbit, Run.* Rabbit, as a boy, had loved to climb telephone poles in order to reach the top "where you could hear the wires sing. Terrifying motionless whisper." You were tempted to fall, but you hung on and had your reward, "Listening to the wires as if you could hear what people were saying, what all that secret adult world was about" (p. 15).

The singing, humming wires, then, contain the secret of what the adult world is all about. But you have to unscramble the twittering message and turn it into English. William Young understands that there is a message to be unscrambled in the humming words "museum" and "women"; yet, though he picks out the "M" 's and the "E" 's as particularly important, he does not go on to decode

the cipher and turn it into English. In "Eros Rampant" what the
town is saying as it communes with itself all night is not decoded
either. Richard is quite evidently frightened by the thought of what
he might hear. He, like William and like Rabbit as a boy, is too
"young" to make a serious attempt at understanding the precise
words spoken in the adult world.

The electrical self-communing of the town remains a humming,
not unscrambled into English, because its inhabitants are asleep.
"Eros Rampant" is very largely concerned to point out the extent
to which the adult world of today remains asleep even in the
daytime, hearing messages which speak to the unconscious mind but
remain unscrambled, and so unread, by the conscious intelligence.
This accounts for the prominence in the story of images of night:
particularly, *dark* and *black*.

The darkness of women in the eyes of men — that is, the male
experience of women as representing the force of the unconscious
— is a prominent element in the story. Richard Junior, who is just
beginning to notice girls and be noticed by them, becomes enraged
with his thirteen-year-old elder sister Judith because she keeps coming in between him and the light of the television screen. Sobbing,
he bursts into his parents' bedroom to complain that she has been
teasing him by this tactic; but his father replies, "She can't help
she's growing" (p. 63). Judith and Richard Jr. wonder why their
parents are dressing in the dark, and Richard explains that they
are saving electricity. Then Judith asks why her mother is crying.
This Richard cannot explain, for he had not noticed that she was.
The process of growth makes males aware — to their consternation
— that there is a "dark" aspect to femininity, one which must
simply be accepted. But, once adulthood is reached, staying in the
dark and saving electricity (that is, not bringing the unconscious
into consciousness) will bring avoidable grief and misunderstanding.

Grief and misunderstanding have been growing in the darkening
bedroom as Richard and Joan discuss Eros, each angrily questioning the other about real or fancied involvement with other loves.
Richard's imagination sees Joan "growing" in a fashion that parallels his daughter's physical growth. "As she moves, her body seems
to be gathering bulk from the shadows, bulk and a dynamic elasticity." The dark that causes this change also increases his inability
to understand her. "In the dim light he hardly knows this woman,
her broken gestures, her hasty voice" (p. 62). Increasing dark means
increasing pain, separation, and ignorance; and only the bursting
in of the children with their less developed troubles brings "shards
of electric light" into the room.

The one new character in this story is also in the dark. Penelope

Vogel (an echo, surely, of Penny Fogleman in *The Centaur*) is a secretary at Richard's office. She is twenty-nine, suffers from a perpetual cold, and has had a succession of unhappy love-affairs with West Indians. Richard thinks of her as a complicated geometrical problem: "find the point at which she had switched from white to black lovers" (p. 61). As with Peter's black mistress in *The Centaur,* the picture is entirely without racial overtones. It is wholly symbolic, telling of a life turned toward the unconscious. Penelope's last love was a snorkel instructor, who used to pull her for miles through the water (the unconscious). And she is unwilling to return to a former lover, an "Afro-American" who is a computer systems analyst and has a nervous stomach. Contact with the analytical aspect of Western civilization means losing the instinctive "black" understanding of love to which Penelope is now devoted. Speaking of the devotion to Eros shown by her West Indians, Penelope says with unsmiling seriousness: "They *work* at it, you know. Those boys are *pros*" (p. 61).

Richard's own attitude to Eros is that of the authentic romantic. Besides trying to hold in his love all the women he has admired since childhood, he "is half in love with death" (p. 60). The echo of Keats is unmistakable here; and it is followed by the equally conventional (and Keatsian) romantic idea of adoring the moon. Surprisingly, perhaps, he also loves President Johnson; but this is largely because Mr. Johnson, like the moon, is inaccessible and remote, and partly because Richard feels that he himself is the only one who appreciates him. The romantic's greatest incentive to love is always the knowledge that his love will be a lonely and hopeless sacrifice.

Richard is jealous of his children's love for their mother because it excludes him. "Joan swims through their love like a fish through water, ignorant of any other element" (p. 60). At night Richard tries "to press her into himself," and wonders whether love can be defined as the refusal to sleep. His pain comes from his wish to possess consciously what lies beyond consciousness — whether the moon or his sleeping wife — and make it his alone. His jealousy comes from realizing that a woman can bestow love without possessiveness, surrendering to the unconscious and living in it as a fish swimming in its natural element. His mind turns to thoughts of the ubiquity of "the libido that, Freud says, permeates all of us from infancy on" (p. 62); and, when Joan confesses that she has a lover and has had others, he forces her to give him precise details. (There is an echo here of Joey Robinson in *Of the Farm,* who used to torment his toys to make them confess.) Once more, like a true romantic, he finds great satisfaction in increasing his pain, and then in having Joan confess that he is a unique lover. Weeping, she praises his "passion," his "male-richness," his "invigorating sadism" (p. 64). At this point he dreams, and afterwards awakes to hear the electrical humming.

Richard's dream is of *descending* to the kitchen, where he finds Joan on the floor, practicing her Yoga exercises in her elastic black leotard. She explains that the point is to find the harmony of everything. Demonstrating the pose called the Lion, she says: "The whole theory is, we hold our heads too high, and the blood can't get to the brain" (p. 64). She thrusts her tongue upward, "as if to touch the ceiling." Richard begs her to tell him of all her lovers. She says that some of the men he will not know — they come to the door selling septic tanks. Richard is appalled to find that Joan's voice is coming from her belly. And then he hears the humming. Terrified, he awakes.

Unscrambled, the dream reveals Richard's fears concerning woman's "darkness" and the state of his marriage. The black elastic leotard Joan wears refers back to his memories of how, earlier that night, his wife in the dark of the bedroom had seemed to gain from the shadows "bulk and a dynamic elasticity." The pose of the Lion echoes the Belloc poem featured in *Rabbit, Run,* for Richard immediately demands that Joan name the men with whom she has shared passion. ("And a good little child will not play with him.") The sexual symbolism of the tongue thrust upward though the lips in the Lion pose suggests that the "harmony" Joan is seeking is to be attained through the libido aspiring to take over the conscious levels of our nature. *Eros rampant,* the Lion of passion untamed and dominant, means a reversal of the natural order: the sexual organs set in the head and speech coming from the belly. The reference to the men who sell septic tanks recalls Richard's conversation with Penelope. One of the secretary's lovers was a West Indian with a goatee who was in the septic-tank business. Richard imagines that, if his wife has been capable of taking lovers, then woman is a being ready to satisfy the lusts of satyrs and content to live in a world of excrement.

But then he goes down to the kitchen, not in dream but in reality. He leaves Joan sleeping, looking as small as Judith "yet infinitely deep, an abyss of secrecy, perfidy, and acceptingness" (p. 64). His wife's revelations have "steepened" the stairs and left the walls "slippery." Searching for traces of his dream he sees only the drawings done by his children and tacked up on the walls, drawings of ordinary objects: houses, cars, cats, and flowers.

"Eros Rampant" ends on the note of the stable realities that impinge upon the "slippery" world of waking or sleeping dreams.

The things men have to do with are unalterably themselves. Man alone, in the exercise of his freedom, can, and does, misuse and pervert his own proper nature. The story shows also how man interferes even with animal nature. The Maples own two cats, a brother and sister, called respectively Esau and Esther. Esther has been "fixed," deprived of her queenly rights. Esau, consequently, has been cheated out of his "birthright" to impregnate her. The Maple's dog Hecuba has also been "fixed." Hecuba (described in *Hamlet* as having "all o'er teemed loins") is the stock figure of the deposed queen left to mourn her former glory. Thus it is that man regulates Eros in the brute creation, causing problems. The animals themselves seem to be puzzled, and the children sense the difference.

Man's handling of his own sexuality is a more far-reaching problem. The third queen in the story is Penelope, a name associated with perfect fidelity and chastity in marriage. Like Ulysses' Queen, the modern Penelope is plagued by a variety of suitors, yet fails to deal with them as cleverly as her classical namesake did. Moreover, the cold in Penelope's nose has an affinity with the cold nose of Hecuba the dog. Hecuba feels herself excluded from family affection, yet is "in love with the smell of love" (p. 60). In this respect, Hecuba is like Penelope — and like Richard, as he himself realizes. On the animal level, there is no problem over Eros so long as nature is left to take its course, for the blood reaches the brain unimpeded. But, where adult human consciousness comes into the picture, everything is changed. Love leads to jealousy and to cruelty (the growing Maple children torment one another). Responsibility shirked brings guilt and tears shed in the dark.

The town communes with itself electrically over these things, for the pattern in the Maples' house is a common one today. But it does so only in the dark, in scrambled fashion. To turn the electric light on so as to illuminate the present human condition constitutes a challenge which the town's inhabitants, individually or corporately, do not care to face.

* * *

In the Eden-like condition presented in "Crow in the Woods," the natural bond between man and nature is seen to be Adam's helpmeet, Eve. "Like her sister the earth, the woman puts forth easy flowers of abundance." In "Eros Rampant," Joan in her role of mother in the house is just such a nourishing figure, gathering love around her and reminding Richard of "the eternal light" in a Vermeer painting (p. 60).[8]

---

[8] Vermeer's paintings are often referred to in Updike's work, where they stand for the perfection of beauty promised in art. See, for example, "Arch-

The setting of "Eros Rampant," however, is not Eden but a fallen world. Joan's clothes are neither royal purple nor Mary-blue, but a black leotard "riddled with runs." Flowers of Eden and wine of Canaan have become "dregs of white wine" tipped into "a potted geranium." In "Your Lover Just Called," Joan had asserted that she had no place for a lover. For, she says, "My days are consumed by devotion to the needs of my husband and his many children" (*Harper's Magazine,* January, 1967, p. 48). But in "Eros Rampant" she has a part-time job at a museum, where one of the assistant directors is her current lover. This man is called Otto, and Richard (playing with the word after the fashion demonstrated in "Museums and Women") says: "Otto. What's the joke? Otto is 'toot' spelled inside out" (p. 63).

In addition, Joan is now trying two expedients to restore the harmony of life she finds lacking in her marriage. The first is Yoga. Yoga is cited by de Rougemont as being one of the attempts to use Eros in order to escape out of life and return to the primal unity of the sexes by means of techniques seeking the abolition of individual consciousness (*Passion and Society,* p. 70). Joan laughs at Richard's suggestion that her Yoga instructor may be one of her lovers, but in his dream she says: "Well, I didn't think it counted if it was part of the exercise. The whole point, darley, is to make mind and body one" (p. 64).

Joan's second expedient is psychiatry. Psychiatry as the answer to the disorder caused by infidelity in marriage is very prominent in Updike's later stories. Alfred Schweigen in "The Music School" says of his wife: "She visits a psychiatrist because I am unfaithful to her. I do not understand the connection, but there seems to be one" (p. 187). Joan tells Richard she went to a psychiatrist because she "kept having these affairs," felt guilty, and needed to get rid of her guilt (p. 63). The solution proposed by psychoanalysis, namely, getting rid of the sense of guilt, disturbs Richard on the deepest level. In his dream, he questions Joan as to why she assented to adultery. The answer of his dream-wife is this: "It's hard, when men ask. You mustn't insult their male nature. There's a harmony in everything" (p. 64). His real wife, confessing her affairs in the dark bedroom, had earlier said that she told him about herself so "he wouldn't feel guilty about this Vogel person" (p. 63).

Only a person in the dark, Updike seems to suggest, would think that adult guilt can be cast off by trying to return to a childish innocence, to that unconscious state in which Eros simply is a part

angel" (*PF,* p. 171); "The Lucid Eye in Silvertown" (*AP,* pp. 188, 194, 199); and *The Centaur* (p. 85).

of our nature that must be allowed to express itself without involving moral judgment and responsible decision. This order, indeed, rules in the animal world. The pets Esther and Hecuba are automatically deprived of their queenly state by being spayed. By contrast, Penelope loses regal dignity by deferring to suitors because they are "pros" in the service of Eros. In the time of Ulysses, the suitors of Queen Penelope were dealt with as rebels who deserved no mercy.

Sinking back into pre-moral unconsciousness, then, is no answer to the problem of guilt. In a waking world, the sexual tongue of Eros Rampant can never reach the ceiling. Throughout the story the image of water, the unconscious element, conveys this message. As the center of love for her children, Joan is a fish swimming in a natural element. But the children are already growing up, ceasing to live wholly in this element. Penelope, the adult seeking to turn back to the *black* element, allows her lover to pull her for miles through the sea, and gains from the experience merely sadness and perpetual cold. In their dark bedroom, Joan and Richard seem to be in an aquarium where they "are swimming, dark fish in ink, their outlines barely visible, known to each other only as eddies of warmth, as mysterious animate chasms on the surface of space" (p. 63). In this darkness, when Richard tells his wife that he is too pale to be accepted by Penelope as a lover, Joan answers with unaccustomed coarseness, "You look pale to me too, buster" (p. 62). At the same time, she kicks off her shoes — as though divesting herself of her adult human status. This is the darkness of male terror and female tears. Neither Richard's romantic quest for the pale moon of disembodied love, which deals cruelly with his actual partner, nor Joan's efforts to be kind to the male ego in order to achieve harmony with nature can make visible the outlines of their real situation.

Twice in the story Richard describes himself as "the watchman of the night" (pp. 60, 64). The biblical phrase comes from a prophecy of Isaiah beginning with the words, "The oracle concerning the wilderness of the sea" (Isa. 21:1), and containing the phrase, "And he cried, A lion" (21:8, King James Version; RSV, a marginal reading). It is a prophecy foretelling disaster:

> *Therefore my loins are filled with anguish.*
>
> *My mind reels, horror has appalled me;*
> *The twilight I longed for*
> *   has been turned for me into trembling.* (vv. 3-4)

This is precisely Richard's experience, when his "twilight" love for Penelope, romantically distant as the pale moon, is met with the appalling revelation by his wife that she has been unfaithful to him with actual men, known and unknown, and that she scorns his paleness. The story ends on Richard's uncertainty about the relation between his terrifying dream of the lion on the one hand and everyday reality on the other. The enigmatic prophecy of Isaiah brings no comfort:

> *"Watchman, what of the night?*
> *Watchman, what of the night?"*
> *The watchman says:*
> *"Morning comes, and also the*
> *night.*
> *If you will inquire, inquire;*
> *come back again." (21:11-12)*

Updike has drawn on this particular prophecy of Isaiah before.[9] Recently, it would seem, he has used imagery from both this chapter and the twentieth chapter in order to epitomize the leading traits of contemporary society. The earlier chapter tells of the dismay of those who shall be confounded "because of Ethiopia their hope and Egypt their boast" (20:5). We have seen how Joey Robinson in *Of the Farm* is linked, through his name and career, with Egypt. The man who wishes to possess and exploit expensive possessions is the man who has made Egypt his boast. In "Eros Rampant" Penelope puts her hope in the black man — in biblical terms, in Ethiopia. In *Couples,* Updike returns to show the fulfilment of Isaiah's prophecy. Although the dominant biblical references in this novel are drawn from elsewhere in the Old Testament, there is a strong echo of the following verse from Isaiah 21:

> For thus the Lord said to me, "Within a year, according to the years of a hireling, all the glory of Kedar will come to an end; and the remainder of the archers of the mighty men of the sons of Kedar will be few; for the Lord, the God of Israel, has spoken." (v. 16)

To this story we now turn. It occupies one year; it is a story about the breakup of a proud, affluent, athletic, Eros-centered community,[10] a story about judgment spoken from heaven.

---

9 "Snowing in Greenwich Village." See above, p. 59, footnote 6.

10 The "tents of Kedar" in the Bible signify blackness, and the community lives in *Tar*box.

14

COUPLES

THE ACTION OF COUPLES *EXTENDS FROM SPRING 1963* to Spring 1964. At one point in the novel, Mrs. Connie Roth remarks to her daughter Elizabeth Whitman that her book circle has been reading Greek mythology — "it seems to be the literary rage this year" (p. 276). The year 1963, of course, was when *The Centaur* was published.

Couples, published early in 1968, gives every indication of having chimed in with the literary rage of its own year even more spectacularly than did *The Centaur* in· 1963. The sophisticated sex-novel apparently was the "in" thing then. *Time* magazine, which some months earlier had run a cover story on the Sexual Revolution, quickly issued a cover story on Updike. Though less than enthusiastic about *Couples* as a piece of literature, and calling it a novel "flawed by overwriting and undercharacterization," the article was unequivocal on the matter of its relevance. It stated: "Updike has taken a particularly American theme, and a highly topical one."[1] Evidently, the public agreed on the question of topicality. *Couples* rose rapidly in the best-seller list and stayed on the list for the whole year. But once again, Updike's surface naturalism has attracted all the attention, leading almost always to the simplistic identification of his theme with his literal subject matter.

Updike's theme remains constant: earth seen in relation to heaven. Only the focus changes. And Updike's technique remains consistent also. Like Kierkegaard, he is adept at indirect communication. Kierkegaard explains that if a writer wishes to talk about religion to those who are immersed in the aesthetic sphere, then the neces-

---

[1] *Time,* April 26, 1968, p. 62.

sary approach is to say: "Let us talk about aesthetics." Updike, in
effect, says: "You think the Sexual Revolution to be highly topical
and a particularly American theme? Well, let's talk about it." This
— directly — he proceeds to do through the four hundred and
fifty-eight pages of *Couples,* and the critics make comments about
the author's self-indulgence and his lack of serious purpose or
sense of responsibility. Meanwhile, the book sells, having been
labeled "the thinking man's *Peyton Place."* Kierkegaard, in his day,
complained that the public took in its right hand what he held out
with his left.

The focus of *Couples* is wider than that of any other of Updike's
works since *The Poorhouse Fair.* As he did in his first novel, so
once more he analyzes the direction in which American society
is moving. His expedient is that of describing a representative part
of American society. In both novels, he has chosen a small group
existing as a self-contained entity in relative isolation from the
larger world of which it forms a part. In *Couples,* however, the action
is not set in the future but is pinpointed in the past. In this respect,
Couples resembles *The Centaur.* It re-creates a patch of Massachusetts in 1963, where *The Centaur* re-created a patch of Pennsylvania
in 1946. Sometimes today the year of John Kennedy's assassination
seems a closed chapter in history, almost as distant from us as
1946. Yet it remains part of our living present. Updike displays
this double perspective in his picture of a little society made up
of ten married couples living in Tarbox, a New England town located thirty miles south of Boston. By the end of the novel the
couples have broken up. But new combinations are forming, and
the middle-class pattern of life in America goes on, modified in
detail, yet essentially the same.

Sex is prominent — virtually omnipresent — in *Couples;* the
topic apparently dominates the conversation, thought, and actions
of the ten Tarbox couples. Nevertheless, *Couples* is not in the least
a sex-novel. Its purpose is neither to celebrate nor to denigrate
sexuality, though it is true that many of the features of the analysis
of Eros which have occupied such a prominent place in Updike's
later short stories are to be seen here. The whole book finds its
focus in precisely that aspect of life which the critics generally have
accused Updike of failing to be concerned about: the social consequences of individual beliefs and choices. As in *The Poorhouse
Fair,* so here Updike asks the question: "How fares America now?"
And, even more pointedly than in his first novel, he gives the answer in terms of accounts left unsettled, talents buried in the ground
of this world, and lines of division ignored until it is too late to
escape judgment.

Couples also continues the argument of *The Centaur* concerning the need to recognize the moral government of the universe. In the earlier novel Peter Caldwell asks his father whether one can steer by Venus rather than by the hard-to-find North Star. *Couples* tells what happens when such an attempt is made, when "few living mortals cast their eyes respectfully toward heaven, and fewer still sit as students to the stars" (*TC*, p. 299). It tells how choosing of pleasure rather than justice leads to slavery instead of freedom. Those who refuse to acknowledge Zeus the All-Ruler find themselves to be puppets in the hands of Chance and Fate.

Technically regarded, *Couples* is the most ambitious of Updike's novels. The lives of the ten couples are linked in an intricate pattern, each involving all the rest. These lives are then taken into the larger pattern of America under the Kennedy dynasty. The private kingdom of marriage is seen to derive its color from the Ruling House. Tarbox society is shown to be the conscious articulation of American values, and thus a microcosm of the whole of Western civilization. Furthermore, behind the complex exterior action, Updike places an equally complex structure of biblical parallelism. The internal action is the announcement of an apocalyptic Day of the Lord, one which comes as darkness and not as light (Amos 5:18), bringing judgment upon individuals and upon nations. Prophecies from both the Old Testament and the New are interlaced and woven into the narrative. It is an ironical comment upon the quality of our educated consciousness that so many critics of *Couples* should think that Updike has written a superficial sex-novel and then dressed it up with a few "pretentious" allegorical motifs. The irony of the situation is the more complete in that Updike has built into his story indications that those who most pride themselves upon being the heirs and interpreters of Western culture are the very people least able to understand the living voice of that culture. These are prodigal sons who chew the dried husks of the wisdom inherited from the past and remain with empty bellies.

* * *

There are two epigraphs to *Couples*. The first is from Paul Tillich:[2]

> There is a tendency in the average citizen, even if he has a high standing in his profession, to consider the decisions relating to the life of the society to which he belongs as a matter of fate on which he has no influence — like the Roman subjects all over the world in the period of the Roman Empire, a mood favorable to the re-

---

[2] *The Future of Religions*, ed. Jerald C. Brauer (New York, 1966), p. 50.

surgence of religion but unfavorable for the preservation of a living democracy.

This quotation is from an essay entitled "The Effects of Space Exploration on Man's Condition." Typically, Updike does not mention the title of this essay or draw attention to the context of the quotation, a context concerning the ideal of education in the West and the deficiencies of that education. Space travel, so Tillich argues, is the logical extension of Renaissance man's concentration upon the *horizontal* exploration of the world. It leaves unsatisfied man's need for a *vertical* or spiritual understanding of the cosmos as a place of ultimate meaning and value. In a society concerned to master the physical universe through a union of scientific research and technological innovation there arises an aristocracy of a few specialists standing apart from the mass of the people. The masses remain entirely dependent upon a knowledge in which they cannot share. There results a vacuum of meaning in everyday life. This, in turn, leads to the tendency to accept fatalistically whatever changes in the shape of our lives the experts may decree for us.[3]

Already in *The Poorhouse Fair* Updike has used the parallel between the Roman Empire and modern America. Hook speaks of both as ages of prosperity and perversity, and this same fatal combination is thoroughly documented in *Couples*.

The second epigraph seems to belong to another world from the first, yet it has underground connections with it through the Rome-America parallel. It comes from Alexander Blok's poem "The Scythians":[4]

> *We love the flesh; its tastes, its tones,*
> *Its charnel odor, breathed through Death's jaws . . . .*
> *Are we to blame if your fragile bones*
> *Should crack beneath our heavy, gentle paws?*

A byword for cruelty, the Scythians were nevertheless praised by Horace for their simplicity, as contrasted with the effeteness of the "civilized" world. The same contrast is used in the poem by Blok, poet of the Russian Revolution; the Scythians stand explicitly for

---

[3] Often this fatalistic attitude is directed towards the process of history itself. In an essay entitled "God and the Spirit of Man," Martin Buber makes this comment: "It is a modern superstition that the character of an age acts as fate for the next. One lets it prescribe what is possible to do and hence what is permitted. One surely cannot swim against the stream, one says" (*Eclipse of God* [New York, 1957], p. 129).

[4] *An Anthology of Russian Literature in the Soviet Period from Gorki to Pasternak*, ed. and trans. by Bernard Guilbert Guerney (New York, 1960), p. 27.

the destructive yet cleansing power of the East destined to succeed the decadent West.

The apocalyptic reference of the second epigraph is reinforced by the biblical significance of "Scythian." In the New Testament the name means simply "barbarian" (Col. 3:11), while in the Old Testament the coming of the Scythians is taken to be a punishment of God signifying the arrival of the terrible "Day of the Lord" (Jer. 1:11-19; Zeph. *passim*). Between the two epigraphs, then, Updike tells his readers that in *Couples* he is presenting the weakness of Western civilization, which, like its Roman predecessor, may fall before a barbarian invader. *Couples* exhibits a trivial society, given over to luxury and to playing games to pass the time — especially the game of tempting fate (p. 288). Moreover, because of the intimate connection between Eros and Thanatos, symbolically this society has already welcomed the barbarian within the gates. Opting for a new religion of Eros instead of strengthening its democratic institutions, it feeds upon cruelty, deceit, and self-destruction. When the Day of the Lord comes, it is likely to find itself totally unprepared.

In all this, there is no frantic despair to be heard in Updike's warning, which is simply the voice of the "watchman."[5] Updike evidently believes that we have not yet entirely lost contact with the wisdom of the past. This wisdom, which is rooted in the Judeo-Christian faith, still persists in the soul of America. It persists today through national virtues that live on, though they are gravely weakened. The root question is this: are we aware enough of our needs to have the virtue (*virtus,* courage) to repossess our heritage?

The challenge facing contemporary America is presented by the local situation existing in Tarbox. The town epitomizes American history. It is not only connected physically to pre-Revolutionary days, through its seventeenth-century saltbox houses and its eighteenth-century farmhouses; but also, through the bones buried in Indian Hill, it is linked to the very origins of America. Updike's first story about Tarbox, indeed, is called "The Indian." It tells how the oldest inhabitant of Tarbox remembers, from her girlhood days, the Indian who, nameless and ageless, loiters perpetually in the center of the town — "And he is no older now than he was then" (*MS,* p. 17). He remains forever, watching and knowing all.

The ten couples around whom *Couples* is written are all recent arrivals in Tarbox. Commuters to Boston began to settle in the quiet town after the Second World War. The last survivor of the

---

[5] The prophecy in Jeremiah concerning the Scythians is preceded by God's announcement that He is "watching over ... [His] word to perform it" (Jer. 1:12).

original Tarbox family (an old lady who lives in rooms lined with unbroken rows of *National Geographics* dating from the first issue of 1888) is taken to the hospital before the novel ends, and her house is converted into offices. But the couples themselves, varied as they are in their ethnic and regional backgrounds, represent a cross-section of modern upper-middle-class America.

The central figure is Piet Hanema, a Michigan-born son of Dutch-speaking parents whose livelihood was raising greenhouse plants. Most of the action of the book is seen through his eyes. Just as *The Poorhouse Fair* was concerned with the soul of America, its *anima,* so *Couples* shows what is happening now to the American *anima* (Hanema) when the ties binding man to the soil and to family traditions have been almost universally broken. Social groupings have become in our day entirely a matter of personal choice. Not only do Americans now decide where they shall live and with whom, but they also make up the rules of social living as they go along, received codes of behavior having become a dead letter.

Piet Hanema, however, is still a believer in rules and codes; and this prevents him from being an intruder into the historical tradition which is Tarbox. He is a carpenter, a carpenter in love with the rules of his craft. So he has a community of feeling with the old carpenters whose work lives on around him. In particular he is at home in the old Congregational Church, the fourth church to be built on the original site of Tarbox's first meetinghouse. At the beginning of the book Piet is the one Protestant among the couples who continues to worship, for the memory of the Calvinistic God of the Dutch Reformed Church in which he was raised has not been extinguished. Thus the American *anima* is not wholly cut off from its roots. But the hold is precarious. Piet ceases his church-going before the book is over.

Insofar as *Couples* is the story of Piet Hanema it is the story of the temptation and fall of an individual soul — and of the soul of a nation — through turning away to strange gods. The physical adultery recorded in the story line refers, at a deeper level, to the spiritual adultery of apostasy against which the Old Testament prophets raised their voices. As Jeremiah cried:

> *Has a nation changed its gods,*
> *even though they are no gods?*
> *But my people have changed their*
> *glory*
> *for that which does not profit.*
> *Be appalled, O heavens, at this,*
> *be shocked, be utterly desolate,*
> *says the Lord.* (Jer. 2:11-12)

What a culture finds shocking is a sure indication of its values. It is noteworthy that there has been a great deal of discussion about whether or not the frankness of Updike's language in *Couples* passes over into obscenity, but very little about the use to which his language is put in showing how the glory of a people can pass over into desolation.

*   *   *

Of the ten men of the couples, two belong to the scientific intellectual aristocracy that Tillich declares to be the controlling agency of our Space Age culture. A third is connected with it. However, only one man is a really prominent member of this elite: John Ong, a nuclear physicist working at M.I.T. Ong is a Korean, while his wife Bernadette (met and married in America) is a product of American fusions. By origin a Euro-Asian, Bernadette is by destiny an American and a Catholic. Ong himself is indifferent to religious belief. The new aristocrats, so Tillich explains, are isolated from the rest of the community because of the extreme specialization of their training. Updike puts this spiritual isolation into physical terms. Although "in love with everything American from bubble chambers to filtered cigarettes" (p. 187), Ong speaks in broken English which no one except his wife understands. And his use of filtered cigarettes does not prevent him from contracting cancer. He dies, a symbol of the fate of "backward" cultures exposed to a Western technology that they can master readily enough, but only at the cost of self-destruction.

The second member of the scientific aristocracy is Ken Whitman, an assistant professor at the University of Boston. Handsome and fastidious, the only son of a successful Hartford lawyer, he is a biochemist who at the age of thirty-two has reached almost a dead-end in his particular line of research. The discoveries of two Japanese scientists have destroyed his prospects of eminence in his chosen field. Being a family man with responsibilities, he cannot start retraining in another area. "He had overreached. Life, whose graceful secrets he would have unlocked, pressed into him clumsily" (p. 95).

The isolated and isolating nature of scientific research stressed by Tillich is thus pictured by Updike on two different levels. John Ong typifies the secular-scientific cultural pattern that obliterates national cultures and destroys traditional religions. Ken Whitman typifies the effects upon the individual of serving the "magnetic Harvard gods" (p. 43). He has learned about life as science knows it until concrete existence has ceased to have much meaning. Ken cannot share his work with his wife. Elizabeth Whitman, known

by her nickname Foxy, has resented having to put off having children during the seven years Ken has taken for his doctorate and
post-doctorate research. She thinks of Ken as being cold, and sees
herself "in terms of a suppressed warmth" (p. 41).

Ken's coldness is not chiefly, as his wife supposes, a selfish complacency. He is rather a *white man,* both in conforming to the pattern of a "waspish" society and in being conditioned by his scientific training to think in terms of rational control. Consequently,
he is insensitive to the "dark" side of life. In practical matters he
is guided largely by the sense of law which he has gained from his
father. Foxy's mother (a worldly-wise woman who had divorced
Foxy's father and made an advantageous second marriage) understands the situation well enough. She tells her daughter: "He's like
your father, he needs a form for everything. But, within the rules,
I think he's remarkable. He's worth treasuring" (p. 282). Mr. Fox,
incidentally, had been a career navy man, on retirement taking a
lucrative job in the shipbuilding industry. Ken is basically a careerist
also, conditioned to live by inherited codes the justification for
which he never thinks of questioning. This inflexibility and un-
imaginativeness infuriates Foxy who, on hearing him in conversation use the phrase "the kingdom of life," asks herself: "Who did
he think was king?" (p. 34).

Ben Saltz is only on the fringe of the scientific aristocracy. He
"miniaturizes" electronic components, and thus is a technician rather
than a scientist. As a Jew he is also on the edge of a theoretically
"open" American society. He and his wife Irene are dropped from
the charmed circle of the Tarbox couples when Ben loses his job
and so is unable to afford to entertain his fairweather friends. It is
as though, like John Ong, he were "mortally diseased" (p. 254).
The Saltzes are drawn to the Constantines, who appear to the other
couples as appealingly dangerous and amoral. Eddie Constantine, an
airline pilot, is a one-time Catholic, though his wife Carol is a
"wasp" — an ex-Presbyterian. A "delicate social line" (p. 226)
separates these two couples from the others.

The core of the Tarbox group is made up of businessmen and
their wives. Roger Guerin is so wealthy he goes to Boston "mostly
to have lunch and play squash" (p. 25). He and his childless wife
Bea live in one of the old saltbox houses so perfectly restored that
it looks rawly new. Harold Smith and Frank Appleby, in securities,
are nearly as well-off. Their wives, Marcia and Janet, though, have
children to look after while their husbands are in Boston. Lower
on the social scale are the Gallaghers. As practicing Catholics they
are also somewhat on the edge of the couples, which may account
for the fact that the Constantines see much of them after the Saltzes

are dropped. Matthew Gallagher manages the Tarbox building firm in which he has taken Piet Hanema as a working "partner." His wife Terry dresses artily, plays the lute, and takes pottery lessons. Carol Constantine shares Terry's musical tastes and also paints coarse oils.

Piet Hanema is accepted in Tarbox because his wife Angela "had been a Hamilton" from nearby Nun's Bay (p. 12). He is the only man in the group who works with his hands. In effect, he is little more than a hired man. Yet he had hoped once to be an architect. His parents' death in a car accident in 1949 put an end to his studies at Michigan State, since there was a younger brother to be set up in business. During the Korean war he met Matt Gallagher, who offered him his present position. The misfortune of having been forced to abandon a dream links him, rather oddly, with the one individual in the group whom he thoroughly dislikes — Freddy Thorne the dentist. Although Freddy, who has his practice in Tarbox, is the only professional man among them, he too has been disappointed in his hopes of a career. Starting out to study medicine with the expectation of being a psychiatrist, Freddy was forced by lack of ability to accept dentistry as a second best. Because of this experience, perhaps, he now works hard to make himself the leader of the group; and in this, in spite of his conspicuous lack of charm, he largely succeeds. As Foxy Whitman guesses when she first comes to Tarbox, Freddy's "being despised served as a unifying purpose for the others, gave them a common identity, as the couples that tolerated Freddy" (p. 32). Freddy Thorne's technique is to voice outrageous opinions — such as disliking Ben Saltz for being a Jew — which the couples can repudiate openly and secretly endorse.

To find any more rational explanation than Foxy's for the cohesiveness of the Tarbox couples is not easy. They are all educated married people who, by the fact of having chosen the same small town to live in, have evidenced somewhat similar tastes. Janice Appleby explains to Foxy that the attraction of Tarbox is that there are no country clubs or servants — "it's so *much* more luxurious to live *simply*" (p. 25). A preference for an elegant simplicity certainly applies as well to the Smiths and the Guerins, who also came to Tarbox in the middle fifties (the Guerins somewhat earlier) and gradually dissociated themselves from an older group of wealthy couples who rode horses, kept servants, and affected a conventional style of "gracious living." Education, however, is the most important bond. Most of the couples are university graduates, making those who are not (Janice Appleby, for instance) feel continually on the defensive. Being married was originally a purely practical bond, allowing the families to arrange their parties and outings at times and places mutually convenient. But, as things turn out, it is the fact of being a group of males and females officially paired that gives specific reason for these very different people to continue to seek one another's company.

The couples are brought together by separate choice converging upon a common center. They stay together because of a common consent, one operating somewhat after the pattern of Rousseau's General Will. "Duty and work yielded as ideals to truth and fun. Virtue was no longer sought in temple or market place but in the home — one's own home, and then the homes of one's friends" (p. 106).

Following the ideals of truth and fun can be viewed, from one angle, as starting a new religion; while, from another angle, it means simply playing a new game. In the Spring of 1963, at the time when the old religion of Christianity celebrates its most central mysteries, the faithful of the new religion are gathered together to perform the new rites, the players of the new game are in their places. A year later they disperse. The ritual has been enacted, the game has been played and the score added up.

*   *   *

Updike tells us that the "final ecology" of the couples was not established until 1958, when Hanema and Gallagher set up their office in Tarbox. Then a continuous round of sports gave the group "an inexhaustible excuse for gathering" (p. 108). In May 1962 Frank Appleby and Marcia Smith started meeting secretly. When the other couples learned of this, truth and fun took on a new meaning. Their games branched out into psychological guessing games over which Freddy Thorne, the least athletic among them, presided as "gamesmaster." "Exposure was, in the games Freddy invented, the danger. The danger and the fruit" (p. 240). Not all the game-playing was formal. The most important way of following the ideal of truth and fun was through in-group gossip about adultery among the couples. "You may tell one other person," Bea Guerin tells Piet, "those are the rules" (p. 316).

There was no lack of opportunity to play the gossip-game. When Janet Appleby found proof of her husband's liaison with Marcia Smith she took Harold Smith as her lover. She had always felt that Marcia's college education had given her an unfair advantage. The other couples, delighted, began to call the foursome the Applesmiths. When a similar situation developed between the Saltzes and the Constantines (rumored to be homosexual as well as heterosexual), they were promptly named the Saltines. The pattern, once established, seemed to offer opportunity for kaleidoscopic shifts and realignments. Piet Hanema started an affair with Georgene, Freddy Thorne's wife.

And soon the couples were talking about his wife and Freddy Thorne.
Fun mattered more than truth.

All this, however, we learn in retrospect. The novel opens with the
welcome given to the Whitmans, the new people whose coming
is to lead to the dissolution of the little society within a year. The
sequence is as follows. Piet, called in to advise about repairs to
the Whitman house, turns to Foxy as a change from Georgene.
The fact that Foxy is pregnant lends allure to their love-making.
After the birth of the Whitmans' son in October 1963, Piet wishes
to discontinue their association. He now has taken up with Bea
Guerin. However, one unguarded encounter, intended to be a farewell, leaves Foxy pregnant with his child. Through Freddy Thorne
an abortion is successfully planned and carried out. Gossip among
the couples, all the same, finally reaches Ken Whitman. Foxy confesses and Ken insists upon a divorce. Angela's reaction is to
banish Piet from the home. Although Foxy says that she does not
wish Piet to feel bound to her, she marries him after Angela gets
her divorce. The new Mrs. Hanema and her husband move to Lexington, "where, gradually, among people like themselves," they are
accepted "as another couple" (p. 458). In Tarbox a new set of
younger couples has already taken over.

For readers who expect dramatic events and the clash of "interesting" personalities, Updike's plot, as usual, has little to offer. The
way into his theme is always through the imagery, which provides
the justification for the story line, not vice versa.

To take a single small example, more than one reviewer of
Couples has singled out as a sample of Updike's stylistic precious-
ness his description of a plate of consommé as "the shallow amber
depths where the lemon slice like an embryo swayed" (p. 26).
Now were these words about any plate of soup, the complaint might
be justified. But in fact they describe what Foxy sees when she
and Ken are at a dinner party at the Guerins. This is a few days
after the party given to welcome them to Tarbox. The Hanemas
are not present. Blushing because she has inadvertently let slip the
fact that she is pregnant, Foxy turns her eyes downward to her plate
in order to escape the mockery of the couples. She sees the lemon
slice in the soup as an embryo because of the nagging of physical
discomfort caused by the fact that her first pregnancy at twenty-
eight has proved unexpectedly burdensome. But her blushes are
also prophetic of her next pregnancy, when the couples will again
mock her, and more cruelly. The embryo in the soup she sees seems
to be swaying. This time it will sway towards life, but the next time
it will be pulled towards death. Soon Freddy Thorne, who is sitting
next to her at the table, is whispering confidentially, "Tummy

trouble?" — as though even now informing her that he is an expert in getting rid of trouble of that sort and she may need his help. But Foxy is also aware of the lemon slice apart from its resemblance to an embryo. Lemon is also *leman* — lover. When she summons Piet to repair her house she will welcome him in lemon-colored clothes and serve him lemonade. At the moment she has seen him only once. Nevertheless, over this table she asks questions about him, preparing the chain of events that will bring them together. It seems all very accidental. Foxy, however, has been looking at soup that is amber, the color of passion. Her own eyes are amber. Piet's hair is amber. The two ambers are to mingle, and then both will be "in the soup."

The coming of the Whitmans as the "new couple" is the natural starting point for the novel because, as the image of the embryo indicates, Foxy brings with her a capacity for life disruptive of the principles upon which Tarbox's little society operates. The Tarbox culture is a sterile one. "The men had stopped having careers and the women had stopped having babies. Liquor and love were left" (p. 12). It is not an accident that this retreat from work and childbearing represents a denial of God's words to the first couple after the Fall. Adam was told then that he must henceforth eat bread in the sweat of his face, and Eve that she must bring forth children in sorrow (Gen. 3:16-19).

Piet's relationship with Georgene Thorne at the beginning of the story illustrates the assumption current among the couples that they have escaped from the consequences of the Fall and have found a way back to Eden. When Piet first went with Georgene and raised the question of contraception, she asked him whether Angela did not use Enovid and laughingly said, *"Welcome to the post-pill paradise"* (p. 52). Here Updike, by putting Georgene's words into italics and by repeating the phrase later in the book (p. 311), follows his usual practice of giving the reader a clue to one of his central images. The belief that we can reenter Paradise is equivalent to the conviction that life can be painless and that our acts carry no fatal consequences. It is as though the fruit of the Tree of the Knowledge of Good and Evil were still untasted and as though mankind still lived in the Garden shaded by the Tree of Life. By taking Piet as her lover, Georgene felt that she had been brought word "of a world where vegetation was heraldic and every woman was some man's queen" (p. 384). Incidentally, William Blake's water-color drawing of "Adam and Eve Sleeping," reproduced on the dust-jacket of *Couples,* supports the reference to heraldic vegetation. Blake portrays the King and Queen of Eden asleep amid formalized flowers and trees, a crescent moon shining down upon the royal couple. But between the guiltless sleep of Adam and Eve in Eden and the furtive meetings between Piet and Georgene in Tarbox there is, after all, a world of difference.

Nevertheless, the appeal of Georgene for Piet lies precisely in her belief in life without guilt. She is described as looking like a Renaissance boy and also as having eyes like those of a Roman portrait bust. Temperamentally she is a pagan, one who in Kierkegaard's terms is not yet awakened to moral consciousness and to the knowledge of guilt that accompanies it. Her love-making is "guileless" and with "the directness of eating, the ease of running" (p. 52). When Piet makes a joke about her not being able to "fall" without him, she replies confidently that she's "not so fallen." She is the best tennis player among the couples, free and forceful. And she worships the sun — "my sun," she claims. When she invites Piet to make love to her on the sunporch above the garage of the Thorne house, he asks: "Won't we embarrass God?" Her answer is: "Haven't you heard, God's a woman. Nothing embarrasses Her" (p. 54). To Georgene both Apollo and Venus are equally divine, to be served in turn or together as the opportunity arises.

But Georgene learns that post-pill paradise is an illusion when Piet leaves her for Foxy. Yet disappointment does not sour her. The corruption that eats away the spirit of others who take the road of adultery does not affect her robustly natural nature. She travels light through life, even in winter scorning to wear a coat, and after this one affair she turns back to sport and to the care of her children. Piet and Foxy follow a far more devious route, one that rises higher and plunges deeper than any known by the pagan consciousness.

* * *

When we first meet Piet, he and Angela are undressing in the bedroom of their eighteenth-century farmhouse home. They have been married for nine years. Piet's chest shows "its cruciform blazon of amber hair" (p. 7). So we know that Piet is both passionate and marked with the sign of a Christian. Angela undresses behind the closet door, which her husband kicks open, disclosing her where "like Eve on a portal she crouched in shame" (p. 10). Her shame, as they both stand naked facing each other, shows that the time is after the Fall. The portal of Paradise has been closed behind them.

Piet feels "with Angela, a superior power seeking through her to employ him" (p. 4). The literal reference is to Angela's father, who employed him to build a pergola at the Hamilton house in Nun's Bay when he was first out of the army and who, after his marriage to Angela, threw business his way. His father-in-law's home had been full of clocks. This identification of Angela's father with the measurement of time makes him a "superior power" — he is even called omnipotent (p. 211) — and explains Angela's fondness for the stars. His wife's presence reminds Piet continually of the fact that the earth is set under the government of heaven. With her in the bedroom during the opening scene of the book Piet is aware of the April night as "a blackness charged with the ache of first growth and the suspended skeletons of Virgo and Leo and Gemini" (p. 10). The human meaning of that moment is revealed to him. In the sky are the emblems of Angela, himself, and their two daughters; and the rising lust he feels within his flesh keeps time with nature's clock. April is the cruelest month, according to T. S. Eliot. Angela tells her husband that he is a bully, "so cruel."

Angela, indeed, is what Piet frequently calls her: *his angel.* Just as Georgene is wholly of the natural world, so Angela is not of it. "Touch Angela, she vanished. Touch Georgene, she was there" (p. 48). Piet's angel brings him messages from heaven. She warns him often of the sickness inherent in their way of life. Speaking of Tarbox, she tells him: "I don't know how to act in this sexpot." When Piet replies that a sexpot is a person, not a place, she retorts: "This one's a place. Get me out or get me a doctor" (p. 210). Her intuition has seized on the corporate evil of their society, one more powerful than the individuals within it. After the exposure of his affair with Foxy, Piet begs: "Don't make me leave you. You're what guards my soul. I'll be damned eternally" (p. 406). But Angela cannot help him, since he refuses to take the path of repentance. A moment later he is ready to strike her. Even angels are powerless to deal with the soul that is hardened through self-will.

After the divorce, Angela returns to her father. She has no place in a fallen world. During the scene in which Ken Whitman calls Piet and her to confront them with his knowledge of Foxy's adultery and abortion, Angela drinks five-star Cognac from a Flintstone jelly tumbler. This is all that the sophisticated culture of Tarbox can provide, its nearest equivalent to the gift of the spirit and the wisdom of the stars. In such conditions Angela resembles Matthew Arnold's beautiful and ineffectual angel, beating in the void [her] luminous wings in vain. On the way back from the confrontation she kneels down in the car and flails her arms and head in a paroxism of futile grief.

Tarbox, so Updike insists again and again, is the fallen world. Kissing Georgene, on the *tar*paper roof of the sunporch, Piet notices a freckle beside her ear. He thinks: "Seed. Among thorns. Fallen" (p. 48).

This reference to the parable of the Sower (Mark 4:7) invites the reader to think of other biblical references to thorns. The first is after the Fall, when God lays down the future conditions of life for the first couple. Cursing the ground, God says: "Thorns and thistles it shall bring forth to you" (Gen. 3:18). As is only to be expected, therefore, Freddy Thorne is already established in Tarbox when the first couples move in. As Piet sees him, Freddy is his evil angel just as Angela is his good angel. Although the novel does not state the obvious, Piet must know St. Paul's words, "a thorn in the flesh, a messenger of Satan to harass me" (II Cor. 12:7), and must apply them, literally, to Freddy. Sitting in church, he recalls his fear of this man "with his hyena appetite for dirty truths," thinking how through his adultery with Freddy's wife he has "placed himself in bondage to him" (p. 21).

The Thorne in the flesh is, unlike Angela, very much at home in a fallen world. His talk is invariably obscene, blasphemous, and cruel. Beside his bed he keeps a collection of pornographic literature. And yet, in a sense, he is not of the world. His interests are wholly spiritual. His work simply confirms him in his belief that the whole of nature is polluted and decaying and that earthly existence is one desperate and futile effort to postpone death. His preoccupation with the idea of sex springs from a conviction that sexuality is the sole distinguishing mark of humanity and the only refuge from despair. For the sex act itself, as distinct from the idea of it, he has little taste or aptitude. Physically, the distinguishing marks of animality are lacking in him. He loses his hair early, and he appears to have no teeth. Because he is drawn to spirituality, he is deeply attracted to Angela; while she, for her part, talks to him in preference to any of the others.

Angela's finding pleasure in Freddy Thorne's company infuriates and puzzles Piet. He himself, the *carnal* man's prototype, despises the other for his lack of animal spirits, while he fears him because, as he tells Angela, "he threatens my primitive faith" (p. 304). Although Piet offers this explanation for feeling threatened by Freddy Thorne as a lie to avoid confessing his involvement with Georgene, it is actually more the truth than the explanation he wants to hide. During a basketball game he intentionally knocks down the dentist, breaking his little finger. This public injury, symbolizing Piet's having made Freddy Thorne a cuckold, calls for retribution. Freddy takes his revenge by making the price of Foxy's abortion a night in bed with Angela. Freddy gains nothing from it personally, except "the nausea of disillusion" when he discovers that under her clothes Angela harbors "the same voracious spread of flesh as other women" (p. 369). Her white skin feels to him "dark," "oily," and "Negroid." He sleeps beside her through the night, but never attempts to possess her, although she offers herself. He is amazed that she should do so. Her unabashed reply is: "He told me I should do it. The Hamiltons are always obedient wives" (p. 368).

Angela, of course, has no fear of Freddy because his diabolism can make no impression upon her, and she sees the essential other-worldliness of the man. Freddy has made himself believe that the couples are a church, a "magic circle of heads to keep the night out" (p. 7). He tells the couples: "We're all here to *humanize* each other . . . . We're a subversive cell. Like in the catacombs. Only they were trying to break out of hedonism. We're trying to break back into it. It's not easy" (p. 148). His "sad lewdness" stirs the couples to further sexual experimentation, as he expects it to do. (The night of his speech about humanizing, Frank and Harold exchange wives openly for the first time.) This is because, already corrupted inwardly, they are looking for an excuse to progress in evil. But when Freddy, in bed with Angela, expounds his theories of the need for a new religion in the time between the death and the rebirth of gods, Angela simply becomes drowsy and falls asleep. The tone of his voice reminds her of "the sterile mild preachiness descended from the pilgrims" which she had heard so often in the past in her father's house. In sleep, angel and fallen angel "parallel, floated toward dawn, their faces slacker than children" (p. 372).

The picture of Freddy and Angela sleeping peacefully together reminds us that though spiritual good and evil cannot mix, yet they can co-exist. It is in the ambiguous realm where flesh and spirit mingle that the two forces are locked in conflict. The life of the couples in Tarbox, and the progressive deterioration of their ideals of "truth and fun," witness to the truth that no coupling of man and woman can bring happiness or restore humanity to paradise, since the essential relationship man must find is the right relationship of flesh to spirit within each individual. Men and women can simply be partners in this quest, to help or to hinder.

* * *

The April opening of Couples, as we have noted, is partly reminiscent of the opening lines of Eliot's *The Waste Land* in their stress upon the cruelty of the month:

> *April is the cruellest month, breeding*
> *Lilacs out of the dead land, mixing*
> *Memory and desire, stirring*
> *Dull roots with spring rain.*

Piet certainly experiences the mixing of memory and desire as he gets into bed and lies down beside Angela on the night after the party to welcome the Whitmans, the new couple. Images of his parents' death alternate in his wakeful mind with images of his adolescent awakening to sexuality, of Bea Guerin at the party telling him she knows about his affair with Georgene and inviting him to sleep with her, and of his five-year-old daughter Nancy's present preoccupation with death. The fact that spring in Tarbox brings no promise of a true renewal of life is what weighs on Piet's mind, keeping sleep at bay. Angela sleeps, as always, deeply and easily, awakening with no memory of her dreams. Piet is haunted by two thoughts that "in the perspective of the night loomed as dreadful: soon he must begin building ranch houses on Indian Hill, and Angela wanted no more children" (p. 14).

During their night together Angela tells Freddy: "Piet spends all his energy defying death, and you spend all yours accepting it" (p. 370). Defying death is Piet's self-imposed task because, like his daughter Nancy, he has never been able to reconcile himself to this intruder into life. Physically, he radiates life. Short and agile, he displays the orange of passion in his flaming hair and in an apricot windbreaker which he constantly wears during working hours. But Tarbox has surrounded him with death. The fact that he will never have a son is connected now in his night reverie with having to carry out "greedy" Gallagher's plan for making money by building on Indian Hill homes for those who will play with life rather than walk through it like men. The town once boasted a hosiery mill. It has been turned into a factory manufacturing plastic toys. Piet's creative powers, whether as a father or as a carpenter, are redundant in this artificial society.

Foxy Whitman is impressed similarly with the sterility of Tarbox. We are introduced to her at the dinner party where she sees the embryo in the soup. The hosts are the Guerins, a sterile couple. It is Easter Eve and they dine off pascal lamb, underdone. Instead of grace "there was the tacit refusal that has evolved, a brief bump of silence they all held their breaths through" (p. 25). In this society where the resurrection season is remembered only by slices of lamb eaten without thanks returned to heaven, nothing is done right.

Foxy is an Episcopalian. Her admission that she attends church causes Freddy Thorne to pronounce her a neurotic, with Piet. Her church-going, like Piet's, is a bond with the past; though in her case it is an attempt to bring back memories that have been shattered by her parents' divorce. She associates Episcopalianism with the social pattern of her father's naval career and his pride in family connections. Although Piet saw her at the welcome party, he remembered her only indistinctly afterwards, apart from her amber eyes — "Eyes the brown of brushed fur backed by gold" (p. 13). He first notices her properly as she leaves Tarbox's Episcopalian Church on Palm

Sunday. He himself is standing outside the Congregational Church holding limply in his hand "the frond welcoming Jesus into Jerusalem" (p. 23). Bridelike, she is dressed in white. He wonders whether, like himself, she comes from a part of the country where spring comes earlier.

Elizabeth Fox is from Bethesda, Maryland. If Piet were in Jerusalem that Palm Sunday, he should have known that Jerusalem's Bethesda is near the Sheep Gate (John 5:2), which is a natural enough place to find a fox wearing white clothing. Bethesda is the pool where the angel comes to trouble the waters. Piet, called in to repair the waterfront home the Whitmans have bought, sees Foxy in her *lemon*-colored smock and "saw she was going to be trouble" (p. 187).

In a lengthy short story entitled "The Wait,"[6] published shortly before *Couples,* Updike tells the story of a wife who is becoming tired of being a mistress and unconsciously scheming to force her lover to marry her. She thinks: "Was she wicked or crazy? How could she possibly take this man away from his blameless wife and helpless children?" (p. 96) — and she waits to be told how! Similarly, Foxy brushes past every obstacle in order to gain her end of marriage to Piet. She is the ruthless predator that features (also in a sexual context) in D. H. Lawrence's *The Fox.* When she proposes to call Piet in to repair the house, Freddy tells her that she will be sorry, and Ken tries to dissuade her. But she persists, just the same. Piet wants to put cabinets in the Whitmans' kitchen, remarking that open shelves are a temptation; but Foxy replies that doors are so self-righteous: "I want open shelves, and open doorways, and everything open to the sea and the sea air. I've lived my whole life in clever little rooms that were always saving space" (p. 187). She tries to make Piet admit that he is building the house for her.

It was the house that Angela had coveted when the Hanemas first came to Tarbox. Piet, who loves the foursquare carpentry of the farmhouse they finally bought, thought that the other structure overlooking the salt marshes would be one impossible to live in. But Angela thought only of the view. She, whose little toes do not touch the ground, disregards the thought of permanence on earth. Foxy wants to have a grape arbor on her house; she is one of those little foxes that spoil the grapes (Song of Sol. 2:15). Piet tells her that it will *spoil* the view. But she says that she cares nothing for the view; she is not like Ken, who always is "looking outward" (p. 198). And looking inward to her own desires, she achieves them. She takes

---

[6] *The New Yorker,* February 17, 1968.

from Angela both her husband and her house. Seeing that Piet will never leave Angela of his own accord, she forces the confrontation that will cause Angela to take the initiative of disowning her husband, using as her tool Ken's predictable sense of legal form. Even the move to Lexington when Piet and she marry is *her* idea. When Ken and she first moved to Tarbox, she thought they ought to have settled in Lexington "among people like themselves" (p. 43).

Piet surrenders to Foxy because, as Angela tells him, he is like a caged animal. He answers, "But Angel, who made the cage, huh? Who? *Who?*" (p. 205). Earlier, there had been a hamster in their house, his daughters' pet. He would hear the squeak of its exercise wheel turning in the night, and, the sound mingling with his thoughts of having come to the edge of a cliff, he would pray, "God help me, help me, get me out of this" (p. 16). One night the hamster, let out of its cage by the girls, was killed by a cat. Burying it, Piet was struck by the fact of its being a male. So he himself, not content to stay within the confines of marriage, likewise is struck down by a hunting animal strong in tooth and claw. When Freddy remarks to Foxy that she has strong teeth, she notes that he says "strong," not "nice" or "good" (p. 289).

Death pervades Tarbox. After Ken's baby is born, Foxy thinks: "How innocently life ate the days. How silly she was, how Christianly neurotic, to feel beneath the mild mixed surface of aging and growing, of nursing and eating and sleeping, of love feigned and stolen and actual, a terror, a tipping wrongness, a guilt gathering toward discharge" (p. 293). She does not want to listen when Freddy hints that he is involved in arranging abortions, imagining that he is trying to make himself seem important. But soon she is seeking Freddy out. She, who once confided to Piet that her life's ambition had been to be pregnant, has to scheme in secret to destroy the life within her in order to safeguard her future. Even her cat, sensing disaster, leaves her. At the time of the abortion, she cries out that her child's father will smash the door down with a hammer and stop it. But at that moment Piet is thinking only of himself, trying to form a prayer: "Rid me of her and her of it and us of Freddy. Give me back my quiet place" (p. 376).

Piet, lacking the courage to act, retains some objectivity in self-knowledge. Waiting for Foxy's abortion to be over, he thinks how her coming into his life had been: "He had been innocent among trees. She had demanded that he know. Straight string of his life, knotted. The knot was surely sin" (p. 376).

Because Piet still carries within him a memory of sin and grace he can move in the older Tarbox with its seventeenth-century relics and learn from it. The hourglass-shaped green with its two churches speaks of a time when God was real to Americans. Foxy would leave her Plymouth beside the rocks below the green when she went to church, trying to recover a history that was now a confused memory. Hope Street and Charity Street meet at right angles. Divinity Street (faced by the churches) moves at right angles to Charity Street. So faith, the third of the theological virtues, was central at first. Now Freddy Thorne, the would-be priest of the new religion, has his office on Divinity Street. Hanema and Gallagher have set up theirs on Hope Street. When Piet hears on the telephone the news of Foxy's being pregnant by him he looks across to Charity Street. It "seemed a sacred space, where one could build and run and choose, from which he was estranged" (p. 341).

Of the four cardinal virtues, Prudence and Temperance survive as streets. But Justice and Fortitude are absent. Piet feels the lack. He feels it when he looks up details of colonial carpentry in order to furnish a local restaurant in antique style. "Trying to turn these ethical old specifications into modern quaintness demoralized Piet" (p. 267). He feels it as he senses his faith ebb away from him. The phrases *Thou shalt not covet* and whoever *lusteth in his heart* merge with a dream of a big new plane, a luxurious jet, plunging to earth while its passengers sit quietly indifferent. "He had patronized his faith and lost it. God will not be used. Death stretched endless under him" (p. 257).

Piet tells Foxy: "I think America now is like an unloved child smothered in candy. Like a middle-aged wife whose husband brings her home a present after every trip because he's unfaithful to her." God is the husband, he insists: "God doesn't love us any more. He loves Russia. He loves Uganda. We're fat and full of pimples and always whining for more candy. We've fallen from grace" (p. 200). Yet at the very moment of speaking he is drinking Foxy's *lemonade* and finding it not sweet enough for his taste. Almost immediately, she invites him to kiss her; so she becomes his *leman*. Sex and candy have become assimilated to each other in Tarbox. After the abortion, as Freddy drives away taking Foxy home, Piet looks downward. "A condom and candy wrapper lay paired in the exposed gutter" (p. 378).

The old station wagon in which Piet goes to work, and which he leaves parked outside the Whitman place, carries drawn into the dirt on its tailgate the legend "Wash Me." Piet carries with him the memory of the stain of sin and the need for forgiveness. When the consequences of his actions finally catch up with him, he is relieved. At the confrontation with Ken he starts to justify Foxy and himself (p. 399):

> But even as he pleaded he knew it was no use, and took satisfaction in this knowledge, for he was loyal to the God Who mercifully excuses us from pleading, Who nails His joists down firm, and roofs the universe with order. (p. 399)

Nevertheless, like Harry Angstrom in *Rabbit, Run,* he quickly tires of feeling guilty. "Nothing will happen," he tells Angela once they are home again. Angela replies: "Something *should* happen, Piet. You've abused me horribly. I've asked for it, sure, but that's my weakness and I've been indulging it" (p. 404). Angela's persistence in seeing that something does happen brings him back to his basic beliefs (p. 415):

> ... he believed that there was, behind the screen of couples and houses and days, a Calvinist God Who lifts us up and casts us down in utter freedom, without recourse to our prayers or consultation with our wills. Angela had become the messenger of this God.

If Piet's sense of the order in the universe verges on fatalism, Foxy sees the world simply as territory to be plundered. When she meets Piet secretly after finding that she is pregnant by him, she remarks that adultery is silly and "so much trouble." He replies that it is a way of seeking knowledge. She asks, "What do we know now, Piet?" He throws back at her, "We know God is not mocked" (p. 343). But she is feeling happy because she is carrying his baby within her. Piet tells her that her God is sex, yet it is more accurately the self-will which, in seeking only its own, is the contrary of Christian Agape (I Cor. 13:5). Piet has found that Foxy's slow response in love-making is really a form of greed. He realizes that she thinks herself to be perfect, and yet her underclothes are not always clean. She would not understand the message, "Wash Me." She consents to the abortion because she knows that refusing it would mean losing Piet. When she goes away to get her divorce from Ken she writes to her lover, "When you desire to be the world's husband, what right do I have to make you my own?" But she has already answered this question earlier in her letter: "To be mastered by your body I would tame you with my mind" (p. 450).

The single vulnerable place in Foxy's tough skin is her pride. She is reduced to tears of shame when, during a game of Impressions during the summer of 1963, she is cast as Christine Keeler. It is not the couples knowing that she has been seeing Piet that she minds, but the fact that they compare her with "that ... tart" (p. 184).[7]

---

[7] Similarly, Sally the adulterous wife in "The Wait" sees herself as desired by well-groomed strangers in the streets of Washington, D.C., and as a queen in the staring eyes of a statue of Charles V. She is mortified to find that a re-

Foxy, who is not particularly concerned about mocking God, cannot stand up before the mockery of others as guilty as herself. But Piet's Calvinistic upbringing makes him aware of another dimension to the situation. Unconsciously, perhaps, he recalls the words of St. Paul that declare:

> Do you suppose, O man, that when you judge those who do such things and yet do them yourself, you will escape the judgment of God? Or do you presume upon the riches of his kindness and forbearance and patience? Do you not know that God's kindness is meant to lead you to repentance? But by your hard and impenitent heart you are storing up wrath for yourself on the day of wrath when God's righteous judgment will be revealed. (Rom. 2:3-5)

The day of God's wrath comes to Tarbox. It is introduced by the words: "Then the supernatural declared itself" (p. 439). It is prepared for by a biblical setting which Updike has carefully built up.

Foxy, who had a Jewish lover before marrying Ken, sees Piet as a Jew. Piet is jealous of her undisguised admiration for Ben Saltz, because Ben is a true Jew. On the night of John Kennedy's assassination the couples have a black-tie party at the Thornes' house. (They had thoughts about cancelling it, but Freddy had already "bought the booze.") Piet misses Foxy and Ben, and imagines that they may be outside making love. He thinks sourly about Foxy's preference: "Abram over Lot" (p. 310).

Piet, like Lot, has been raised in the knowledge of the God of Abram. Like Lot, he has a wife and two daughters. Like Lot, he has left the tents of Abram and gone to live among the heathen in the Cities of the Plain.[8] The fourteenth chapter of Genesis tells how four kings (including Tidal, King of Goiim — that is, of the barbarians) fought against the kings of Sodom and Gomorrah and took Lot captive. The battle was in the valley of Sidim, the Salt Sea. This valley was full of bitumen pits, into which some of the kings of Sodom and Gomorrah fell. The bitumen pits in the valley of the Salt Sea strongly suggest Tarbox,[9] which looks out over salt

---

mote acquaintance of her husband, meeting her with her lover, regards her as a tart.

[8] In the *Paris Review* interview, after giving other examples of his working in the "mythic mode," Updike adds: "And in *Couples,* Piet is not only Hanema/anima/Life, he is Lot, the man with two virgin daughters, who flees Sodom, and leaves his wife behind" (*Art,* p. 104).

[9] Lot makes his home in Sodom. In popular tradition Sodom is linked with homosexuality. Tarbox may qualify as a modern Sodom if Freddy is to be trusted when he tells Angela that Piet alone among their circle of couples is properly heterosexual (p. 370). But Updike makes another identification. Once when Angela asks, her eyes flashing, whether Piet wishes her to practice

marshes. And, just as the Cities of the Plain are destroyed by fire from heaven, so Tarbox's Congregational Church is burned at the end of the novel. "God's own lightning had struck it" (p. 441).

This event parallels the account of the Day of the Son of Man as given in the Gospel of Luke:

> Likewise as it was in the days of Lot — they ate, they drank, they bought, they sold, they planted, they built, but on the day when Lot went out from Sodom fire and brimstone rained from heaven and destroyed them all — so will it be on the day when the Son of man is revealed . . . . Remember Lot's wife. (Luke 17:28-30, 32)

The passage is preceded by a comparison with the days of Noah, when the floodwaters came. In Tarbox, the lightning is preceded by a torrential rain driving everyone from the beach. Then, as Piet sees the church burn after the lightning has struck it, he "watched his wife walk away, turn once, white, to look back, and walk on, leading their virgin girls" (p. 444). *Remember Lot's wife.* She, too, turned back to look once at Sodom, and was turned into white salt.

As the action in *The Centaur* takes place under the eye of Zeus (Zeus-Zimmerman, the Carpenter-God), so the action in *Couples* takes place under the gaze of the golden rooster on the spire of the Congregational Church. The bird has a copper English penny for an eye, and it has stood atop each new church building since colonial times. ". . . If God were physically present in Tarbox, it was in the form of this unreachable weathercock visible from everywhere. And if its penny could see, it saw everything, spread below it like a living map" (p. 17). As Piet drives away from the single time of love-making with Foxy after the birth of her baby, he feels happy, "Exhilarated once again at having not been caught" (p. 335). But the golden weathercock is peeking through the leafless trees, and he is caught in a net of consequences he had never imagined possible.

---

fellatio, he replies: "No, no, no. Good heavens, no. That's sodomy" (p. 248). But this practice he follows constantly with Foxy, and it is particularly emphasized in the last days he spends with her in Tarbox before she leaves to get her divorce.

The interviewer in the *Paris Review* (*Art*, p. 102) asks Updike about "oral-genital contacts" and why these are treated in *Couples* differently from in *Rabbit, Run,* where only one such incident takes place and there seems to be more devastating. Updike replies that he is noting the "change in sexual deportment" in the intervening years that has made pornography so universal. "In *Rabbit, Run* what is demanded, in *Couples* is freely given." He points out that the sterility of the lovers in the Tristram and Iseult story is emphasized by de Rougemont. Piet and Foxy, following the Tristram-Iseult pattern, take the way of sterility. "It's a way of eating, of eating the apple," Updike explains, "of knowing." He does not add — although he might have done so — that it is a way of falling into the mores of Sodom.

Because the All-Seeing Eye is the eye of a weathercock, there is also a link with St. Peter and the cock who announced the disciple's denial of his Master. Piet is a Peter who does not repent of his denial, a Rock unfit for founding a lasting church upon. After the Congregational Church burns to the ground, the weathercock is retrieved. Piet, watching the operation, knows "that his life in a sense has ended" (p. 457). He realizes also that he is standing in the spot where he first glimpsed Foxy coming out of church.

* * *

As the church burns, Piet sees that the fire hoses trained on the exterior are accomplishing nothing. "The only answer was immediate ax-work, opening up the roof, chopping without pity through the old hand-carved triglyphs and metopes" (p. 441). Shortly after, Piet notices at his feet a water-soaked pamphlet. It is a sermon, dated 1795, containing the statement that the United States of America has cause, above all other nations, for acknowledging the power and goodness of God. The American nation, so this scene implies, has come to a crisis where only the most drastic measures can preserve its structure. Tarbox represents an acute stage of moral and spiritual degeneration.[10]

At the beginning of the book, Angela, in reply to Piet's remark that he wonders what stage the new couple (the Whitmans) are in, says: "You're hoping they're at our stage?" And he answers: "That's right. The seventh circle of bliss" (p. 4). The seventh circle in Dante's *Paradiso* is the Heaven of Saturn. Thus Piet's sarcastic remark is parallel to George Caldwell's statement in *The Centaur* that we are not living in the Golden Age.[11] The seventh circle in the *Paradiso* is also the circle of the ascetic life and of the virtue of temperance. On reaching it Dante is informed about the mystery of God's predestination and hears of the judgment pronounced upon those who, through love of luxury, have turned away from the service of God. Tarbox, then, represents the antithesis of the seventh circle of bliss. Incidentally, Angela accepts Piet's statement as though, "remotely, ready to believe it." She who comes from Nun's Bay (*seven* miles distant from Tarbox) and who belongs among the stars is not really aware of the corrupt state that life in Tarbox has reached.

That Piet's progress in the book is partly a parody of Dante's

---

[10] Another image presenting the seriousness of Tarbox's moral decline is Frank Appleby's indigestion. "It's like a ball of tar in there I can't break up," he explains (p. 153). His wife Janet's family made their money through manufacturing laxatives. But Frank's condition (he has developed an ulcer) — and Tarbox's — requires more than this easily available remedy.

[11] According to Hesiod the Age of Gold on earth was under the rule of Saturn.

progress to the white rose of Paradise[12] is shown by the fact that, after Piet thinks he has broken with Foxy, he turns to Bea Guerin as his mistress. He realizes that Bea's attraction for him lies in her barrenness. As Beatrice is Dante's guide as he ascends from Hell through Purgatory to Heaven, and points him to life, so Bea reconciles Piet to the descent into death. Piet finds that he enjoys striking Bea, as she tells him others always seem to want to do — and she had hoped that he would be different. Instead of finding his way to paradise, Piet, whose sign in the sky is the Lion, is down in Nether Hell within the circles dominated by the "sins of the Lion," that is, by violence.

Nevertheless, however much Tarbox has turned away from heaven and towards hell, it continues to exhibit the ambiguities of flesh. In their search for new games the couples explore the further reaches of duplicity and perversity, but one night at the Constantines they play the game Wonderful. Freddy proposes the game, the object of which is to name the most wonderful thing in the world, in order to show that life is meaningless. He himself suggests as his choice the human capacity for self-deception. His summing-up is this: "You're born to get laid and die, and the sooner the better." Piet objects that a greater wonder is human ingenuity in creating unhappiness: "We believe in it. Unhappiness is in us. From Eden on, we've voted for it. We manufacture misery, and we feed ourselves on poison. That doesn't mean the world isn't wonderful" (p. 242). In spite of his brave words, Piet himself chooses for his most wonderful thing a woman asleep, exhibiting his fear of conscious, responsible existence. The others suggest various alternatives: Carol Constantine, a baby's fingernails; Foxy, the Eucharist; Terry Gallagher, the music of Bach; and Angela, the stars.

The capacity for wonder, and so the acceptance of life rather than death, is still in them. The question remains as to how this capacity can be creatively channeled when no religious faith is available to focus those scattered hopes that life can be wonderful. Terry Gallagher, who retains a formal relation to a church, *recites*: "Hope isn't something you reason yourself into. It's a virtue, like obedience. It's given. We're free only to accept or reject" (p. 243). When Piet drives away at the end of the evening, he sees "beyond the backstop screen his church bulking great, broad and featureless from the rear, a stately hollow blur" (p. 244). How can hope be accepted as a grace beyond willing when for these Catholics grace is a formula

---

[12] In "The Wait" Sally's lover compares the lights of Washington, viewed from the airplane in which he is traveling with his mistress, to Dante's dream of the Rose.

learned by rote and when for these Protestants the community mediating grace is a hollow blur rapidly receding from sight?

The problem, as Piet senses during the game, is that "the world hates the light" (p. 239). This echo from the Gospel of John (3:19) recalls how judgment is pronounced on those whose works are evil. Freddy Thorne, in seeking to make the couples into a church with himself as priest, can only play nihilistically with the trappings of Christianity in order to contrive his new religion. Explaining to Angela that he believes in a God, Big Man Death, Freddy details his views of their friends, but he excludes Ben Saltz and Ong. "They don't count, they're not Christian" (p. 371). At the party at his house on the night of Kennedy's assassination, while Carol carries "two bottles of burgundy black as tar in the candlelight," Freddy carves ham and intones: "Take, eat. This is his body, given for thee" (p. 319). Yet, though they enjoy pretending to be shocked, the couples are not Christian enough even in memory to accept Freddy's blasphemies as a new faith.[13] The music that plays as they dance as though "gliding on the polished top of Kennedy's casket" is more convincing in its description of their attitudes. "*Castles* may *tumble,* that's *fate* after *all,* life's really *funny* that *way*" (p. 310). Tarbox's little society tells itself that the party is a compliment to Kennedy, an Irish wake. The couples gossip, backbite, and display or invite jealousy as they play off one married partner against another. Ken Whitman stands aloof, formally correct in black even to his onyx cufflinks. Bea Guerin alone displays any sign of grief. Her rather theatrical cry that she *"loved"* Kennedy seems to Piet to contain within it "a woe calling from an underworld" (p. 305).[14]

---

[13] Piet is the only one likely to respond to Freddy's perverted manipulation of Christian motifs, and this fact constitutes one strand in his dislike of the dentist. During the confrontation with Ken Whitman, Piet flares up when Ken says that he is considering bringing criminal charges against Thorne. "For God's sake, why? That was probably the most Christian thing Freddy Thorne ever did. He didn't have to do it, he did it out of pity. Out of love, even." "Love of who?" "His *friends*" (p. 398). At the moment he says this, Piet feels that he and Freddy "at last comprehend each other with the fullness desired. . . . Hate and love both seek to know."

In the Christian story the fullness of love is for a man to lay down his life for his friends (John 15:13). Freddy's religion of death culminates in a man destroying innocent life for his friends.

[14] Bea, who pulls Piet down to the Nether Hell dominated by violence, is in her symbolic guise a fit person to be the mouthpiece of this cry of woe. Those whom the gods "love" die young, and Kennedy has been pulled by violence out of life by the gods of the underworld. The short reign of King John and Queen Jacqueline is indeed marked by woes until its untimely end. The news early in the book of Mrs. Kennedy's miscarriage is one of the reasons for Nancy's fear of death; and it makes a deep impression on her

When faith in the moral government of the universe is absent, and responsibility for good and evil in the public or the private realm is not recognized, then fate and chance become the sole gods. Piet, after he is put out of his home, dreams of building something that will not stay either joined or erect. He also dreams of standing beneath the stars and trying vainly to change their pattern by an effort of will. These dreams show how far he has passed into the stage of despairing of living according to the order of things. During three "slavish days" with Foxy he finds respite in making love, and takes pleasure in making loud groans and pretending he is dying. "I'm in the pit," he cries (p. 437). "We are all exiles who need to bathe in the irrational," is Updike's gloss (p. 438).

Piet's dreams at the time when he knows that he will marry Foxy make an interesting contrast with the earliest dream of his that we are told about. He thought himself then to be an elderly minister making calls in the country. He stood for a long time on the meridian strip of a superhighway, and then crossed. He was relieved "when a policeman pulled up on a motorcycle and, speaking German, arrested him" (p. 10). In today's world there is no tolerance of the old faith that sustained an earlier America. It is a relief not to have to try to communicate it.

As the Congregational Church burns, Piet explains to the minister that, even if they save the shell, the walls are so weakened that they will have to tear it down anyway. The minister has just been telling him: "This church isn't that old stump of a building. The church is people, my friend, people. *Human beings*" (p. 444). The minister's cliché, with its horizontal, humanistic emphasis, misses the point of which Piet is subconsciously aware, namely, that we are God's building and the temple within which God's Spirit dwells (I Cor. 3:6, 16). The Day of the Lord tests with fire what sort of work each one has done (I Cor. 3:13). That is why Piet realizes that the burning of the building signifies the end of his life. The carpentry work of this edifice cannot be duplicated. The golden weathercock, God's presence in America, can be raised on another building, but not on this one.

Foxy, holidaying at Charlotte Amalie in the Virgin Islands before

---

father also. Updike comments: "Piet's first step at seducing Foxy is clearly in part motivated by the death of the Kennedy infant" (*Art*, p. 106).

Updike's belief that the tone of the "reigning house" communicates itself to the American nation is very evident in *Couples*. As death marks down its victims in the White House, both unborn child and father, so it claims for its own both Piet's unborn child and Piet's spiritual self. The "New Frontier" of the Kennedy era is to be equated with Piet's acceptance of the life of Tarbox and Lexington. Piet accepts the mores of the Cities of the Plain; he is Lot, "pitching his tent towards Sodom" (Gen. 13:12).

her divorce, writes to Piet of her meeting Negroes and — greatly daring for a Southern girl — dancing with them:

> They are a very silky people, and very innocently assume I want to sleep with them. How sad to instinctively believe your body is worth something. After weeks of chastity I remember lovemaking as an exploration of a sadness so deep people must go in pairs, one cannot go alone. (p. 451)

This is the explanation of the title of *Couples* and the key to the entire work. Because there is no understanding of the essential coupling of flesh and spirit in each individual, in our contemporary Western society lonely halves of couples go around seeking to find the other half that shall make a complete self, as in the myth expounded by Aristophanes in Plato's *Symposium*. The perverse and desperate sexuality of Tarbox is the result of the illusion that man is embarked on the quest to discover an original sexual wholeness lost by the fall into the flesh. From such a perspective life is a pit of sadness out of which there can be no escape except through death, though people try to recover their lost innocence either by pretending that they can enter post-pill paradise or by traveling to the Virgin Islands.

Couples begins in April, the season of life's renewal in nature and for mankind the season of mocking images blending life and death. Either man discovers the Christian message of the way of resurrection through death, or else Freddy Thorne's vision alone remains, the vision of death ruling life: "You're born to get laid and die, and the sooner the better." And if a whole nation loses its understanding of earth being set under the rule of heaven, then, like Piet Hanema, its soul is given over to death. As he was crushed under the heavy, gentle paws of a predator, a lusty, cunning Fox, so America may one day lie defenseless before the barbarian invader.

AFTERWORD

THE VITALITY, SENSITIVITY, AND INTELLIGENCE OF Updike's writings are generally admitted. The principal objection raised against them is that they are too slight and decorative, too narrowly restricted in range, and too concerned with the private world of feelings and with life's little problems to engage in full seriousness with the human situation and with the heights and depths of good and evil in our apocalyptic age. It has been the purpose of the present study to point out that on the contrary, Updike's refusal to be heavily pretentious is the sign of his genuine seriousness. Because he sees the smallness of all earthly things set under heaven's jurisdiction, he also knows that nothing is too small to reflect the radiance of eternity. No event can be trivial in a universe ordered by truth and justice. So his scenes of American middle-class life are set in a perspective ranging from early Greek speculation to the thinking of the Space Age — from Hesiod to Paul Tillich — and illustrate mankind's perennial problem: how to reconcile the ambiguities of flesh with the vision of the spirit. The problem, he suggests, can never be solved out of the human spirit thinking itself to be self-sufficient. Man either finds his true freedom in knowing himself to be the creature of his Creator called to the upright life, or else he destroys himself by serving idols of his own creation.

Being a writer — a "maker" in the old sense of that word — Updike does not tell his stories out of a sense of mission to proclaim general truths.[1] Yet, in spite of himself, he gives evidence of having sprung from a line of preachers and teachers. His belief that man is indeed the being who stands on the boundary between heaven and earth informs all he writes. If we consider his novels to date we can see there a progressive delineation of how death

---

[1] Saying that his work "is meditation, not pontification" Updike explains: "I tried not to force my sense of life as many-layered and ambiguous, while keeping in mind some sense of transaction, of a bargain struck, between me and the ideal reader. Domestic fierceness within the middle class, sex and death as riddles for the thinking animal, social existence as sacrifice, unexpected pleasures and rewards, corruption as a kind of evolution — these are some of the themes I have tried to objectify in the form of narrative" (*Art*, p. 117).

triumphs over life wherever earth is not understood in the light of heaven. *The Poorhouse Fair* exhibits the bankruptcy of a social creed that thinks to build a heaven on earth while at the same time it considers the universe a meaningless absurdity. *Rabbit, Run* traces the disintegration of a consciousness in which inner feeling tries to assert its self-sufficiency. *The Centaur* celebrates a victory of faith achieved in the sacrificial life where heaven and earth are "married" — and also explains how hard it is to follow such a life. *Of the Farm* shows the consequences for an individual of choosing the horizontal dimension of existence and ignoring the vertical, a choice resulting in the displacement of right order in the horizontal. Finally, *Couples* displays the catastrophic social effect when disorder is regarded as the norm because the human has usurped the place of the divine.

The focus of each novel is different (and a corresponding change of emphasis is to be found in the short stories) because of Updike's concern to catch the changing tone of the American consciousness at each particular moment of history. Freddy Thorne of *Couples* exemplifies the false creed which Updike sees as beguiling America today, just as Stephen Conner of *The Poorhouse Fair* exemplified the false creed current in the fifties. But, whereas Conner deceived himself in imagining that a paradise on earth could replace the righteous rule of heaven over earth, Thorne has no such illusions. Leaving to others dreams about a post-pill paradise, Freddy hopes for nothing more than a brief respite on the way to final dissolution. He tells the couples: "In the western world there are only two comical things:[2] the Christian church and naked women. We don't have Lenin so that's it. Everything else tells us we're dead" (*C*, p. 146). Christianity is not a live option for Freddy, and so: "People are the only thing people have since God packed up. By people I mean sex" (p. 145).

Freddy's companions call him sick. Yet they follow his prescription for living, repelled yet fascinated by his dedication to obscenity. Already in "You'll Never Know, Dear," Ben knew that the delight of nice women in dirty jokes took away the foundation of the world, leaving treacherous mud and straw alone supporting it. Conner's optimism about the future was futile because it was based on the assumption that life was an "obscene horror." As T. S. Eliot makes

---

[2] *Comical* here refers to the notion of comedy (as in Dante's *Divine Comedy*) as opposed to tragedy, the realm of life over against the realm of death. When dominated by a vision of despair, George Caldwell spoke of man as a *tragic animal*. Freddy Thorne lives in this despair, in the condition described by Kierkegaard as "the sickness unto death."

clear in *Murder in the Cathedral,* obscenity is one of the terrifying faces of the Void.

The explicit descriptions of sexual intercourse and the constant use of four-letter words in *Couples* have drawn a great deal of comment and criticism. Updike's procedure in this novel, however, is consistent with his previous attitude towards both sexuality and obscenity. Sexuality and obscenity are very different things, of course, in spite of their focus upon the same area of human experience. Updike never goes back upon his belief that sex is both central to man's existence and one of the better things of life; but he is also keenly aware of how, in a fallen world, this good thing is widely perverted and brought into the service of death — when it appears as the obscene. Freedom to speak about all aspects of sexuality without restriction is a loudly-proclaimed achievement of the "sexual revolution," one that in the past few years has removed every limit to what can be said in print and also to the language used to say it. Updike takes full advantage of this new freedom; and, presumably, he is glad not to be restricted. Yet his use of the latitude now granted writers to range over areas formerly forbidden does not indicate that he thinks prudery to be the sole vice in connection with things sexual, or that he ignores the fact that obscenity often disguises itself as sexual frankness.[3]

Clearly, Updike welcomes the liberty to report without circumlocution how present-day society thinks, speaks, and acts in relation to sex. This liberty permits him to follow his preference for allowing his readers to draw their own conclusions about the scenes he describes rather than being told in so many words what the author himself thinks. An example of this can be seen in *The Centaur,* when George Caldwell gives a lift to the hobo (Hermes). In the short story "On the Way to School" Updike writes that the hitchhiker used a phrase "so obscene" that, remembering Peter's presence, he felt compelled to add "Sorry, boy." But in *The Centaur* Updike simply records the remark: "That's just what the fucking sucker did. Sorry, boy" (p. 83). The "moral" emphasis is surely better presented in the novel than in the short story, just because no comment

---

[3] "About sex in general, by all means let's have it in fiction, as detailed as needs be, but real, real in its social and psychological connections. Let's take coitus out of the closet and off the altar and put it on the continuum of human behavior.... In the microcosm of the individual consciousness, sexual events are huge but not all-eclipsing; let's try to give them their size" — Updike (*Art,* pp. 102-03). Speaking of "the change in sexual deportment" between the appearance of *Rabbit, Run* and *Couples,* Updike remarks: "... now you can't walk into a grocery store without seeing pornography on the rack. Remember Piet lying on Freddy's bed admiring Freddy's collection of Grove Press books?" (p. 102).

is intruded. The direct approach must be always superior to the indirect, unless the whole territory of the profane and the obscene is to be excluded from literature.

Updike leaves us in no doubt that he believes this territory to be far too important to be either passed over or else suggested by oblique hints. The direct approach is not so necessary where society itself imposes standards of "decency" and abides by these. For example, in *The Poorhouse Fair* Gregg alone consistently affronts the accepted norms of social politeness. He appears there as a grown-up small boy who uses profanity to shock his elders much as Johnny Dedman in *The Centaur* flaunts his deck of dirty cards at Minor's Place. Updike abbreviates Gregg's more vulgar words ('f.ing bastard," "this is p."), but in his later books he drops the rather artificial convention in favor of plain speaking. Here, too, moral values are served rather than flouted. A timid censorship accomplishes little.

Words in themselves reflect chiefly our attitude towards them. In *Of the Farm* Updike tells how Joey's mother mentions to the boy Richard the "very little difference" between men and women. She is shocked when Richard replies, "You mean the penis?" (p. 69). Here there is simply a change of attitude towards words, for Richard is being as serious in terms of his generation as is Joey's mother in terms of hers. But words also carry the weight of our attitudes and become clean or dirty on that account. There are two illuminating passages in *Rabbit, Run,* in which Janice reflects first upon her husband's angrily saying to her "Screw you" (pp. 12-13), and then upon his habit of speaking of her "ass" (pp. 250-51). The latter occasion is shortly before she allows her baby to drown. Updike is always alert to the intimate connection between our choice of language and the quality of our lives. Crudity and cruelty are not identical, but neither are they unrelated.[4]

It is in *Rabbit, Run* that Updike first makes extensive use of sexual description. In order to present Harry Angstrom's dilemma as he is caught between his inner feelings and the unattractive world to which his limited education has condemned him, Updike has to make his readers enter into the circle of Rabbit's imagination. He has to describe in detail Rabbit's sexual talk; not only the conver-

---

[4] Interesting contemporary confirmation of this fact is to be found in the Walker Report of the Chicago troubles during the 1968 Democratic National Convention: "We have, with considerable reluctance, included the actual obscenities used by participants — demonstrators and police alike. Extremely obscene language was a contributing factor to the violence described in this report, and its frequency and intensity were such that to omit it would inevitably understate the effect it had" ("About the Report," in *Rights in Conflict,* a report submitted by Daniel Walker [New York, 1968]).

sation in the dubious society to which Tothero introduces him, but also the sexual imagery by means of which he continually interprets his experience. Using the direct approach, Updike simply records his story and does not moralize. Yet the moral dimension is consistently emphasized. Rabbit's choice of the way of hardness of heart instead of the way of grace is also the choice of obscenity instead of purity.

Couples describes a society where crude language is no longer the mark of the insecure adolescent, or of the uneducated, or of those trying to be noticed. There is a kinship of spirit between Gregg and Freddy Thorne. But Gregg counts for nothing in the poorhouse (except in the eyes of the purblind Conner), while Freddy Thorne is gamesmaster among the sophisticated, college-trained couples of Tarbox. The contrast is no doubt an indication of Updike's estimate of the increasing spiritual debility of Western culture. A society that chooses for its leader an individual it professes to despise condemns itself by its choice. In the Old Testament we are told of a parallel situation when Gideon's son Jotham denounced the men of Shechem in his parable of the trees electing their king (Judg. 9:7-15). Because no worthier tree would accept the position, said Jotham, the bramble (thorn!) became king. Freddy's chief attraction for the couples is that he will use language in public which the others will admit only in private.

In *Rabbit, Run* Harry Angstrom is furious at finding his young sister in a restaurant where he has been listening to dirty stories told by one of Tothero's protégés. Similarly in *Couples,* Piet is annoyed at Angela's using language reminding him of Freddy Thorne. The inconsistency of both Rabbit and Piet here is patent — recalling the incident of Rabbit leaving Janice for Ruth but going back to his apartment to get a clean shirt. Yet, in each case the intuition linking decency of language with decency of behavior is sound enough. In the scene in *Couples* where Angela grants Freddy his night in bed with her there is a revealing sentence. Angela replies to a question by Freddy about their love-making: "Piet and I don't — she couldn't manage the word, out of consideration, it seemed, for *him* —as often as he'd like, but of course we do" (p. 369). That love-making is natural and good, both in itself as an act and as something to speak about, is something Updike takes for granted. But, if you happen to live in Tarbox, then you know (if you are an Angel) that language relating to sex has been debased and must be safeguarded. If you touch pitch, you are defiled (Ecclus. 13:1).

The language used in Tarbox is the language of people dedicated to truth and fun. Because duty and work are neglected, the frankness on which the couples pride themselves becomes a vehicle of deceit and corruption. Updike's sole contact with his readers is through language. He uses the language of Tarbox directly and without comment. If his readers notice only the words and remain fascinated with them, thinking the thoughts of the couples after them, then they will see only the obscenity and miss the point of why Updike has introduced them to Tarbox in the first place. Concerning themselves with asking such questions as whether Piet's multiple adulteries are credible, they will overlook the fact that the really important question is the unfaithfulness of the soul of America to the God of righteousness.

Updike has directed our attention to the essay by Paul Tillich that discusses how education in our modern Space Age stresses the horizontal line of existence to the neglect of the vertical line. If Tillich's thesis is correct, it is not surprising that Updike's own writings have been viewed almost entirely from a horizontal stand-point that never looks for their vertical meaning. The teller of para-bles has been judged by the canons of naturalism — and the verdict returned is that he seems to have nothing to say!

Parables are always, as the Greek word *parabolē* suggests, a plac-ing of one thing beside another. Biblical parables are stories of ordinary life conveying some truth of the spiritual life. In other words, they place earth beside heaven in order to show how the heavenly gives meaning and direction to the earthly. Updike's fiction is fully parabolic both in intention and in execution. Our age, which is moving so rapidly along the horizontal line, believes itself to be a totally new world facing problems that mankind has never before encountered. Thus the past can give us no guidance, and our hopes must be set upon learning to change with a continually changing world. Yet Updike's parables remind us that the quantitative and the qualitative are forever distinct. Quantitative change in the hori-zontal line, even if it takes us to the moon and beyond, gets us nowhere at all in the vertical dimension where quality rules. Travel as far into space as we may, we are not a step nearer heaven; press forward into the future as eagerly as we can, we do not leave behind what we are and have always been. For we are still in the creation conceivable to us, which is earth. In relation to the vertical line we are no different from our ancestors or ourselves of yesterday.

So Updike directs us to those aspects of earth which can speak to us of heaven and show us how to relate ourselves qualitatively to it. He gives us scenes from childhood, adolescence, young man-hood, maturity, and old age — specific scenes set in one particular place at one particular time. He turns us from generalizations about a New Age to the concrete situations confronting us from day to day. And he lets us see that, behind the shifting surface of the experiences life brings us, there is one constant question which each of us must answer for himself: Does the universe, blindly ruled by chance, run downward into death; or does it follow the commands of a Living God whose Will for it is life?

Updike's answer to that question is unambiguous and given in Christian terms. Whether we agree with him or not is our own concern, for no man can answer for another or choose for him. But the elements of Updike's world are displayed before us so that we can enter imaginatively into his vision of the reality of things, a vision of earth set under heaven. If man views himself not merely as a hairless ape but principally as a child of God called to the upright life in a world governed by eternal laws and visited by divine grace, then he can affirm with George Caldwell: "Only goodness lives. But it does live."

SELECTED BIBLIOGRAPHY

A complete bibliography of Updike's works to 1967 is C. Clarke Taylor's *John Updike: A Bibliography* (Kent, Ohio: The Kent State University Press, 1968). The present list is intended chiefly to supply general references in connection with the works mentioned in the text. However, other titles published recently (up to February, 1969) have been included. The list of Critical Essays makes no pretense to completeness, but represents a cross-section of critical opinion.

I. Works by John Updike

Unless otherwise noted, all cloth editions have been published by Alfred A. Knopf, New York, and all paper editions by Fawcett World Library, New York (Crest Books).

Novels

The Poorhouse Fair, 1959; paper, 1964.
Rabbit, Run, 1960; paper, 1966. *Rabbit, Run* and *The Poorhouse Fair*. New York: Modern Library, 1965.
The Centaur, 1963; paper, 1964.
Of the Farm, 1965; paper, 1967.
Couples, 1968; paper, 1969.

Collected Short Stories

The Same Door, 1959; paper, 1964.
Pigeon Feathers and Other Stories, 1962; paper, 1963.
Olinger Stories: A Selection. New York: Random House (Vintage Books), 1964. Paper only.
The Music School, 1966; paper, 1967.

Uncollected Short Stories Since January 1, 1966

"Marching Through Boston," *New Yorker*, 41 (Jan. 22, 1966).
"The Witnesses," *New Yorker*, 42 (Aug. 13, 1966).
"The Pro," *New Yorker*, 42 (Sept. 17, 1966).
"Bech in Rumania," *New Yorker*, 42 (Oct. 8, 1966).
"Your Lover Just Called," *Harper's*, 234 (Jan., 1967).
"The Taste of Metal," *New Yorker*, 43 (March 11, 1967).
"Museums and Women," *New Yorker*, 43 (Nov. 18, 1967).
"The Wait," *New Yorker*, 43 (Feb. 17, 1968).
"Man and Daughter in the Cold," *New Yorker*, 44 (March 9, 1968).
"Eros Rampant," *Harper's*, 236 (June, 1968).
"The Slump," *Esquire*, 70 (July, 1968).
"Bech Takes Pot Luck," *New Yorker*, 44 (Sept. 7, 1968).

Collected Poems

The Carpentered Hen and Other Tame Creatures. New York: Harper and Brothers, 1958.
Telephone Poles and Other Poems, 1963.
Verse, 1965. (The collected poems of *The Carpentered Hen* and *Telephone Poles.*) Paper only.

Uncollected Poems

"The Azores," *Harper's,* 228 (Jan., 1964).
"Lamplight," *New Republic,* 150 (Feb. 29, 1964).
"Sea Knell," *New Yorker,* 40 (March 28, 1964).
"The Vow," *New Yorker,* 40 (May 23, 1964).
"Fireworks," *New Yorker,* 40 (July 4, 1964).
"Roman Portrait Busts," *New Republic,* 152 (Feb. 6, 1965).
"A Poem For a Far Land," *New Republic,* 152 (March 13, 1965).
"Sunshine on Sandstone," *New Republic,* 152 (April 17, 1965).
"Dog's Death," Harvard Yard: The Adams House and Lowell House Printers, May, 1965.
"Postcards From Soviet Cities: Moscow; Kiev; Leningrad; Yerevan," *New Yorker,* 41 (May 29, 1965).
"Decor, *Poem," American Scholar,* 34 (Summer, 1965).
"Home Movies," *New Republic,* 154 (Jan. 8, 1966).
"The Lament of Abrashka Tertz, A Russian Song Rendered by John Updike," *New Leader,* 49 (Jan. 17, 1966).
"Amoeba," *New Republic,* 154 (June 25, 1966).
"The Seal in Nature," *New Republic,* 155 (Oct. 15, 1966).
"The Amish," *Saturday Review,* 49 (Oct. 22, 1966).
"Air Show," *New Republic,* 155 (Dec. 17, 1966).
"Elm," *Polemic,* 11 (Winter, 1966).
"Antigua," *New Yorker,* 42 (Feb. 11, 1967).
"Subway Love," *New Republic,* 156 (May 20, 1967).
"Memories of Anguilla, 1960," *New Republic,* 157 (Nov. 11, 1967).
"Bath After Sailing." Monroe, Connecticut: Pendulum Press, 1968.
"Angels," *New Yorker,* 43 (Jan. 27, 1968).
"The Naked Ape," *New Republic,* 158 (Feb. 3, 1968).
"The Origin of Laughter," *Atlantic Monthly,* 221 (June, 1968).
"An Average Egyptian Faces Death," *New Republic,* 159 (July 6, 1968).
"Topsfield Fair," *American Scholar,* 37 (Summer, 1968).
"Dream Objects," *New Yorker,* 44 (Oct. 26, 1968).
"America and I Sat Down Together" by Yevgeny Yevtushenko, translated by John Updike and Albert C. Todd, *Holiday,* 44 (Nov., 1968).
"The Dance of the Solids," excerpts from *Midpoint and Other Poems, Scientific American,* 220 (Jan., 1969).
"Report of Health," *New Yorker,* 45 (Feb. 22, 1969).

Collected Essays

Assorted Prose, 1965.

Uncollected Essays

"Death's Heads," *Books, New Yorker*, 41 (Oct. 2, 1965).

"The Author as Librarian," *Books, New Yorker*, 41 (Oct. 30, 1965).

"The Fork," *Books, New Yorker*, 42 (Feb. 26, 1966).

"The Mastery of Miss Warner," *New Republic*, 154 (March 5, 1966).

"Two Points on a Descending Curve," *Books, New Yorker*, 42 (Jan. 7, 1967).

"Nabokov's Look Back: a National Loss," *Life*, 62 (Jan. 13, 1967).

"Behold Gombrowicz," *Books, New Yorker*, 43 (Sept. 23, 1967).

"Grove Is My Press, and Avant My Garde," *Books, New Yorker*, 43 (Nov. 4, 1967).

"My Mind Was Without a Shadow," *Books, New Yorker*, 43 (Dec. 2, 1967).

"Questions Concerning Giacomo," *Books, New Yorker*, 44 (April 6, 1968).

"Letter from Anguilla," *New Yorker*, 44 (June 22, 1968).

"Indifference," *Books, New Yorker*, 44 (Nov. 2, 1968).

For Children

Updike and Warren Chappell. *The Magic Flute*, 1962. (An adaptation, with tunes from Mozart's opera.)

Updike and Warren Chappell. *The Ring*, 1964. (An adaptation of the Siegfried Idyll, with tunes from Wagner's *Ring*.)

A Child's Calendar, 1965.

II. Critical Essays on Updike

Aldridge, John W. "The Private Vice of John Updike," *Time to Murder and Create: The Contemporary Novel in Crisis*. New York: McKay, 1966.

Brenner, Gerry. "Rabbit Run: John Updike's Criticism of the 'Return to Nature,' " *Twentieth Century Literature*, 12 (April, 1966).

De Bellis, Jack. "The Group and John Updike," *Sewanee Review*, 72 (Summer, 1964).

Detweiler, Robert. "John Updike and the Indictment of Culture-Protestants," *Four Spiritual Crises in Mid-Century American Fiction*. Gainesville: University of Florida Press, 1964.

Doner, Dean. "Rabbit Angstrom's Unseen World," *New World Writing*, 20 (1962).

Doyle, P. A. "Updike's Fiction: Motifs and Techniques," *Catholic World*, 199 (Sept. 1964).

Duncan, Graham H. "The Thing Itself in *Rabbit, Run*," *English Record*, 13 (April, 1963).

Finklestein, Sidney. "Acceptance of Alienation: John Updike and James Purdy," *Existentialism and Alienation in American Literature*. New York: International Publishers, 1965.

Galloway, David D. "The Absurd Man as Saint: The Novels of John Updike," *The Absurd Hero in American Fiction, Updike, Styron, Bellow and Salinger*. Austin: University of Texas, 1966.

Geismar, Maxwell. "The American Short Story Today," *Studies on the Left,* 4 (Spring, 1964).

Hamilton, Alice. "Between Innocence and Experience: From Joyce to Updike," *Dalhousie Review,* 49 (Spring, 1969).

Hamilton, Kenneth. "John Updike: Chronicler of the 'Time of the Death of God,' " *Christian Century* (June, 1967).

Hamilton, Alice and Kenneth. *John Updike: A Critical Essay.* Grand Rapids: Eerdmans, 1967.

Harper, Howard M., Jr. "John Updike," *Desperate Faith — A Study of Bellow, Salinger, Mailer, Baldwin and Updike.* Chapel Hill: University of North Carolina Press, 1967.

Hicks, Granville. "Generations of the Fifties: Malamud, Gold, and Updike," *The Creative Present,* ed. Nona Balakian and Charles Simmons. New York: Doubleday, 1963.

——. "Mysteries of the Commonplace," *The Saturday Review,* 45 (March 17, 1962).

Howard, Jane. "Can a Nice Novelist Finish First?" *Life* (November 4, 1966).

Kauffman, Stanley. "Onward with Updike," *New Republic,* 155 (Sept. 24, 1966).

LaCourse, Guerin. "The Innocence of John Updike," *Commonweal,* 77 (Feb. 8, 1963).

Mizener, Arthur. "The American Hero as High-School Boy: Peter Caldwell," *The Sense of Life in the Modern Novel.* Boston: Houghton Mifflin, 1964.

Murphy, Richard W. "John Updike," *Horizon,* 4 (March, 1962).

Novak, Michael. "Updike's Quest for Liturgy," *Commonweal,* 78 (May 10, 1963).

O'Connor, William Van. "John Updike and William Styron: The Burden of Talent," *Contemporary American Novelists,* ed. Harry T. Moore. Carbondale: Southern Illinois University Press, 1964.

Podhoretz, Norman. "A Dissent on Updike," *Doings and Undoings: the fifties and after in American Writing.* New York: Farrar, Straus, and Giroux, 1964.

Samuels, Charles Thomas. "The Art of Fiction, XLIII: John Updike," *Paris Review,* 45 (Winter, 1968).

Stubbs, John C. "The Search for Perfection in *Rabbit, Run,*" *Critique,* 10.2 (1968).

Tate, Sister Judith M. "John Updike: Of Rabbits and Centaurs," *Critic,* 22 (February-March, 1964).

Time: "View from the Catacombs," April 26, 1968.

Ward, J. A. "John Updike's Fiction," *Critique,* 5 (Spring-Summer, 1962).

Yates, Norris W. "The Doubt and Faith of John Updike," *College English,* 26 (March, 1965).

GENERAL INDEX

INDEX OF UPDIKE'S CHARACTERS
AND FICTITIOUS PLACES